ASTROLOGY THE NEW GENERATION

Coming soon from Flare Publications:

New Voices in Astrology by various contributors (2013)

New Perspectives: The Planetary Bodies by various contributors (2013)

New Perspectives: The Zodiac Signs by various contributors (2013)

Synastry, A New Introduction by Frank Clifford (2013)

The Midheaven: Spotlight on Success by Frank Clifford (2013)

Humour in the Horoscope: The Astrology of Comedy by Frank Clifford (2012)

The Complete Guide to Solar Arc Directions by Frank Clifford (2012, published by Starcrafts/ACS)

Also published by Flare Publications:

The Draconic Chart by Rev. Pamela Crane (1st ed., 2000; 2nd ed., 2012)

The Frank Guide to Palm Reading by Frank C. Clifford (2012, revised ed. of *Palm Reading*, Hamlyn, 2004)

The Astrology of Love, Sex and Attraction by Frank C. Clifford and Fiona Graham (2012, revised edition of *Venus* and *Mars* booklets, 2000)

Using Astrology to Create a Vocational Profile: Finding the Right Career Direction by Faye Cossar (2012)

From Symbol to Substance: Training the Astrological Intuition by Richard Swatton (2012)

Getting to the Heart of Your Chart: Playing Astrological Detective by Frank C. Clifford (2012)

Solar Arc Directions by Frank C. Clifford (booklet, 2011)

Palmistry 4 Today by Frank C. Clifford (2010, fully revised ed. of *Palmistry 4 Today*, Rider 2002)

Kim Farley's Astro Mind Maps by Kim Farley (2010)

Jane Struthers' 101 Astrology Questions for the Student Astrologer by Jane Struthers (2010)

The Astrologer's Book of Charts by Frank C. Clifford (2009)

The Twelve Houses by Howard Sasportas (2007)

The Contemporary Astrologer's Handbook by Sue Tompkins (2007)

Jupiter and Mercury: An A to Z by Paul Wright (2006)

Astrology in the Year Zero by Garry Phillipson (2000)

The Sun Sign Reader by Joan Revill (2000)

The Essentials of Hand Analysis by Frank C. Clifford (booklet, 1999)

Shorthand of the Soul: The Quotable Horoscope by David Hayward (1999)

British Entertainers: The Astrological Profiles by Frank C. Clifford (1st ed., Flare, 1997; 2nd ed., 1997; 3rd ed., 2003)

Essays from 14 Rising Stars of Astrology

TNG Project Manager Demetrius Bagley
TNG Editor Nan Geary

Flare Publications
The London School of Astrology

LSA

The London School of Astrology

First edition published in 2012 by Flare Publications
in conjunction with the London School of Astrology
BCM Planets, London WC1N 3XX, England, UK
Tel: 0700 2 33 44 55
www.flareuk.com and www.londonschoolofastrology.co.uk
email: admin@londonschoolofastrology.co.uk

A CIP catalogue record for this book is available from the British Library

ISBN: 978-1-903353-21-9

Managing Editor: Frank C. Clifford
Editor: Nan Geary
Project Manager: Demetrius Bagley
Charts: Solar Fire (Esoteric Technologies)
Cover: Craig Knottenbelt

Frank Clifford would like to extend his sincere thanks to:

All the contributors for their essays, talent, and their dedication throughout the editing process to make this project the best it could possibly be

Demetrius Bagley for supervising the project with great efficiency and humour

Nan Geary for her editing expertise and tremendous support

Craig Knottenbelt for his inspired cover design

Wendy Stacey and Michael Nile for their support and encouragement

*Real generosity toward the future lies in
giving all to the present*

– Albert Camus

Back in 1987 astrologer Tad Mann edited *The Future of Astrology*, a collection of essays from some towering figures in modern astrology (including Dane Rudhyar, Robert Hand, John Addey, Michel Gauquelin, Dennis Elwell, Alan Oken, Charles Harvey, Bruno and Louise Huber and Karen Hamaker–Zondag). Twenty-five years on, with Uranus in Aries, it feels like the perfect time to publish a volume that introduces new members of the astrological community. *Astrology: The New Generation* is an eclectic compendium of essays from some truly stellar astrologers who are emerging as strong voices in the field.

On board from the beginning have been Nan Geary, the treasured editor of *The Mountain Astrologer*, and Demetrius Bagley, an experienced networker, promoter and organizer of all things astrological. Nan's expertise in editing the essays has proven invaluable, and Demetrius has provided the 'glue' for the project – insights and promotional tips, as well as gentle nudges and humour to keep authors happy and the project ticking along.

Each writer was asked to contribute an essay of between 5,000 and 7,000 words – a new piece of work in their field of expertise. In total, over two dozen astrologers were approached who had astrological specialisms in branches as diverse as traditional, Vedic, psychological, esoteric, mundane, electional, transpersonal, archetypal, mythological, horary and evolutionary astrology. Twelve writers were available and submitted proposals. Eventually the number expanded to fourteen.

Let's meet the contributors. First up, we have teachers–writers–consultants Wendy Stacey, John Green and Frank Clifford, each of whom directs courses at a major astrology institute in the UK (the Mayo School of Astrology, the Centre for Psychological Astrology, and the London School of Astrology, respectively). Then there's Gary Caton and Nick Dagan Best, who are making their names investigating planetary cycles and sharing their findings at major conferences. Other contributors include Maurice Fernandez, Mark Jones and Eric Meyers, all of whom are offering important contributions to the field of evolutionary and spiritual astrology with books, articles and seminars. Another member of that team is Tony Howard, who is a force behind online enterprises FindAnAstrologer.com and Astrology University. A respected and leading traditional astrologer, Branka Stamenkovic from Serbia, lends her talents and experience to the book, as does Benjamin Dykes, who is carving a reputation by translating, publishing and lecturing on techniques from medieval texts. Astrologers may remember the Blast Astrology Conferences of 2007 and 2008, which were spearheaded by Moses Siregar III, who joins the team with insights into locational astrology. The lineup also includes counselling astrologer Rebecca Crane and Keiron Le Grice, who lectures in philosophy, cosmology, Jungian and archetypal studies at institutes in California.

Achieving the right balance of astrological approaches, perspectives and voices was always going to be a challenge and the response we received resulted in fewer women contributors than we'd expected and no essays on Vedic astrology. But we look forward to presenting Volume 2, which will bring together additional members of this exciting generation.

For the time being, we offer you a compendium of thought-provoking ideas and intriguing views; insights into where astrology stands now; issues facing consultants; and some of the various techniques employed by astrologers today.

We hope this volume inspires, teaches and entertains. It is offered to you in the spirit in which it was conceived: to celebrate some of the new talent in our special, diverse community.

Part I

Celestial Cycles:
Tracking the Mundane

Wendy Stacey
A Personal Biography

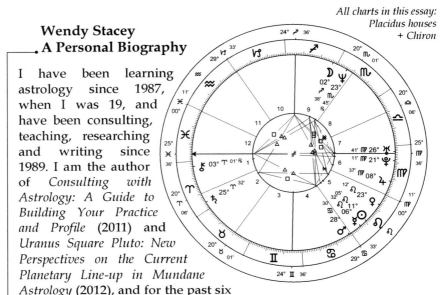

All charts in this essay:
Placidus houses
+ Chiron

I have been learning astrology since 1987, when I was 19, and have been consulting, teaching, researching and writing since 1989. I am the author of *Consulting with Astrology: A Guide to Building Your Practice and Profile* (2011) and *Uranus Square Pluto: New Perspectives on the Current Planetary Line-up in Mundane Astrology* (2012), and for the past six years I have written a regular column for students in *The Astrological Journal*. Currently I hold the position of Chair of the Astrological Association of Great Britain, held since 2002 (Treasurer from 1999–2002), and have been the Principal of The Mayo School of Astrology since 2007, when I facilitated the re-write of both the certificate and diploma course and wrote much of the modernized syllabus material. I also tutor for the London School of Astrology (from which I hold the diploma) and taught voluntarily for the Astrological Lodge of London from 2007–10. I have a first degree in Sociology and was also one of the first students and graduates to complete the Master of Arts in Cultural Astronomy and Astrology at Bath Spa University in 2003. At the time of publication I am in my final year at Southampton University, completing a PhD in Sociology exploring changing birth methods and, consequently, birth times. My lecturing experience extends to talking at astrological conferences and schools in many countries, including the UK, the USA, New Zealand, Greece, Norway and Turkey. Media experience includes speaking on several radio stations in the UK, USA and Canada and television appearances on *Quarter Life Crisis* and *Spirit and Destiny* (USA). I covered William and Kate's royal wedding on ABC's *Good Morning America,* and my article on it was syndicated in over 2,000 newspapers around the world. I live with my husband and two daughters in Buckinghamshire, UK, where I run my astrological consultancy and property development business (since 1998), study, research, write and watch too many movies.

www.wendystacey.com • www.mayoastrology.com
wendy@wendystacey.com

Chapter One

PLANETARY CYCLES & CINEMA TRENDS

WENDY STACEY

With Neptune now in the sign of Pisces, it should be an exciting time for film. Not forgetting a touch of Leo for drama, costume and casting, cinema is essentially a Neptunian/Piscean phenomenon, inviting the audience to escape and immerse themselves into an illusory, fantasy experience. Movies evoke emotion; they stretch our imagination, take us on narrative journeys and entertain us. As Alexander Walker puts it, 'Movies give us the myths we worship and the metaphors that simplify our existence'[1] Although the previous ingress of Neptune into Pisces coincided with the development of photography, which paved the way for cinematography, the recent ingress of Neptune into Pisces offers us the first chance to watch movies made in this new Neptunian era. As Neptune travels through its own sign we can be sure that we are in for a treat with the development of all things cinema.

Cinema can be analysed from various perspectives, from cinematic genres to eras such as the 'Chaplin Years', the 'Marilyn' period, the 'Disney Age' or Spielberg's blockbusters of the 1980s; from films that have won Oscars to those that have been mauled by critics but fared well at the box office. We can also look at technology, the introduction and use of colour, sound, music or costume in film. What makes cinema so interesting is that is represents a medium *for the masses.* Hollywood is one of the largest industries in the world and provides for one of the biggest economies ever known. Hollywood is power and money, and it is difficult for young innovators to get their work 'out there'. The relatively few movies that reach the box office are the ones that have the chance to shape a generation; these are the films with the power to influence people *of that particular time.* Subsequently, astrology offers a fascinating inside track into the various meanings of these times.

This essay will take a look at some pivotal dates in cinema and examine how these are reflected in astrological placements in actors' charts and in major planetary ingresses of the time. It will also focus on key outer-planet aspects and cycles and link these to the times of movie releases. There will also be correspondences made between film titles/plots and the signs/planets involved at the time of their release. For example, to the astrologer it is not surprising to see a movie about a man who is born elderly only to get younger as time passes – *The Curious Case of Benjamin Button* (2008) – released as Saturn opposed Uranus, a planetary combination that suggests a *reversal* of *time*. It is amusing to see movies with titles such as *The Headless Horseman* (1922) hit the screens as Jupiter and Saturn in Libra opposed Chiron in Aries. (Some fifty years later, when Chiron returned to Aries, the memorable scene involving a decapitated horse was featured in *The Godfather*, which we'll look at later.)

The first cinema to open was in Frankfurt am Main in Germany on 21 February 1906. On that date, there was a T-square: Neptune in Cancer was exactly opposite Uranus, and both were square to Mars in Aries. There was a tight stellium of the Sun, Mercury, Venus and Saturn in Neptune-ruled Pisces – befitting the occasion.

The first projection room was opened by William Fox in New York City on 1 May 1907 (no time known; the chart on the right is set for noon) and here we have the two rulers of Pisces in aspect: Jupiter at 7° conjunct Neptune at 10° Cancer, accentuating the illusion, the projection, the imagery and mammoth scope of 'something magical'. These planets oppose an exact conjunction of Mars and Uranus at 12° Capricorn, which suggests the pioneering, technical quality of this moment. The opposition forms a T-square to Venus at 4° Aries, again emphasising the pioneering characteristics of this day, and perhaps Aries indicates the flickering of images merged into *one*.

A monumental moment would have to be the first onscreen kiss. This was filmed early in the day on 15 June 1896 in West Orange, New Jersey. At the time, public kissing was frowned upon, so this was controversial; it was considered loathsome and created a major scandal. In the chart for the day of filming, there's a stellium in Gemini of Pluto, Mercury, Neptune, Venus and the Sun. The Moon and Jupiter were in Leo that day, and Saturn was widely conjunct

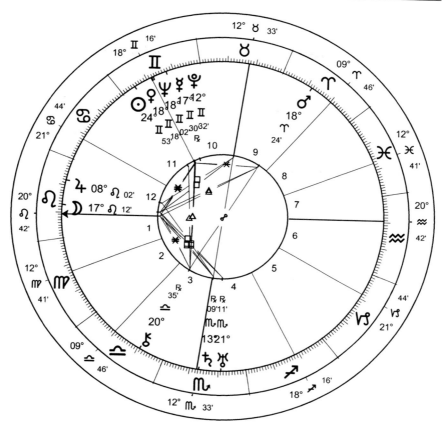

The Filming of the First Onscreen Kiss (chart set for 9am)

Uranus in Scorpio. Rampant Mars in Aries was opposing Chiron in Libra. This is a 'daredevil' horoscope and the event itself broke ground in the area of onscreen intimacy. One would normally expect to see more Libra, but Venus is locked in a romantic interlude with Neptune, along with the several other planets in Gemini (duality). While saucy Scorpio describes the intimacy and 'greediness' of the kiss,[2] Leo suggests the exhibitionism and – along with Mars in brazen Aries – the audacity in filming it.

During a series of Saturn in Pisces oppositions to Neptune in Virgo in 1936, movies of a Neptunian nature were released, such as *Mutiny on the Bounty* (the sea), *The Invisible Man* (the elusive and unseen), and Bette Davis won an Oscar playing an alcoholic (drink, escapism) in *Dangerous*.

Snow White and the Seven Dwarfs was the first full-length production from Walt Disney. Its release date was 21 December 1937;

Pluto had just made its first entry into Leo and had retrograded back into Cancer. This release was legendary in children's entertainment, bringing cinema alive for children (Leo) and spearheading Disney's remarkable career.

'Frankly, my dear, I don't give a damn' and 'After all… tomorrow is another day' would have to be two of the most memorable lines from the early Hollywood period. *Gone with the Wind* premiered on 15 December 1939 at 8.15pm in Atlanta.[3] This film adaptation of a novel set in the mid 19th century on the eve of the American Civil War is lauded as one of the epic movies of all time. The movie was controversial at the time; some considered it incredibly racist and compared it to *The Birth of a Nation* (which was about the Ku Klux Klan). One newspaper critic was sacked for not being harsh enough in his reviews, as many felt this movie was an apology for slavery.[4] The chart has an opposition of Neptune in Virgo to Jupiter in Pisces, which suggests the enduring plight of the underdog.

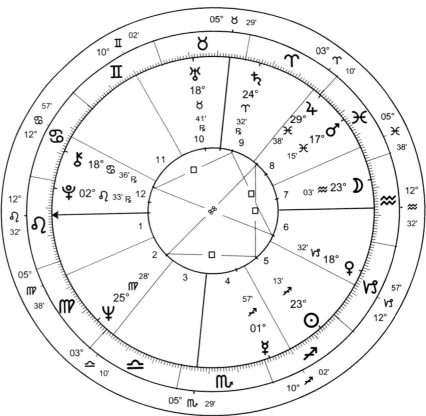

The Premiere of Gone with the Wind

There is a cardinal T-square with Chiron in Cancer in the 12th House opposing Venus in Capricorn in the 6th House, both square to an elevated Saturn in Aries, which highlights class distinction and the weight of war. What makes this relevant to planetary cycles is that *Gone with the Wind* embraces the despair and hope and the loss and gain of an anticipated war, as depicted by the T-square and the Jupiter–Neptune opposition. It was December 1939 and America, in the Great Depression itself, was watching Europe plunge into war. However, the movie's social and political aspects are eclipsed throughout by the monumental love story between Scarlett O'Hara (Vivien Leigh) and Rhett Butler (Clark Gable). This is depicted in the chart by the exact Venus–Chiron opposition and Pluto having risen in Leo. Like the premiere, Leigh had the Moon in Aquarius and this is conjunct her natal Uranus and Midheaven. Gable had an Aquarius Sun (conjunct Leigh's Moon) and Mercury. Their chemistry/synastry with each other and with the film's chart reflects the success of the movie. The drama of the movie is second to none and was attractive to audiences as one of the first feature films made in Technicolor.

The year 1939 saw several other classics hit the screen, including *Wuthering Heights* (13 April 1939) and *The Wizard of Oz* (17 August 1939). Pluto made its final ingress into Leo in June 1939. This is a significant moment as, besides Neptune, Leo plays a major role in the astrology of cinema. Leo is about drama, being on stage and entertaining an audience, and here the movie industry was given a new lease on life with vibrant colour.

Comparing movies to astrological phenomena at any time is fascinating, and the title often reflects the astrology of the times. An example of this can be seen during the early 1940s as Jupiter, Saturn and Uranus travelled through Taurus. There were releases such as *How Green was My Valley* (1941), a title that depicts the characteristics of Taurus. *The Postman Always Rings Twice*, a *film noir* about an illicit, sado-masochistic love affair, a *femme fatale* and the murder of a spouse, was released on 2 May 1946. On this day Mars was conjunct Pluto and there was a T-square between Mercury in Aries, Chiron and Jupiter in Libra, and Saturn in Cancer. Venus and Uranus were in Gemini.

During the early 1950s, as Saturn and Neptune united in Libra, musicals moved to new heights, first with Gene Kelly's appearance in *An American in Paris* (4 October 1951) and *Singin' in the Rain* (27 March 1952), then with Fred Astaire's *The Belle of New York* (1952). This was an interesting era, as Libra is linked to dance and couples; along with Pluto in Leo, this period saw the launch of several dancing musicals, which reflected a post-war period of celebration and hope for the future. Marilyn Monroe (Venus in Aries on a Taurus MC) adorned the screen with *Don't Bother to Knock* (1952), *Niagara* (1953) and, playing to the Libra theme, in *Gentlemen Prefer Blondes* (18 July 1953), with the Moon conjunct Saturn–Neptune in Libra trine Venus–Jupiter, and *How to Marry a Millionaire* (5 November 1953), with Venus–Neptune in Libra trine Jupiter in Gemini.

In the second half of 1953, Uranus in Cancer was opposite Chiron in Capricorn and square to Neptune in Libra. Films with rivalry, war, gangs or fighting as themes included *The Wild One* with Marlon Brando (30 December, with Saturn in Scorpio), *From Here to Eternity* (5 August) and H.G. Wells' *The War of the Worlds* (26 August), all reflective of the social conflict between different groups.

Rebel Without a Cause was premiered in New York on 26 October 1955 and tells the story of the cowardly and the brave. With Jupiter

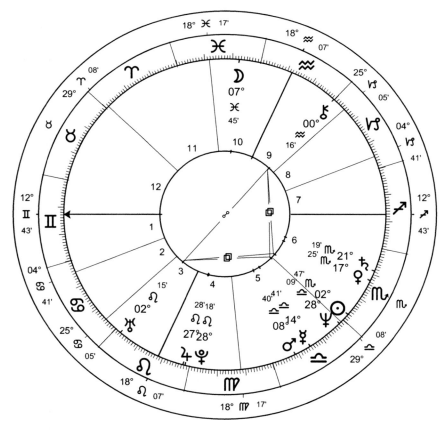

The Premiere of Rebel Without a Cause (chart set for 8pm, New York)

conjunct Pluto in Leo, this film embraces romance and loyalty, as well as bullying. A teenager (played by James Dean, in his final film) goes to a new school, meets a girl and a new best friend, whom he protects from bullies. There is also the theme of difficult relationships and power plays between parents and children here, picking up the Jupiter and Pluto in Leo theme, too. The story is a tragic one and in the chart we see a T-square between Uranus in Leo, Chiron in Aquarius and Neptune in late Libra. Leo and Aquarius are the signs associated with 'acting up' and rebelling and the film is brilliantly titled to reflect this. *Rebel Without a Cause* is ultimately about friendship, relationships within the family and the difficulty of relating to others. It is a story about teenagers (Leo) and the personal and social issues they face as they grow into adulthood. Uranus in Leo opposing Chiron in Aquarius echoes the theme of friendship, and with Neptune as the apex conjunct the Sun in early Scorpio, we see a violent ending and a crazy, unexpected sacrifice. The Neptune apex and the Pisces Moon suggest a sense of loneliness, a turn to alcohol in hard times and a run-in with authority – all themes in the film. This movie received much acclaim as it was pertinent to the changing times in society: the way teenagers adapted to, and coped with, their environment. Dean's meaningless and tragic death one month before the film's release adds to its iconic status and his cinematic immortality (Neptune). His own chart reveals a cardinal T-square with rebellious Uranus in Aries as the apex.

Uranus is linked to the ideas of friendship and detachment, Leo is about royalty and romance, and together their polarity addresses individuality. Two weeks after Uranus's final ingress into Leo (10 June 1956), *The King and I* (28 June 1956) was released. A story of love, but also estrangement and the breaking of class boundaries, is depicted by this astrological configuration.

In 1958 as Pluto retrograded back to the final degrees of Leo the lion, *The Young Lions* (1958) starring Marlon Brando and *Cat on a Hot Tin Roof* (1958) with Elizabeth Taylor and Paul Newman were released.

One would be remiss to not mention the wonderful *Breakfast at Tiffany's*, released on 5 October 1961. Audrey Hepburn does a splendid job playing a young woman new to the big city of New York and struggling to find her place in work and society. This is befitting the astrology of the day as the Moon–Pluto–Venus conjunction in Virgo opposes Chiron in Pisces, and Jupiter and Saturn make a conjunction in Capricorn.

The first James Bond movie, *Dr No*, was released on 1 October 1962, as Uranus was building to a conjunction with Pluto (and opposing Jupiter and Chiron in Pisces). Bond was played by Sean Connery, who went on to do another six Bond movies. The Cuban missile crisis at the time provided a perfect plot for the movie and the adventures of 007 formed the thematic basis for another twenty-three movies (to date); a further six actors starred as Bond. The period and the movie were concerned with the threat of espionage, fatalities and mass destruction on a global level. In *Dr No* Ursula Andress's emergence from the water in a white bikini has been judged as one of cinema's sexiest-ever moments.[5]

The magical movie *Mary Poppins* was released on 27 August 1964. A delightful and heartwarming children's musical, it was the most popular of its year. Julie Andrews starred as the enchanting nanny who is employed temporarily to look after two children. In the chart we see a stellium of the Sun, Uranus, Pluto and Mercury in Virgo. Here, witchcraft is seen as a permissible and good-spirited activity. True to the characteristics of Virgo, Mary Poppins announces on

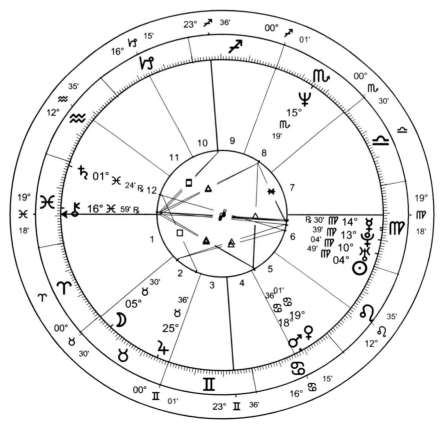

The Release of Mary Poppins (chart set for 8pm, Hollywood)

several occasions that she is 'practically perfect in every way'. The stellium in Virgo opposite Chiron and Saturn in Pisces shows the polarity between practicalities and magic – and one of Mary's first jobs as nanny is to use her witchcraft to move the children's toys and tidy up their messy bedroom. The magical theme is also seen in Neptune in Scorpio in the 8th House, which suggests the magical umbrella she travels with.

The Moon and Jupiter in Taurus are fitting for Mary's bottomless carpetbag of possessions and the Taurus attraction to sweet things, as expressed through one of the film's songs, 'A Spoonful of Sugar'. The conjunction of Venus and Mars in Cancer suggests the nurturing of the children, the position of nanny, and the efforts in bringing a family back together. The tight Grand Trine in water between Venus–Mars, Chiron and Neptune brings a feel-good quality and affirms the beauty of imagination. When Uranus and Pluto came together in the mid 1960s in Virgo, the Virgin maiden and all that goes with her were unleashed.

This movie introduced children to witchcraft and magic in such a wonderful and new way that these things were suddenly permissible. It paved the way for TV shows such as *Bewitched*. It is not surprising to find that Julie Andrews has Venus and Neptune in Virgo with Virgo rising – apt for a magical maiden witch. The movie was produced by Walt Disney, who has an elevated Neptune (in Cancer) and Virgo rising. Another very successful film released that year also had a Virgo/Virgin maiden title and theme, *My Fair Lady*, which was about the transformation and reconstruction (Uranus–Pluto) of a young flower seller from the slums into an elegant 'duchess'.

The Uranus–Pluto conjunction period in the mid 1960s also marked a time when revolutionary and evolutionary themes were portrayed in film. *2001: A Space Odyssey* is an example of this, as it addresses technological change, space travel and artificial intelligence. It was pioneering and set the scene for future sci-fi movies.

On 15 March 1972 after much controversy, the movie *The Godfather* premiered. The story is set around an Italian–American Mafia family where gambling and criminal activities are rampant. Before the film's release, the Italian–American civil rights movement held a rally and raised £600,000 to stop the film, there were bomb threats and the producer's car was shot at. The producer negotiated the removal of the word 'Mafia' from the movie (substituted with 'family' – the film's release chart has a Cancer MC) and donated proceeds from the film to a hospital fund.[6]

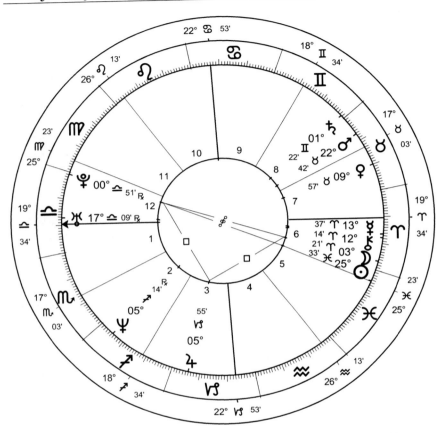

The Premiere of The Godfather (chart set for 8pm, New York)

In *The Godfather* the dialogue is slow but the pauses and language are potent and pregnant with anticipation. In the chart we have the Sun in Pisces making an out-of-sign opposition to Pluto in early Libra. The Sun–Pluto aspect suggests the power plays, the literal opposition between people and the repeated demonstration of conflict and threats ending in death. Pisces is strong here, denoting the mystery, the sabotage and the hidden enemy theme that permeates the movie. The opposition creates a T-square to Jupiter (*God*) in Capricorn (*father*). This film is predominantly about Mafia and the criminal operations and underworld, as well as the institutionalization of authority (Saturn opposite Neptune). Along with hidden agendas, violence, murder and the laundering of money, we would expect to see an emphasis on Pluto, Neptune and Saturn. This film has it all and the chart doesn't disappoint.

In the premiere's chart, the Moon in Aries opposes Pluto, apt for the psychological trip that the audience is put through, as well as the ruthlessness and rash acts of violence in the movie. The Aries stellium suggests rawness, blood and sweat – components that give the film fire, zest and an unrivalled edge of anticipation. Aries has links to cutting and severing, and with the Moon's conjunction to Chiron (the centaur – half horse, half man) in Aries, we even witness a severed horse's head left in a bed (the Moon).

From a social perspective, the film depicts a darker side to society (Pluto) and reflects the uglier sides of existence – not just of society but of the psychological make-up inherent in us all. The film displays violence on a large scale; it brings attention to the underworld of corruption, manipulation and murder. Even then, it doesn't fail to encourage the audience to have respect and admiration for the Godfather (Marlon Brando) himself.

The 1970s was a great decade for cinema. We saw the release of *Star Wars* (25 May 1977) at a time when Saturn in Leo sextiled Pluto in Libra, which sextiled Neptune in Sagittarius, offering hope and optimism. *Saturday Night Fever* (14 December 1977) was released when Pluto in Libra was exactly sextile Neptune, and Jupiter in Cancer sextiled Saturn in Virgo. *Grease* (16 June 1978) continued the Neptune–Pluto sextile aspect plus Jupiter trine Uranus at 12° Cancer-Scorpio. Both were feel-good movies offering dance, humour and a great soundtrack. Jupiter–Uranus suggests an uplifting time, and the brilliant Monty Python comedies (including *The Life of Brian* [1979]) and *Airplane* (aka *Flying High*, 1980) followed.

Back to the Future, a zany and entertaining film, was released on 3 July 1985. The movie is riveting and very clever; with Uranus in Sagittarius opposite Chiron in Gemini, it takes the audience on a *breathless spin of adventure*, demanding they keep up with the non-stop twists and turns throughout the movie – the audience sits on the edge of their seat throughout. Gemini and Sagittarius play a large theme here as two people – the science academic and the teenage student – travel (Sagittarius) through time in a car in order to save the future from indefinite ruin. It is also very witty and, although light-hearted, it does warn of unknown danger (Saturn in Scorpio). At the time of the film's release, Neptune in Capricorn was sextile Pluto in Scorpio (only one minute apart). Together, these planets give the illusion of not knowing what is around the corner, or what fate might bring. The Moon and Jupiter in Aquarius give the film its futuristic and science fiction bent. Michael J Fox who stars in the movie has his Ascendant at 18° Aquarius, close to Jupiter of the film's chart. Fox's MC sits on the film's Uranus –

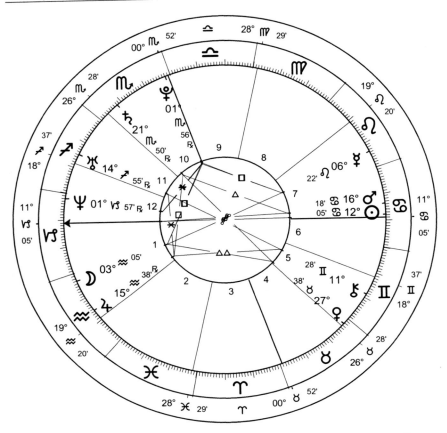

The Release of Back to the Future (chart set for 8pm, Hollywood)

this Uranus–MC transit in his chart brought instant film stardom to this TV actor. Christopher Lloyd, who played the scientist, has Jupiter at 22° Aquarius and his Sun conjoins the film's Pluto, again emphasising the eccentricity and power of his character. The film was so successful it went on to have two sequels.

Another movie to capture a large audience this same year was Steven Spielberg's *The Colour Purple*. The movie was released (18 December 1985) with Chiron in Gemini as the handle of a Bucket-shaped chart (and opposing Uranus in Sagittarius); this film told the tale of two sisters (Gemini) who were painfully separated by lies and distance.

On the 12 April 1988, *The Big Blue (Le Grand Bleu)* was released. It chronicled the lives of two divers and their ambitions to compete in the world diving championships. The focus of the movie is the ocean, and it was released as Neptune was in a wide conjunction with Saturn and Uranus in Capricorn. Neptune was also trine Jupiter and sextile Pluto, and the movie takes the audience on a magical journey to the depths of the sea, as the two men compete for the title. The action is divided into two timelines (Capricorn and Saturn link to time and chronology): the early friendship as children and then their rivalry as adults.

Pulp Fiction is considered one of the most brilliant films ever to hit the big screen. An evening chart of the film's US general release (14 October 1994) has the Moon conjunct Saturn in Pisces. The film demands that its audiences have a thick skin and a strong stomach (Moon–Saturn). The plot addresses religious dogma, and drugs are in abundance. With Mercury, Jupiter, Venus and Pluto in Scorpio, the film was not without its share of violence, along with mental and sexual torture. Death is a recurring theme, as are underground crime and power plays. Through the mind-tripping smokescreens, the weird and wonderful scenarios, the violence, the

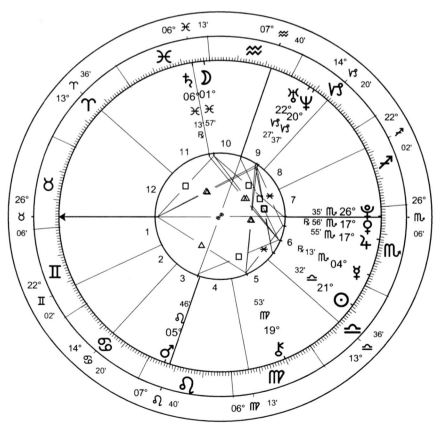

The US General Release of Pulp Fiction (chart set for 8pm, Hollywood)

genius dialogue, the film seeks to show meaningful connections (the Pisces and Scorpio emphasis, and Uranus conjunct Neptune) between time and between people. It achieves this through shock and humour. At first it looks exaggerated but upon reflection it actually demonstrates the horror and the excitement of how times have changed, showing many of the sordid aspects of the society in which we live. Released at the Uranus–Neptune conjunction in Capricorn, the film uses a rollercoaster of events to address the challenge to authority and the status quo and the need for personal responsibility. Almost every character in the movie is over-ambitious but has suffered loss or fallen from grace in some way.

The strong Saturn and Capricorn theme reflects how the issue of *time* dominates throughout the movie. The movie offers a different perspective on the linear nature of time and aims to connect time outside of the normal time-conscious and time-measured world we live in. It does this brilliantly, taking the audience on a wild ride of anticipation. Director Quentin Tarantino has the Sun and Mercury in Aries trine Mars in Leo; he is a pioneer and master of his field. Saturn in Aquarius square Neptune in Scorpio describes his renowned skill for turning time upside down and challenging the audience's perception.

One of the most fascinating films to reach the cinema in the 1990s was *The Matrix* (released on 31 March 1999). This movie gave audiences a taste of an alternate reality, as the plot reveals that human existence is merely a simulation. With Uranus and Neptune in Aquarius, we experience the rebellion against authority and the status quo. The recognition of the warrior and the special 'one' is depicted by the movie's Sun at 10° Aries trine Pluto at 10° Sagittarius.

In 2001, Saturn and Pluto opposed each other in the sky and made it an interesting year for cinema, as the dark and threatening characteristics of these planets were played out in movies such as *Hannibal*. The very literal brink of war was captured by the movie *Pearl Harbour*. With Uranus and Neptune travelling through Aquarius, technology lifted films to new heights and this year also saw the release of *Shrek* and *Monsters Inc.*

Both Saturn and Pluto can be seen astrologically as lords of darkness. They are concerned with power plays and dread. In Gemini and Sagittarius during 2001, they suggest the mastery of information and knowledge, learning and philosophy, and the perils of short- and long-distance travel. *Harry Potter and the Philosopher's Stone* (the first of eight *Harry Potter* movies) was premiered on 4 November 2001. *The Fellowship of the Ring* (the first film in *The Lord of the Rings* trilogy) was premiered five weeks later on 10 December. Both films premiered in London.

The charts of both of these movies are very similar as they have the Saturn–Pluto opposition. *Harry Potter* has it exact at 13° – and even the title of this movie is apt: philosopher's (Sagittarius) stone (Saturn). Interestingly, *Harry Potter* received the Saturn Award that year.[7] *Harry Potter* is not just about magic and witchcraft but also about wizardry, which is more attributable to the Gemini-Sagittarius axis than the Virgo witchcraft of *Mary Poppins*. The opposition resides across the 6th House and 12th House, echoing the craft, the alchemy and the fantasy sides to the movie. In both films, journeys are a theme throughout. In the chart of *The Lord of the Rings*, there is a large stellium of Venus, Pluto, Sun, Mercury and Chiron in Sagittarius and the entire movie is about a journey and the learning process along the way. As we would expect

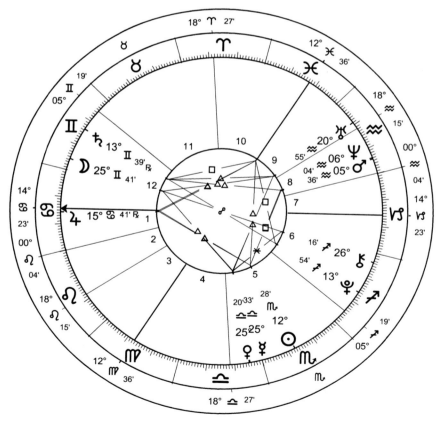

*The Premiere of Harry Potter and the Philosopher's Stone
(chart set for 8pm, London)*

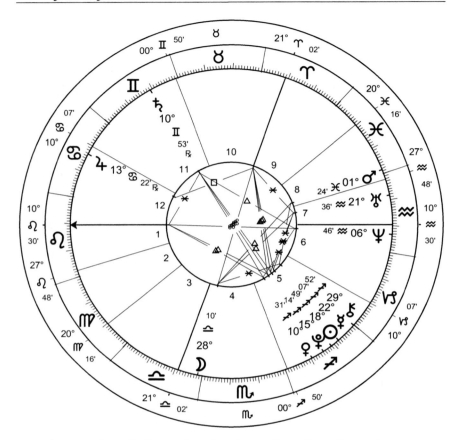

The Premiere of The Lord of the Rings: The Fellowship of the Ring
(chart set for 8pm, London)

with such a strong emphasis on Sagittarius, we marvel at the use of the bow and arrow (particularly by Orlando Bloom who, aptly cast, has Neptune at 15° Sagittarius – exactly conjunct the film premiere's Pluto).

The Sagittarius theme in these movies is accentuated by the strong position of Jupiter in both charts. In *Harry Potter*, Jupiter in Cancer trines the Sun in Scorpio: following the mysterious death of his parents, orphan Harry discovers that Hogwarts school (Jupiter) is home (Cancer). He finds comfort in friends Hermione Granger and Ron Weasley, who form the main part of his magical circle (Mars–Neptune in Aquarius). In *The Lord of the Rings*, Jupiter is unaspected, making it a maverick, dominant planet that operates alone. Here, Jupiter is the dispositor of the large stellium in Sagittarius and being exalted in Cancer depicts the mysterious journey to protect the ring and return it to its rightful home. An unaspected planet is both a curse and a gift, which is depicted well in the movie by whoever is the ring carrier. With Mars in Pisces and an unaspected Jupiter, the travellers are aware of a cause greater than themselves but have little sense of the fate that lies ahead of them; they are guided by guardian angels, teachers and strange creatures of Middle Earth.

The *Harry Potter* film has the Sun in Scorpio, which is shown through the deeper, mysterious and investigative qualities of the plot. In contrast, the Saturn–Pluto opposition in the chart of *The Lord of the Rings* brings in Venus and the Sun, perhaps here the link to the 'lord' (Sun) of the 'ring' (the unity/circle of the Sun and the jewellery of Venus). This film also has a Leo Ascendant, which suggests the dramatic epic, the landscapes in the film, the Herculean effort with costumes and casting.

At the time of writing (spring 2012, when Uranus and Pluto are coming to square each other), *The Artist* has just won the Best Picture Academy Award for 2011. The film is set from 1927–1932, a time when the Uranus–Pluto squares last occurred. It is interesting that this movie won the Oscar as Neptune moved into Pisces (the artist). Resonating with the Neptunian times, *Salmon Fishing in the Yemen*, *The Deep Blue Sea* and *Mirror Mirror* were released in the early degrees of Neptune in Pisces.

The last time Neptune was in Pisces was in the mid-19th century, and two men that played instrumental roles in changing society were Charles Darwin (whose *Origin of Species* changed people's worldview on the evolution of humankind) and Abraham Lincoln (who led the Civil War in the US with the aim of abolishing slavery). It is remarkable that over 150 years later, as Neptune moves back into Pisces, we are seeing movies being made such as *Natural Selection* and *Abraham Lincoln: Vampire Hunter*. These are variations of recurring themes, which were evident from the last Neptune in Pisces era.

The films and charts listed in this essay give examples of how planetary cycles are markers of history, played out through the lens of cinema. These cycles and aspects are pivotal points in time; through film, they reflect and influence the consciousness of the masses.

References and Notes

1. Alexander Walker, Preface, *Chronicle of the Cinema, 100 Years of the Movies*, Dorling Kindersley, London 1995, p 10.

2. *Ibid.*, p. 20.

3. Herb Bridges, *Gone with the Wind: The Three-Day Premiere in Atlanta*, Mercer University Press, 2011.

4. Walker, *Chronicle of the Cinema*, p. 296. The paper was *The Daily Worker*.

5. http://news.bbc.co.uk/1/hi/entertainment/3250386.stm

6. Walker, *Chronicle of the Cinema*, p. 619.

7. The Saturn Award honours the best movies in science fiction, fantasy and horror.

Film release dates have been retrieved *Chronicle of the Cinema* and set speculatively for 8pm at their release location. All locations are Hollywood, CA (34n06, 118w20), unless otherwise noted.

Chart Data *(courtesy of Sy Scholfield, unless stated otherwise):*

Julie Andrews: 1 October 1935, 06:00 BST(-1.00), Walton on Thames, England (51n2, 0w25). Source: From the biography *Julie Andrews* by J. Cottrell (1969, p. 14), 'approximately 6.00 am'. RR: B

Orlando Bloom: 13 January 1977, 09:15 GMT, Canterbury, England (51n17, 1e05). Source: The date and place are from various biographies and websites. The time is from Bloom's mother (as given by letter) to a trusted source of Frank Clifford. RR: A.

James Dean: 8 February 1931, 02:00 or 09:00 CST (+6), Marion, Indiana, USA (40n33, 85w39). Source: Birth certificate quoted by Steven Przybylowski for 09:00. Sy Scholfield cites the biography, 'James Dean' by George Perry (DK ADULT, 2005; 'Authorised by the James Dean Estate') for a reproduction of Dean's baby card: 'Feb. 8th 9. a.m.' (p.21), yet with regard to the time of birth Perry states that 'the birth certificate says it was at 2 am, rather than the more civilized 9am that was given on the announcement card' (p.20). Friend Elizabeth Taylor is quoted as saying they were both born at 2 am. RR: DD.

Walt Disney: 5 December 1901, 00:35 CST (+6.00) Chicago, Illinois (41n51, 87w39). Source: Marion March quotes Disney Studios. RR: A

Michael J Fox: 9 June 1961, 00:15 MST (+7.00) Edmonton, Canada (53n33, 113w28). Source: From Fox to Jean Berlow. RR: A.

Clark Gable: 1 February 1901, 05:30 CST (+6.00) Cadiz, Ohio (40n16, 81w00). Source: Sy Scholfield quotes data from a newspaper article citing a doctor's receipt for Gable's birth, which is located at the Clark Gable Birthplace Museum and Gift shop (http://www. clarkgablefoundation.com). RR: AA.

Vivien Leigh: 5 November 1913, 17:30 (-5:53) Darjeeling, India (27n02, 88e16). Source: From a biography *The Oliviers*, 'not long after the sun had disappeared'; sunset calculated at 5.16pm. RR:B.

Christopher Lloyd: 22 October 1938, birth time unknown.

Marilyn Monroe: 1 June 1926, 09:30 PST (+8), Los Angeles, California, USA (34n03, 118w15). Source: Birth certificate obtained by Bob Garner. RR: AA.

Quentin Tarantino: 27 March 1963, Knoxville, Tennessee, USA (35n58, 83w55). Source: Frank Clifford quotes a note from the Tennessee Vital Registry Office. Birth time unknown. RR: X.

Gary P. Caton
A Personal Biography

All charts in this essay:
Whole Sign houses
7 visible planets

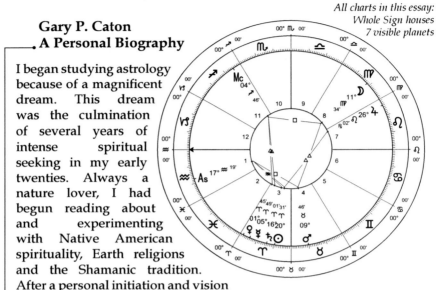

I began studying astrology because of a magnificent dream. This dream was the culmination of several years of intense spiritual seeking in my early twenties. Always a nature lover, I had begun reading about and experimenting with Native American spirituality, Earth religions and the Shamanic tradition. After a personal initiation and vision quest, I left college to 'see the world'. Along the way I was given a deck of Tarot cards. After studying and practicing the Tarot for a while, my connection with what Jung calls the 'collective unconscious' became clear enough to receive a communication which changed my life forever. I began to have a series of very vivid, symbolic dreams. In the final one I was lying on my back in an enormous field of green grass with the Sun directly overhead. Emblazoned in the solar disk was the symbol for Venus. I instinctively knew this dream was telling me something very important, so I obtained an ephemeris and gradually deduced that the planet Venus had been transiting in conjunction with the Sun on that very day! I began studying astrology in depth and I was extremely fortunate to be living near the offices of Project Hindsight in the mid '90s. What really sparked my imagination in the classical tradition was a handful of techniques that seem to be relics from the even earlier Mesopotamian and Egyptian observational traditions. After realizing that the *observable phenomena* of the planets matter greatly in our understanding of their qualities, I became an avid amateur astronomer and researcher of the visual cycles of Venus and the other planets. My essay here represents my best attempt to communicate the *philosopher's stone* of a twenty-year journey to understand my dream. It is my hope that it may serve as the 'call to adventure' for further discoveries.

www.DreamAstrologer.com
gary@dreamastrologer.com

Chapter Two

THE VISUAL JOURNEY OF VENUS
As Heroine and Goddess of Death/Re-birth

GARY P. CATON

Counting stars by candlelight, some are dim but one is bright
The spiral light of Venus, rising first and shining best
Oh, from the north-west corner, of a brand new crescent Moon
from 'Terrapin Station'
by Robert Hunter and Jerry Garcia

As the lyrics to this popular song allude, Venus is by far the brightest of the five visible planets and easily outshines all the stars in the sky except the Sun and Moon. In her brightest phases, Venus can cast shadows and can even be seen in broad daylight. Many have seen the star and crescent formation mentioned in this song – a frequent celestial occurrence known as a conjunction of Venus to the Moon. A star and crescent in some combination form the basis of symbols widely found across the ancient world, and remain potent symbols to this day. They are featured on the flag used by many Muslim-majority states, for instance.

It should come as no surprise, then, that records of fairly complex observations of Venus date back to the very origins of civilization. The observations recorded in what is known as the Venus tablet of Ammisaduqa date somewhere around the 17th century BCE. Long before the Common Era, Mesopotamian astrologers were well aware of, and even able to predict, the intricate movements of Venus in the sky. In particular the first visual appearances of any planet (or star) were considered extremely important. This event, known as the heliacal rise, was religiously and meticulously followed by Egyptian and Mesopotamian astrologers. In fact regular observations of heliacal risings form the most important records for the later development of mathematical planetary theory. The diaries of the Mesopotamian astronomer/astrologers, which were compiled over several centuries of observations before the Common Era, have been described by scholars as being 'among the most extraordinary achievements in the entire history of Science'.[1]

Some time after the Hellenistic era, with the advent of horoscopic (chart-based) astrology and the Ptolemaic world-view, astrology began to lose touch with some of its early observational traditions. As an abstraction the horoscope or chart hides a great deal of nuance regarding the planets as *observable phenomena*. Only in the hands of an experienced stargazer and astrological scholar are these nuances revealed. The result is that, despite a very long and rich tradition of observation, there is very much more to Venus than many if not most modern astrologers realize. At any gathering of astrologers you will hear someone saying something to the effect of: 'My Venus is in this or that sign/house and in aspect to this or that planet in my chart.' Being an avid stargazer, my response is always: 'Were you born while Venus was the Morning Star, Evening Star or Invisible in the Underworld?' You would be very surprised at how few astrologers can understand, much less answer, that question! In this essay I hope to demonstrate not only how important these visual distinctions are but also that this is just the tip of the iceberg in terms of deepening our awareness of this most crucial planet.

Planets have sidereal cycles, which track their motion through the zodiac, as well as synodic cycles, which track their relationship to the Sun. Synodic cycles also track the nature of a planet's visual appearance in the sky. Most astrologers know that the sidereal cycle of Venus is one year, as she will generally return to any given zodiac sign once yearly. However, the synodic cycle of Venus lasts 1.6 years (19 months or 584 days) between any two similar events. The synodic cycle tracks the visual appearance of Venus as Morning Star, her disappearance from view and then her return as Evening Star.

Visually speaking, Venus has three incarnations: Morning Star, Invisible (or Underworld) and Evening Star. Her eastern appearance as Morning Star is separated from her western appearance as Evening Star by 60 days of darkness (invisibility). As she slowly passes through the crucible of the solar fire, during her superior or exterior conjunction with the Sun, she is invisible to the outer vision of humans for approximately 60 days and nights. The ability of an astrologer to distinguish in a chart or horoscope the Morning Star appearance of Venus from her Evening Star appearance and invisible journey through the underworld gives another, important layer of interpretive ability, which is crucial to individualizing any reading of this important planet.

In 2010 while I was on a speaking tour in the American Southwest, shamanic astrologer Daniel Giamario[2] shared with me an extremely fascinating book. In *Star Trek to Hawa-i'i,* archaeoastronomy scholar H. Clyde Hostetter documents his attempts to discern the meaning of intricate markings on an ancient chalice. What Hostetter found was that the ancient Mesopotamian myth of Inanna is intimately tied to the actual visible (synodic) cycle of the planet Venus.[3] In this essay we shall see how the entire process of Venus's visual cycle is intricately related to her earliest mythology. I will also demonstrate how this mythology is a classic version of what Joseph Campbell has called the Monomyth, or Hero's Journey. Finally I will use the chart of President Barack Obama to give examples of how the information gained from this merger of ancient and modern views can inform and greatly add to the depth and richness of an astrological analysis of Venus.

Mythology Explains Astronomy

It is through the visual, phenomenological and astronomical model of the synodic cycle that Venus offers a rich heritage and mythic tapestry for modern astrologers to uncover. Scholars have often made the connection between the movements of the Goddess Inanna and the astronomy or visual phenomena of the planet Venus.[4] According to some very learned minds, parts of the mythology of Inanna seem to clearly be correlated with the astronomical/ visual cycle of Venus.[5] For scholars, the most obvious linkage seems to be that the tale of Inanna's descent to the Underworld describes the setting of the planet Venus in the east, followed by a period of invisibility and eventual rising in the west.[6] However, when the myths are strung together with a sound knowledge of astronomy and the phenomenology of the planet Venus, a more complete picture appears and the entire mythology of Inanna can be seen to be an explanation of the astronomical/visual cycle of Venus.

In the early parts of the myth we encounter Inanna as a young, inexperienced queen going to see Enki, the God of Wisdom. Enki welcomes Inanna and then proceeds to get drunk. In this inebriated state he gives her the 'me', the sacred instructions for setting up civilization. Inanna decides to keep them and departs. Later Enki, now sober, wants to take back the 'me'. He sends magical creatures to reclaim them from Inanna. With the help of her faithful servant, Ninshubar, Inanna rebuffs Enki's occult powers and delivers the 'me' – more than was originally handed over – to her city of Uruk.

The granting to Inanna of the 'me' – and her ability to keep them and miraculously deliver more than she was given by Enki – suggests an initiation and her worthiness to assume worldly power.

From this part of the myth we can gather that the Mesopotamians saw the first visible appearance, or heliacal rise in the east, as being near the beginning of the synodic cycle of Venus. Since Ninshubar means 'Queen of the East', scholars see this part of the myth as a clear reference to Venus in her Morning Star appearance.[7] Furthermore we can see a loop within this part of the myth which corresponds to a loop in the astronomy of Venus. The granting of powers, the attempt to re-take them and the ultimate success of Inanna in not only defending them but in miraculously and spontaneously producing more 'me' than were actually given her appear to be an explanation of the first 60 days of the visual journey of the planet Venus. The events of heliacal rise or first visible appearance in the east (during retrograde motion), station direct, resumption of forward motion and subsequent achievement of maximum brightness all happen during the early part of the 584-day cycle during the first two (of twenty) lunar cycles.

The next part of Inanna's myth holds the clearest evidence that it is an account of the astronomical movements of Venus's exterior or superior (direct) conjunction. This is the famous descent of Inanna to the Underworld.[8] At mid-life, after gaining her queenship and becoming married to her husband Dumuzi, Inanna turns 'from the great above to the great below'.[9] Similarly, after reaching maximum brilliancy as Morning Star, the planet Venus reaches her maximum elongation or separation from the Sun and begins to move back towards him, thus appearing gradually lower and dimmer in the sky. On her way to the Underworld Inanna passes through seven gates where she is removed of her royal regalia. Likewise the planet Venus makes seven conjunctions with a waning crescent Moon between her maximum brilliancy and eventual disappearance. Upon entering the Underworld Inanna is killed by her dark counterpart, her sister Ereshkigal, and hung on a hook. Through divine intervention from Enki, Inanna is resurrected. Enki sends magical beings who sprinkle the water and bread of life on Inanna 60 times. Hostetter notes that this correlates with the (approximate) 60 days that the planet Venus is invisible while near superior or exterior conjunction on the far side of the Sun.[10]

The next part of the myth and astronomy reveals a remarkable symmetry which portends the true essence of this myth/cycle. As Inanna made her *descent* to the Underworld, her husband Dumuzi made an *ascent*, taking her place on the throne. When Inanna is reborn she is told that someone must replace her in the Underworld. When she finds Dumuzi absorbed in his role as King rather than mourning her, she decides that he will be the one to replace her. Now

Inanna ascends the throne and Dumuzi must make the descent. The roles are reversed.[11] Similarly, while the planet Venus makes seven conjunctions with a *waning* crescent Moon as she descends on her way to invisibility, she makes seven conjunctions with a *waxing* crescent Moon as she climbs towards maximum brightness as Evening Star in the west.

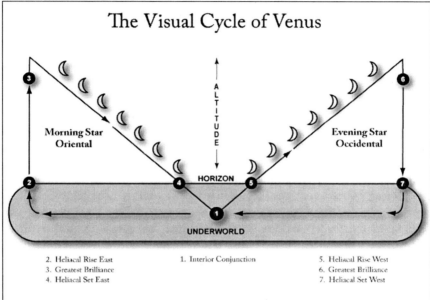

The Visual Cycle of Venus

Morning Star
Oriental

Evening Star
Occidental

ALTITUDE

HORIZON

UNDERWORLD

2. Heliacal Rise East	1. Interior Conjunction	5. Heliacal Rise West
3. Greatest Brilliance		6. Greatest Brilliance
4. Heliacal Set East		7. Heliacal Set West

The Visual Cycle of Venus, part 1 (rendered by Vanessa J. Keys, 2011)

Venus has 3 distinct visual phases: Morning Star, Underworld and Evening Star. As Morning Star she rises in the east before the Sun each morning. After 36 days she reaches maximum brightness. Then over seven months she slowly descends, becoming lower and dimmer each morning before she sets in the east, disappearing altogether into the Solar glare. Venus remains invisible in the Underworld phase for about 60 days before re-appearing, this time in the west as Evening Star. After seven months of slowly climbing higher and brighter, Venus reaches maximum brightness before stationing retrograde and then sets in the west, disappearing again briefly, before starting the whole 584-day cycle over again.

After Inanna returns to her throne and re-assumes her power as Queen, she takes pity on her husband Dumuzi and agrees to let his sister Geshtinanna split his time in the Underworld. Hereby Inanna formalizes the opening between above–below, conscious–unconscious and sets up a divine balance between masculine–feminine by establishing the annual ritual of ascent and descent for Dumuzi and his sister Geshtinanna in accord with the seasons. The King now enters the Underworld once a year and will emerge every six months, renewed by feminine wisdom and strength. In doing this Inanna has set up a Divine Order which brings lasting balance and harmony to her world.

A Classic and Universal Story

Inanna's return to power after facing an ordeal is a familiar part of many stories we encounter to this day. Wolkstein and Kramer call the collected myths the 'Cycle of Inanna'.[12] Other scholars[13] have noted that this cyclical nature makes Inanna's myth a clear example of what Joseph Campbell has called the Monomyth, or Hero/ine's adventure.[14] Campbell notes that across time, geography and culture, certain mythological elements remain constant. He divides the Hero/ine's journey into three basic parts: Separation, Initiation and Return.[15] In both the cycles – of the planet Venus and the goddess Inanna – we can clearly see these basic elements.

It should be noted that some modern astrologers do recognize the need to differentiate between the Morning Star and Evening Star incarnations of Venus. However, it is only by recognizing the 60-day invisible phase between them that we can see the parallels to the Hero/ine's Journey. These three phases together clearly mark Venus/Inanna's cycle as a classic early example of the Monomyth.

After retrograde conjunction, as the planet Venus passes between the Sun and Earth, she then moves out (separates) from the Earth (from a heliocentric point of view). This is like the heroine setting off for adventure. The Morning Star phase thus represents the 'day force' or yang/active nature of Venus and her role as seeker of power through relationships and connections. Likewise the young, acquisitive Inanna sets off on her adventure and seeks out relationships with Enki, Dumuzi and Ereshkigal.

After visually dimming and descending, Venus then disappears from view, lowering below the eastern horizon as she passes behind the Sun (from a chart-based, geocentric point of view) for 60 days. The longer invisible or 'combust' phase of Venus marks a time of extended darkness where the brightest star in the heavens (next to the Sun or Moon) cannot be seen. Likewise at mid-life Inanna undergoes an initiation into the death/rebirth mysteries of the Underworld.

After exterior or direct conjunction, as Venus passes on the far side of the Sun from Earth, she moves back towards the Earth (from a heliocentric point of view). This is like the heroine who returns with her boon. The Evening Star phase of Venus thus activates

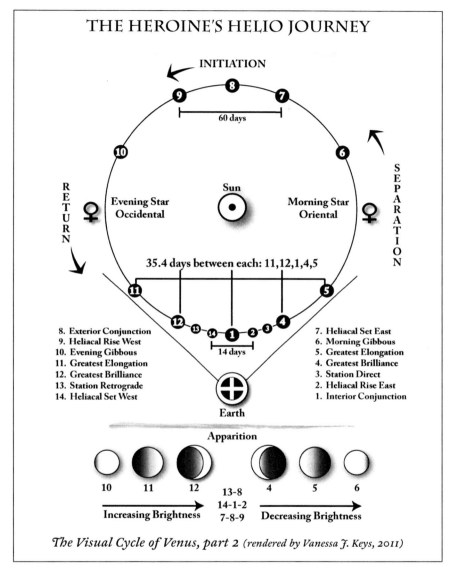

THE HEROINE'S HELIO JOURNEY

INITIATION

60 days

SEPARATION

RETURN

Sun

Evening Star
Occidental

Morning Star
Oriental

35.4 days between each: 11,12,1,4,5

14 days

8. Exterior Conjunction
9. Heliacal Rise West
10. Evening Gibbous
11. Greatest Elongation
12. Greatest Brilliance
13. Station Retrograde
14. Heliacal Set West

7. Heliacal Set East
6. Morning Gibbous
5. Greatest Elongation
4. Greatest Brilliance
3. Station Direct
2. Heliacal Rise East
1. Interior Conjunction

Earth

Apparition

10   11   12   13-8   4   5   6
                  14-1-2
Increasing Brightness   7-8-9   Decreasing Brightness

The Visual Cycle of Venus, part 2 (rendered by Vanessa J. Keys, 2011)

the 'night force' or yin/receptive nature of Venus as harmonizer and bestower of blessings. Likewise an older, wiser and initiated Inanna is resurrected and returns as Queen. She brings order to the kingdom by setting up an annual ritual of descent/ascent.

Modernizing a Classic: Applying a Modern Template to an Ancient Myth

This three-fold division of the myth/cycle mirrors a profoundly archetypal process of transformation which is clearly universal and can be seen in such varied examples as the triple way of mysticism (purgation, illumination, union), the three classic phases of alchemy (nigredo, albedo, rubedo), the way of the shaman (training, initiation, re-birth) and even in the phases of birth labor (contractions, pushing, reunion with mother). The psychiatrist Stanislav Grof has theorized that the processes of birth are so profound that they form structures or matrices in the psyche.[16] Thus when we experience significant change, or re-birth in our lives, these basic structures are spontaneously re-activated.

In fact this three-step process of transformation is so psychologically inherent that it forms the basic literary structure of many stories, books and movies. In his *Poetics* the Greek philosopher Aristotle put forth this three-part view of a plot structure, saying 'a whole is what has a beginning and middle and end.'[17] Aristotle called these the protasis, epitasis and catastrophe. The three acts serve the functions of setup (of the location and characters), confrontation (with an obstacle) and resolution (culminating in a climax and a dénouement). Aristotle was also the first to use the term *catharsis* with reference to the emotions. In drama catharsis describes the 'emotional cleansing' sometimes depicted in a play as occurring for one or more of its characters, as well as the same phenomenon as (an intended) part of the audience's experience. In astrology, by offering clients the opportunity to re-frame their life experiences in parallel with this basic structure, we can assist them to experience the liberation of catharsis in the theatre or dramaturgy of their own lives.

I have often found that a profound process emerges when I apply these basic stages of the Hero/ine's Journey to the astronomical turning points of the planet Venus, as well as the myth of Inanna, and simply describe them to a client. I have consistently seen clear correlations with the patterns and stories of the lives of living people: readers, listeners, clients and public figures. Quite often when I speak of these turning points and phases it brings up extremely visceral experiences which constitute major life events and themes for the person.

Obviously the basic three-act structure can be expanded and/ or elaborated upon. In the mid 1980s, expanding on the ideas that Joseph Campbell introduced, Christopher Vogler wrote a paper[18] on mythic structure in the popular media in such films as *Star Wars*.[19] Vogler's paper evolved into an international, best-selling book *The Writer's Journey*,[20] which outlines the more subtle shifts and phases within the story and expands upon the basic three-act structure, as well as describing the archetypal characters who navigate them.

Sometimes in consultation I will use these more subtle and nuanced dramatic elements to describe the mythological and archetypal elements of a particular part of the story within which a client seems to be living. But this is also usually re-framed within the basic three-act structure for the purposes of simplicity, consistency and ease of understanding and navigation.

In a consultation it is important for the astrologer to be able to take on the role of storyteller. Upon hearing these stories many clients will leap at the connections without any further help from the astrologer/storyteller. For others it may take the astrologer to make the connection and ask the client if it rings true for them. By understanding the connections between the astronomy and mythology of Venus and applying them to a person's chart and life experiences we can frame these within an archetypal journey of growth and transformation. This has tremendous potential to give people a sense of meaning, purpose and direction in their lives.

Taking It to the Next Level: Accessing the Hidden Venusian Treasure

Beyond the relationship between Venus as a visible phenomenon and the mythology of Inanna, I would also like to convey to the reader that when the natal placement of Venus stands out, astrologers have an additional set of tools for deepening their awareness and delineation of this planet. To explain how Venus might stand out in a chart, it is necessary to briefly outline how I prepare for a chart reading.

When preparing for a reading I have come to divide my analysis into three categories. I call these: Structural Considerations, the Mixing Board of the Soul, and Spiritual Considerations. These correspond roughly to the alchemical trinity of body (corpus), soul (anima) and mind (spiritus). This was also inspired by the physical, astral and 'causal' planes which Robert Blaschke used to organize the three types of progressions in his classic book on the subject.[21]

What I call structural considerations is what you are used to seeing discussed in modern astrology, which is notable for its 'cookbook' renditions. These represent the basic parts and pieces of the psyche/personality. Analogous to Aristotle's *material cause*[22] these exist only *in potentia* – that is, they are potentials of which the person may or may not be fully aware. I have found that individual parts and pieces of the chart are more likely to be high in awareness and active use under any of the following conditions:

1. The planet is located on or near the solstice or equinox (0° cardinal) or cross-quarter points (15° fixed) of the tropical zodiac.

2. The planet is located on or near a bright fixed star (especially the Royal Stars: Aldebaran currently near 10° Gemini, Regulus currently near 0° Virgo, Antares currently near 10° Sagittarius, and Fomalhaut currently near 4° Pisces).

3. The planet is located on or near an angle of the horoscope.

4. The planet is in close aspect to the Sun, Moon or Ascendant.

5. The planet is in a sign the element of which is either highly or sparsely represented in the horoscope.

6. The planet is the only planet in a hemisphere or quadrant.

7. The planet is the focal point of an aspect formation such as a T-square, or midpoint formation, especially the Sun–Moon midpoint.

What I call the mixing board of the soul is an estimate of the 'charge' or intensity of a planet. This is analogous to Aristotle's *formal cause* and is an attempt to discern the soul's *desire level* or intention to fully actualize a particular archetype. Planets stand out on this level via:

1. Essential dignity/debility.

2. Dispositorship (being the ruler of many other planets).

3. Connection to the nodal axis (mainly via aspect to, or dispositorship of the lunar nodes).

What I call spiritual considerations are the hidden factors in the chart which can only be accessed via awareness of synodic cycles. These are analogous to Aristotle's *final cause* and represent the *purpose* of a particular archetype being actualized. The natal horoscope is but a momentary snapshot of the heavens. Each of the planets within a horoscope came from somewhere and is going somewhere else. The place from which it originated is the pre-natal conjunction with the Sun. Like the pre-natal eclipse, the pre-natal conjunction of a planet with the Sun is an unseen area of the chart which is often very important and accentuated.[23] If the pre-natal conjunction stands out as a structural consideration and/or is on the mixing board of the soul (see above), then that planet is seen as highly important to the person's spiritual purpose.

Putting It into Practice: Venus in the Astrology of President Barack Obama

On the level of structural considerations, President Barack Obama's Venus is at 1° Cancer. Right away this should tell us that Venus will be a crucial planet for understanding this man. This is because Venus dwells on the Mundane Cross (or cardinal axis) which is formed by the solstice and equinoctial points. These are the very foundation of the tropical zodiac and represent critical turning points. Any planet at one of these points should not be underestimated in its importance to the chart and life of the individual. In fact it is quite interesting that any chart of the USA which is cast for either 2 or 4 July 1776 will have Venus near this same point (as well as Jupiter).

In *Horoscope Symbols* Robert Hand describes Venus as an attractive or unifying force which arises from within and makes people more aware of their true nature, more fully realized and more in tune with their world.[24] Obama's consistent appeals for us to recognize a unity of common principles, to realize and live up to our founding ideals and to forge new beginnings in world relations all share strong Venusian themes.

On the mixing board of the soul Venus stands out in Obama's chart via the sextile to the North Node. It is important for this soul to actualize Venus as a helpful tool in realizing the soul's main focus as a leader (North Node and its dispositor, the Sun, in Leo). Because Venus is low on the dispositor chain or tree (Venus does not rule any planets), it may be an archetype which seems to be at work behind the scenes, supporting many others. In other words it is generally important to and helpful for this soul to be of a loving nature, someone who is peaceable and sociable.

Given the importance of Venus in this chart, in my practice it is imperative to look at the pre-natal conjunction of Venus. For some time I have worked with the zodiacal position of the pre-natal Sun–Venus conjunction to establish the 'theme' within which the individual or natal Venus is operating. In her excellent, ground-breaking and comprehensive work on the subject, Arielle Guttman recently described the pre-natal conjunction of Venus, what she calls the Venus Star Point (VSP), as relating to the concept of Eros: 'An energy of creation... that existed before anything else... a deeply moving creative life force.'[25] It is as if the pre-natal conjunction (or VSP) is the Imum Coeli of Venus – a deep inner reservoir of Venusian energy from which the individual may draw strength and sustenance.

Obama's pre-natal conjunction is in the sign of Aries, the warrior. This is the perfect archetype to signify the political 'campaign' and winner-take-all contest of American politics. In addition to the emphasis placed on the Venus theme by sign, we can also expect to see more emphasis on the house of the pre-natal conjunction. Obama's pre-natal conjunction is in the natal 3rd (Whole Sign) House.[26] This indicates that he will be able to use communications skills as a writer and orator to activate and support his Venus theme of the warrior. It also shows his passion for local and grass roots community activism. We may also expect to see more emphasis on the sign and house of the *ruler* of the pre-natal interior conjunction. Pre-natal Mars, the ruler of Obama's pre-natal interior conjunction in Aries, is himself in the natal 6th House (Whole Sign), where natal Venus resides. This deepens and activates the emotional (Cancer) urge for public service indicated by the natal Venus position in the 6th.

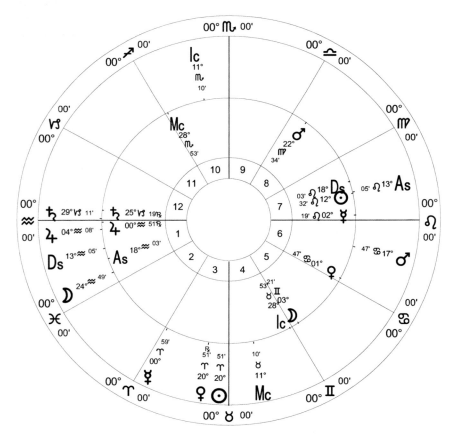

Inner Wheel: Barack Obama's Birth Chart
Outer Wheel: Obama's pre-natal Sun–Venus conjunction

Venus Themes by Transit

Venus has a very dependable and predictable cycle. Every 1.6 years (19 months or 584 days) we see the same kind of event – for instance, the interior/retrograde conjunction with the Sun. However, these successive events occur in different regions of the zodiac until five synodic cycles have been completed over the course of eight years. For example, Venus currently makes her conjunctions with the Sun in only five signs: Aries, Scorpio, Gemini, Capricorn and Leo. Interior/retrograde conjunctions recur in each of these signs every eight years. This forms the fabled pentagram of Venus in the sky.

Just as the pre-natal conjunction sets the Venus 'theme' for a nativity, the transiting interior conjunction can be seen to set the Venus theme for the following 19 months of Venus transits. We can clearly see this phenomenon at work in Obama's chart. Every eight years, when there's an interior/retrograde conjunction of Venus with the Sun in Gemini, we can see a repetitive theme in the events of his biography. We might call these 'Venus theme recurrences'.

The transit Venus theme of Gemini appears to be very important for Obama. It is interesting that when Venus is in her 19-month transit cycle, which begins with an interior conjunction in Gemini, Obama makes attempts to advance his political career to the next level. This illustrates the importance of the Gemini–Venus theme for Obama. He was elected to the Illinois Senate in 1996. The previous interior conjunction that year was at 20° Gemini (with Mercury in Taurus). Obama was elected to the United States Senate in 2004. That year's previous interior conjunction was at 17° Gemini (with Mercury in Gemini). So Obama made significant advances in his political career in the previous two cycles which began with an interior conjunction in Gemini – the sign of his natal Moon. He was elected State Senator after the first, and then US Senator following the second. In 2012 Obama will be seeking to become part of an elite group of two-term presidents. There have been only thirteen two-term presidents. The interior conjunction leading up to the 2012 US Election is at 15° Gemini, with Mercury also in Gemini. So Obama's attempt to advance his political career in Gemini-themed Venus cycles is a clear pattern. While this may not necessarily guarantee that he will succeed for a third time, it does seem to bode well.

A Closer Look at the Venus Phase

At 40 degrees of separation from the Sun, and earlier in the zodiac, Obama's natal Venus is shining high and bright as Morning Star.

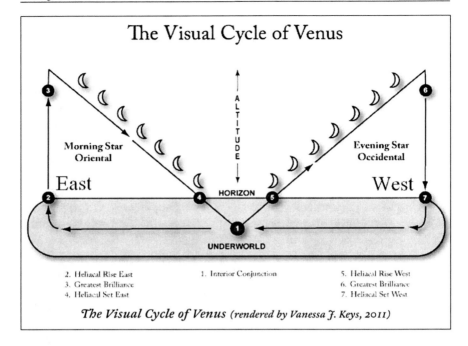

The Visual Cycle of Venus (rendered by Vanessa J. Keys, 2011)

This incarnation of Venus is like the heroine who sets off for adventure and emphasizes the yang/active nature of Venus as seeker and initiator of relationships, connections and power. We have certainly seen Obama make consistent appeals for a working relationship between people and government, between political parties, between nations and even between faiths.

Looking closer, we see that Obama's natal Venus is also in what we might call the 'descent phase' – that is, between maximum brightness (where Inanna is crowned Queen) and heliacal set in the east (where Inanna enters the Underworld). Being born during the descent of Venus signifies an 'ordeal' which the Hero/ine must face, like Inanna's famous descent to the Underworld. Here Venus gradually lowers and becomes dimmer before disappearing altogether for 60 days. During this descent Venus makes seven conjunctions with a waning balsamic phase crescent Moon. These can be seen as the seven gates through which Inanna passed where she was forced to surrender her royal regalia and enter the Underworld naked and humbled.

Very much like Inanna, Obama made his descent into Washingtonian politics at mid-life, while married with two children. Since arriving in Washington he has faced several ordeals, including speaking out against an ill-advised war, shepherding the country from the brink of economic collapse and working to create an historic law to provide basic health care as a right for all citizens. He has done all of this in the face of tremendous irrational anger and ill will from conservatives, whose refusal to deal with him makes it seem that they are only interested in bringing him down personally, much like Ereshkigal did to Inanna.

Shamanic astrologer Cayelin Castell writes that the spiritual purpose of this descent is like a fall from grace.[27] It helps us to see ourselves anew and rediscover our true center by forcing us to learn what needs to be let go. Seen in this light, it is as if Obama (or anyone born in this part of the Venus cycle) is 'destined' (or perhaps chose) to experience the ordeal of descent as a karmic or spiritual lesson.

Synodic Returns in Transit Analysis

Jungian analyst Sylvia Perera writes of the descent as an initiation into the Id – the dark chthonic and instinctive parts of human nature.[28] In that light it is very interesting that during the most recent return by transit of the descent phase of Venus, during the spring of 2011, Obama was responsible for the death of Osama bin Laden and at least partially responsible for the fall from power and death of Muammar Gaddafi. In fact Gaddafi was also born and came to power under this same phase of Venus.

When two planets, such as the Sun and Venus, return to the same relationship as at birth, astrologers call this a recurrence transit, phase angle return or synodic return. It's pretty remarkable that both Obama and Gaddafi were born near the same phase of Venus and that Gaddafi's coup and Obama's ultimatum for Gaddafi to step down all occurred relatively close to the same part of their respective Venus cycles. There are nearly 20 lunations in the 584-day Venus synodic cycle. Mathematically, the odds of four seemingly unrelated events to all occur within one lunation of the same point in a cycle seem pretty long.[29] Add in the fact that both men are leaders of countries and it boggles the mind. This is the hidden power of synodic awareness which astrologers can reclaim. These returns are a powerful opportunity to activate and actualize the natal potential.

Knowledge of the synodic cycle of Venus can greatly enhance our understanding of timing the emergence of personal destiny. When the natal placement of Venus stands out we have an additional set of tools for deepening our awareness and delineation of this planet. By understanding the astronomy of Venus and applying it to a person's chart and life experiences, we can frame these within a series of cycles which repeat predictably over time. This has tremendous potential to give people a sense of purposeful timing and direction in their lives.

Transits to Previous Sun–Venus Conjunction Degrees

We've seen how the theme of a transit Venus cycle showed up in Obama's chart and life, and how the transit return of the natal Venus phase can be a powerful window. Now let's examine a couple of specific and notable events. As we do so, it is important to remember that in addition to setting the archetypal theme for any transit Venus cycle of 19 months, the degree of the interior conjunction remains active or 'hot'. Thus any transit planets making conjunctions, either to the pre-natal or previous transit interior conjunction or the ruler of those signs, will be expected to give extra emphasis to that transit.

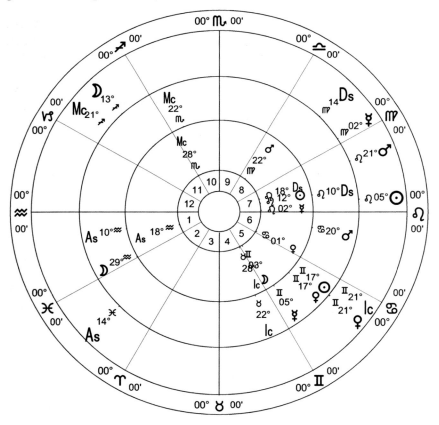

Inner Wheel: Barack Obama's Birth Chart
Middle Wheel: Sun–Venus conjunction of June 7, 2004
Outer Wheel: The Speech, July 27, 2004
(Inner planets and angles only)

In 2004 Obama delivered the Democratic National Convention Keynote Address. This is now known as 'The Speech' and it served to catapult him into national politics. The transit Venus cycle for this event began with an interior conjunction at 17° Gemini, with the ruler Mercury at 5° Gemini (conjunct his natal Moon). At the time of the Speech Venus was near maximum elongation (and brightness) as Morning Star (heroine seeking adventure) at 21° Gemini (near the previous interior conjunction degree). Also at the time of the Speech Mercury, the dispositor of Venus, was at 2° Virgo (square natal Moon). And at the time of the Speech the Sun was at 5° Leo (conjunct natal Mercury). Many modern astrologers dismiss Venus and other transits from personal planets as too quick and of minor importance. However, when viewed through a more nuanced lens, this transit seems to clearly stand out in what was a monumental event in this man's life.

We can see a similar process at work in the charts for Obama's election as President. When we chart the pre-natal Sun–Venus conjunction along with the previous Sun–Venus conjunction to the election and Venus in the election chart itself, we see a Grand Trine in Fire signs. While I certainly recognize that there were other astrological factors in play, I do think this is most noteworthy and we will see later that I am not the first astrologer to analyze US Presidential elections from a Venus-centric perspective.

Yet again we can see a similar process at work in another important time in Obama's life. For better or worse, the passage of Health Care reform is an extremely important event, as Obama achieved what other presidents had not come close to achieving in many decades. President Obama himself seems to consider this a very significant accomplishment.

As we noted before, Obama's pre-natal interior conjunction of Venus was 20° Aries (with Mars in Cancer in the 6th). The transit Venus cycle within which the passage of Health Care Reform is framed began with an interior conjunction at 7° Aries (with Mars in Pisces conjunct natal Chiron). At the time Obama signed the bill into law the Sun was at 2° Aries (near the previous interior conjunction degree). Venus had recently emerged as Evening Star (bestower of blessings) and was at 20° Aries (conjunct Obama's pre-natal interior conjunction of Venus). The ruler of Aries, Mars, was at 1° Leo (conjunct natal Mercury – ruler of Sect Light, the Moon). Once again, when viewed through a more nuanced lens, this Venus transit seems to clearly stand out in what was one of the most important events in this man's life.

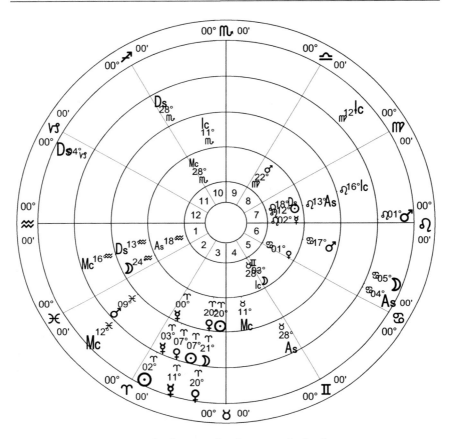

Inner Wheel: Barack Obama's Birth Chart
Middle Inner Wheel: Pre-natal Sun–Venus conjunction, April 10, 1961
Middle Outer Wheel: Sun–Venus conjunction, March 27, 2009
Outermost Wheel: Obama signs Health Reform Bill, March 23, 2010
(Inner planets and angles only)

Besides Obama's natal Venus being in the descent phase, there is another very interesting link to Venus and the difficulties of the second half of his first term. Regarding visibility as a phenomenon which flavors a planet's expression, we have a vivid example in the case of Venus and the US Presidential elections. Due to the synchronicity of the four-year election and eight-year Venus cycles, currently these happen with Venus shining brightly – either as Morning Star in the sign of Libra, or as Evening Star in the sign of Sagittarius. Two years later, at the time of mid-term elections, Venus is close to one of her conjunctions with the Sun in Scorpio, unable to be seen. Thus the mid-term Venus is in the Underworld incarnation. So the brightest planet in the sky at the time when any President is elected then becomes hidden when they face mid-term elections. With the President's party usually faring poorly in mid-terms, this visual disappearance of Venus every two years seems to correlate with the vagaries of voter opinion. It is almost as if the American voting public suffers from a kind of 'buyer's remorse' and they decide to take back the support they gave only two short years ago.

So what does the future hold for Obama? In the short term there are a couple of good Venusian reasons to think he will be re-elected. By secondary progression Obama is experiencing a Full Moon at 1° Aries–Libra, forming a T-square to his natal Venus on the cardinal (or World) axis. This does not look to me like the chart of a man leaving power. When we look at the previous Sun–Venus conjunction to the election, in Gemini, and Venus in the election chart itself, we see another trine relationship. Granted, it is not the Grand Trine of the 2008 election, but then again an incumbent does not need quite as much energy to get re-elected and Obama has succeeded with this placement before. Bernadette Brady has documented the power of Venus in US Presidential elections. By far, most upsets of incumbents or the incumbent party have been under the Morning Star Venus. Since 2012 is an Evening Star Venus election, this favors Obama.[30]

In conclusion, despite the sometimes myopic focus on the outer planets in modern astrology, I hope that it has become evident to the reader that Venus is an extremely complex archetype that is more than worthy of the astrologer's deep and close attention. The key to this new world of Venusian insight rests with an understanding of the basic astronomy of the synodic cycle of Venus. The power of this synodic awareness should not be underestimated. Much of science and thus the world as we know it today has its foundations in the millennia-old synodic awareness of the Mesopotamians. When harnessed and put into practice by the modern astrologer, this has tremendous potential to give people a deeper sense of meaning, purpose and direction in their lives. Upon deeper inspection, we discover that Venus is more than just an indicator of our urge for sex, love and/or money. We begin to see that it can be an extremely important planet for understanding the emergence of personal destiny.

References and Notes

1. Noel M. Swerdlow, *The Babylonian Theory of the Planets*, Princeton University Press, 1998, p. 16.

2. Daniel Giamario published a groundbreaking article on this topic in *The Mountain Astrologer* in 1997, which can also be found in the booklet *A Shamanic Investigation of Venus and Mars*, JCA Unlimited (Tucson, Arizona), 1997.

3. H. Clyde Hostetter, *Star Trek to Hawa-i'i*, The Diamond Press, 1991, chapters 7 and 8.

4. J. Cooley, 'Inana and Šhukaletuda: A Sumerian Astral Myth', *KASKAL* 5 (2008): 161–172, and 'Early Mesopotamian Astral Science and Divination in the Myth of Inana and Šukaletuda', *Journal of Ancient Near Eastern Religions* 5 (2008): 75–98.

5. According to the Cooley references above, these include the scholarship of Samuel Kramer, Jerrold Cooper, Clyde Hostetter, Konrad Volk and Bendt Alster, as well as Wilcke, Heimpel and Buccellati.

6. Being interior planets, Venus and Mercury rise and set over both horizons. Venus rises in the east, achieves maximum brightness and then sets in the east. This is followed by a 60-day period of darkness and then her rise in the west, followed by maximum brightness and setting in the west.

7. D. Wolkstein and S. Kramer, *Inanna, Queen of Heaven and Earth: Her Stories and Hymns from Sumer*, Harper & Row, 1983, p. 150.

8. *Ibid.*, p. 162. Wolkstein notes that Inanna's descent occurred during mid-life, while she was married with two children.

9. *Ibid.*, p. 52.

10. Hostetter, *Star Trek to Hawa-i'i*, p. 62.

11. Wolkstein and Kramer, *Inanna, Queen of Heaven and Earth*, p. 166.

12. *Ibid.*

13. S. Nicholson, 'The Perennial Philosophy of the Goddess Inanna', *International Journal of the Humanities*, Vol. I, 2003.

14. Joseph Campbell, *The Hero with a Thousand Faces*, MJF Books, 1949.

15. *Ibid.*, p. 30.

16. See, for instance, S. Grof, 'The Shamanic Journey: Observations from Holotropic Therapy', in *Shaman's Path: Healing, Personal Growth and Empowerment*, ed. Gary Doore, Shambhala, 1988.

17. See http://www.perseus.tufts.edu/hopper/text?doc=Perseus%3Atext%3A1999.01.0056%3Asection%3D1450b

18. See http://www.thewritersjourney.com/hero%27s_journey.htm

19. Joseph Campbell & Bill Moyers, *The Power of Myth*, Doubleday, 1988.

20. C. Vogler, *The Writer's Journey: Mythic Structure for Writers*, Michael Wise Productions, 2007.

21. R. Blaschke, *Astrology: A Language of Life, Volume I – Progressions*, Earthwalk School of Astrology, 1998.

22. See Robert Hand's article, 'On Matter and Form in Astrology', for a discussion of Aristotle's Causes in relation to astrology: *ARHAT Journal*, http://www.arhatmedia.com/Matter&FormArticle.htm

23. R. Blaschke, *Astrology: A Language of Life, Volume V – Holographic Transits*, Earthwalk School of Astrology, 2006. Robert Blaschke is one of the few astrologers I know of who looked at these pre-natal conjunctions. See his excellent Volume V for an in-depth look at his approach to synodic work with all the planets.

24. R. Hand, *Horoscope Symbols,* Para Research (Gloucester, MA), 1981, pp. 58–61.

25. A. Guttman, *Venus Star Rising: A New Cosmology for the 21st Century,* Sophia Venus Productions (Santa Fe, NM), 2010.

26. The chart for Barack Obama is cast for August 4, 1961 at 7:24pm, Honolulu, Hawaii. This data receives an 'AA' rating as it is based on the birth certificate published by the Obama campaign (http://static. politifact.com.s3.amazonaws.com/graphics/birthCertObama.jpg) which was deemed authentic by fact check dot org (http://www. factcheck.org/elections-2008/born_in_the_usa.html).

27. http:// shamanicastrology.com/astro-news/the-first-venus-gate-december-2-2010/

28. S. Perera, *Descent to the Goddess,* Inner City Books (Toronto), 1981.

29. All four events happened during a 30-day time frame within the 584-day cycle of Venus:
    (1) Gaddafi was born June 7, 1942 – 125 days after the Sun–Venus conjunction of February 2, 1942.
    (2) Obama was born August 4, 1961 –116 days after the Sun–Venus conjunction of April 10, 1961.
    (3) Gaddafi's rise to power via coup occurred on September 1, 1969 – 146 days after the Sun–Venus conjunction of April 8, 1969.
    (4) Obama's ultimatum to Gaddafi was delivered on March 18, 2011 – 141 days after the Sun-Venus conjunction of October 28, 2010.
    For Gaddafi's birth date, see http://www.guardian.co.uk/ world/2011/oct/20/muammar-gaddafi-timeline/ and http://www. astrotheme.com/portraits/w5pb54Q9t475.htm

30. B. Brady, 'Standing in the Radiance of Venus – A visual astrology view of the US presidential elections and its self-imposed union with Venus', http://www. zyntara.com/VisualAstrologyNewsletters/ van_Sept2008/VAN_Sept2008.htm

Nick Dagan Best
A Personal Biography

I feel blessed to be a 21st-century astrologer. Before I knew astrology I used to think most people were irrational lunatics. Now that I have learned astrology I've managed to figure out how some of them got that way. Since 1999 I have been developing my own database of natal and event charts for a great variety of historical and biographical subjects using specialized astrology software, a collection that now totals well over 40,000 pieces of data. It allows me to observe astrological phenomena at a capacity that would have been impossible before I started doing this. Prior to discovering astrology I was one of the peculiar history buffs who memorizes a lot of calendar dates, a fact-happy chronology fanatic. Astrology brings a whole new platform to that kind of interest. Every astrological chart can be seen and used as being part of a vast and complex calendar, one that gives every day of recorded history a unique and distinguishable value that it wouldn't otherwise have. It is my contention that the studies of recorded history and astrology belong to the same, greater, discipline.

Chapter Three

HIGHLIGHTS AND ECHOES
The Venus Synodic Cycle in Mundane Astrology

NICK DAGAN BEST

In modern astrology the simple archetypal delineation of the planet Venus associates it with matters like social peace, love, harmony and feminine values. However, the astrological Venus is hardly one-dimensional. Venus, like Mercury, has a two-sided nature by virtue of its alternating role as both a morning star (preceding the Sun in zodiacal order) and evening star (following the Sun in zodiacal order). If identified within the context of its complete cycle, Venus can also be linked to social discord, dishonesty, betrayal, defiance and rebellion.

The eight-year synodic cycle of Venus – the time it takes to return to the same position relative to the geocentric position of the Sun – is as useful to an astrologer for observing patterns of renewal and change as Solar and Lunar cycles are. Every nine months there is a geocentric conjunction between the Sun and Venus. However, these conjunctions alternate between what are called 'inferior conjunctions' and 'superior conjunctions'. Simply put, inferior conjunctions involve the Sun conjunct retrograde Venus, while superior conjunctions involve the Sun conjunct direct Venus. Inferior conjunctions mark the transformation of Venus from evening star to morning star, while superior conjunctions mark the opposite, from morning star to evening star. The interval between every two Venus inferior conjunctions or every two Venus superior conjunctions is eighteen months.

The focus of this article is going to be the Venus retrograde phase, and more specifically, just one of the five Venus retrograde phases that occur in the overall Venus synodic cycle. The period between the retrograde station of Venus – when it appears to stop and then start moving backwards through the zodiac – and the direct station of Venus – when it appears to stop again and start moving forward again – is about forty days. Transiting Venus goes retrograde five times every eight years, in pretty much the same five spots in the zodiac. With every successive eight-year cycle, the retrograde and direct stations occur about two-to-three days and two-to-three zodiacal degrees earlier than the previous time, so that every 120 years the Venus retrograde wanders back to the preceding Tropical sign. For example, on May 15, 2012 transiting Venus stations retrograde at 23° Gemini; eight years earlier on May 17, 2004 it stationed retrograde at 25° Gemini; eight year prior to that on May 19, 1996 it stationed retrograde at 28° Gemini; another eight years before that on May 22, 1988 it stationed retrograde at 0° Cancer, the Tropical sign in which Venus had been stationing retrograde every eight years until then for the preceding 120 years.

The Venus retrograde period itself is preceded and followed by the planet's greatest elongation from the Sun, days when the planet is at its brightest in the sky because it is at its farthest possible distance from the Sun. The greatest elongation of Venus as evening star occurs about fifty days prior to the retrograde station, while the greatest elongation of Venus as morning star occurs about fifty days following the direct station. For the purpose of this article, I will be referring to the 'Venus retrograde phase', which includes the entire approximately **140-day period it takes from the greatest elongation as evening star, to the retrograde period, to the greatest elongation as morning star**.

Part One: Venus and U.S. Presidential Inaugurations

Since George Washington's first presidential inauguration in 1789, the United States has kept a tight schedule of four-year intervals between every presidential election/inauguration. Ironically, for a country that uses a five-pointed star to represent every state in the Union on its flag (from the original thirteen to the present fifty), the five-pointed star design, deliberately or otherwise, is an accurate pictorial depiction of the eight-year Venus synodic cycle.

Washington's first inauguration occurred in New York City on April 30, 1789.[1] Following that, presidential inaugurations were always held on March 4, unless that date fell on a Sunday (as it did in 1821, 1849, 1877 and 1917), in which case it was held on Monday, March 5. As of 1937, however, the date of presidential inaugurations was moved up to January 20, so as to cut down the waiting time for new administrations to take office. Again, if that date fell on a Sunday, as it did in 1957 and 1985, the ceremony was held the following day instead.

The peculiar thing about this change in schedule is how it relates to the date of Venus' greatest elongation as evening star. On the day of Washington's second inauguration – the first one that was held on March 4[2] – Venus was at 0° Taurus (otherwise known as the first degree of Taurus), fourteen days prior to its greatest elongation as evening star and sixty-two days prior to its retrograde station at 15° Gemini. Curiously, Venus had been at 2° Taurus at the time of Washington's first inauguration four years earlier in 1789, approaching a superior conjunction with the Sun. It is almost as if the nation's early lawmakers deliberately chose the March 4 date for future inaugurations for the select purpose of having a Venus zodiacal return to the first one. Since the Venus synodic cycle repeats itself every eight years, every second presidential inauguration often occurred with Venus transiting at 0° Taurus, although it could sometimes be found at 29° Aries, as it was at the first inaugurations of Thomas Jefferson in 1801,[3] James Madison in 1809[4] and James Monroe in 1817.[5]

With every successive eight-year cycle, the presidential inaugurations got closer and closer to both the date of Venus' greatest elongation as evening star and its retrograde station in Taurus. On March 4, 1841, the very day William Henry Harrison was inaugurated the 9th president of the United States,[6] Venus was at 0° Taurus and at its greatest elongation from the Sun as evening star. On that day Harrison famously delivered what still stands as the longest presidential inaugural address in U.S. history, nearly two hours long, while underdressed for the cold rainy day. He died of pneumonia exactly one month later, April 4,[7] marking the shortest presidential term in the nation's history. On the day of his death transiting Venus was now at 25° Taurus and only nineteen days away from stationing retrograde at 2° Gemini.

Twenty-four years later, Abraham Lincoln was inaugurated for his second term as the 16th U.S. president on March 4, 1865,[8] with transiting Venus once again at 0° Taurus, forty-three days prior to its retrograde station. His assassination on April 14 that year,[9] the first in the nation's history, occurred while transiting Venus was one day away from its retrograde station at 25° Taurus, the same degree it had been on the day of William Henry Harrison's death in 1841. Sixteen years after that, James Garfield was inaugurated the 20th U.S. president on March 4, 1881,[10] with transiting Venus yet again at 0° Taurus, now eleven days following its greatest elongation as evening star and thirty-eight days preceding its retrograde station. He was shot on July 2 that year,[11] thirty-eight days following the Venus direct station. Transiting Venus on that day was again at 25° Taurus, the same degree where it had been on the days Harrison and Lincoln died. However, Garfield himself did not die from his wounds until September 19,[12] probably due more to infections caused by unsanitary doctors than from the actual bullet that pierced his body.

As the years went by, presidential inaugurations gradually wandered further away from the date of Venus' greatest elongation as evening star, while wandering closer to the date of its retrograde station. Not only that, but precession had shifted presidential inaugurations away from the 0° Taurus position. In 1889 Benjamin Harrison was the last president to be inaugurated with Venus at 0° Taurus.[13] McKinley in 1897, (Theodore) Roosevelt in 1905,[14] Wilson in 1913,[15] Harding in 1921[16] and Hoover in 1929[17] were all inaugurated while transiting Venus was in late Aries. By the time of Hoover's inauguration on March 4, 1929,[18] transiting Venus was now only twenty-five days away from its retrograde station.

The following Venus synodic cycle, in 1937, coincided with the year of Franklin Roosevelt's second inauguration as 32nd U.S. president (his first inauguration occurred at the other part of the Venus cycle, the one not discussed in this article). Had things remained unchanged, he would have been inaugurated on March 4 that year, with transiting Venus now at 26° Aries, twenty-three days away from its retrograde station. But this was not the case. As mentioned earlier, the date of presidential inaugurations was moved ahead to January 20, as it was no longer necessary to allow as much time for the changeover of administrations. With this new date, January 20, 1937,[19] Roosevelt was inaugurated while transiting Venus was at 16° Pisces, a safe sixty-six days away from its retrograde station. Amazingly – possibly by design but probably unwittingly – the new date moved the inauguration to a day that preceded Venus' greatest elongation as evening star by sixteen days, pretty much as it had been in the days of George Washington. Astrologically, it was almost as if Congress had changed the date as a symbolic gesture to realign the country with its historical principles and intentions.

Every eight years following 1937, transiting Venus was at 16°–17° Pisces on inauguration day, edging closer and closer to the date of its greatest elongation as evening star. Dwight Eisenhower,[20] John F. Kennedy,[21] Richard Nixon,[22] Jimmy Carter,[23] Bill Clinton,[24] George W. Bush[25] and Barack Obama[26] all began their administrations under this transit. Ronald Reagan's second inauguration occurred with transiting Venus at 18° Pisces, due to the fact that it was held on Monday, January 21, 1985,[27] instead of the 20th, due to its being a Sunday. Bill Clinton's first inauguration, on January 20, 1993,[28] occurred on the very day Venus was at its greatest elongation as evening star. Since then, as it was after 1840, transiting Venus on inauguration day has been slowly receding from its greatest elongation and slowly moving closer to its retrograde station, which now happens in Aries instead of Taurus. Perhaps at some point in the future, American lawmakers will again see fit to move the date of inauguration ahead.

Part Two: Venus and the State of Empires
Mundane astrologers are rather attached to the idea of using national charts as the central axis by which they study the past, present and future of a given nation. Certainly, as events in the history of regions, the establishment of a new kind of organized government is a major affair, and inception charts for these states are far from useless or irrelevant. But they don't do anything to connect the successive types of regimes that govern regions from revolution to revolution. Each inception chart specifically addresses the state that began at the time the chart was cast, and presumably stops being relevant once that state comes to an end and the nation becomes something else. Countries are constantly re-invented, and it is hard to argue that the inception chart of, say, the Russian Federation is going to be useful for studying the earlier histories of Tsarist Russia or the Soviet Union. Of course, since the native population of most countries grew gradually over millennia, any true notion of an 'inception chart' is lost to pre-history. The astrologer has little apparent choice but to study every inception chart independently for every new state.

However, there is another approach to studying the astrology of nations. The observation of recurring planetary synodic cycles enables the astrologer to transcend the beginnings and endings of governmental regimes. These cycles are a means to see a society grow and change in its own natural time, for which the establishment of a new state is merely a milestone in a much greater journey. Planetary synodic cycles are easy to learn and follow, but their simplicity allows one to explore history in its complexity, without trying to tie a nation down to its political definition.

The eight-year return of the Venus retrograde phase in tropical Taurus-to-Aries (or Gemini-to Taurus, as it was in the early 1800s, the same segment of the cycle examined in Part One of this article) has an interesting relationship to the recent history of Russia and Germany. In both cases we can 'look in' on what was going on in both countries for a specific 140-day period (from the greatest elongation of Venus as evening star preceding the 40-day retrograde cycle, to the one as morning star that follows it) that occurs once every eight years, and find a striking number of major events and nativities related to the history of those countries.

Every date listed below falls within this one specific Venus retrograde phase that occurs once every eight years, accounting for approximately only one-twentieth of total time. Included in the following are three events that fall just outside the 140-day phase, by no more than ten days, but I have included them for consideration within the context of the larger story. Instead of introducing these events as one long chronological list, I have divided them into smaller lists by general topic. In some topics the Russian and German dates are separated; in others they are combined into one list.

Births
Deaths
Royal Weddings
National Pride
Administration
Diplomacy
Military
Dissidents

BIRTHS: Russia

Sergei Witte
June 29, 1849[29] – Venus at 24° Taurus, 26 days following direct station, 22 days prior to greatest elongation as morning star
Witte was the first Prime Minister of Imperial Russia, appointed in 1905 after he had negotiated the Russian side of the Treaty of Portsmouth that ended the Russo-Japanese war, and then convinced Tsar Nicholas II to issue the October Manifesto in the wake of the 1905 Russian Revolution. This led to the adoption of the first Russian Constitution and the creation of an elected Duma (parliament) the following year. However, Witte was forced to resign within seven months of taking office.

Grand Duke Sergei Alexandrovich
May 11, 1857[30] – Venus retrograde at 18° Taurus
Grand Duke Sergei was both the uncle and brother-in-law of Tsar Nicholas II, and served as Governor of Moscow until shortly before his assassination in 1905, which occurred during the same 140-day Venus period as his birth (see **Deaths**). His brother, Tsar Alexander III, had trusted him more than any of his other siblings, and he enjoyed a close relationship with Nicholas, thanks in part to the fact that their wives were sisters.

Pavlo Skoropadskyi
May 15, 1873[31] *– Venus retrograde at 9° Taurus*
Skoropadskyi was a Ukrainian general in the Imperial Russian Army who took power in a German-backed coup against the Bolshevik-backed Ukrainian People's Republic government in 1918. His reign lasted less than a year, until the end of World War I. Like Grand Duke Sergei Alexandrovich and Adolf Hitler, Skoropadskyi was both born and killed during this same 140-day Venus period, as he died following an Allied bombing in Bavaria on April 26, 1945.

Alexander Kerensky
May 4, 1881[32] *– Venus retrograde at 12° Taurus*
Kerensky was the second Prime Minister of the Russian provisional government, which came into power after the abdication of Tsar Nicholas II in March 1917. He took over from Georgy Lvov, who had been appointed by the Tsar but couldn't muster support for his administration. Kerensky was responsible for arming the Bolsheviks, who ultimately opposed him and took control during the 'October Revolution' of November 1917.

BIRTHS: Germany

Alfred von Tirpitz
19 March 1849[33] *– Venus at 13° Taurus, 17 days following greatest elongation as evening star, 33 days prior to retrograde station*
In the years leading up to WWI, German Grand Admiral Tirpitz spearheaded the development of German naval power, from torpedo boats to submarines, with the aim of making Germany a world power. The Tirpitz Plan provoked Great Britain into a naval arms race and contributed to the bad blood between the two nations in the years before the war.

Bernhard von Bülow
May 3, 1849[34] *– Venus retrograde at 27° Taurus*
German Chancellor under Kaiser Wilhelm II from 1900 to 1909, Bülow was generally a 'yes' man to the Kaiser, and spent much of his time covering up for Wilhelm's various gaffes and misfires. He favored a policy of German military and imperial expansion during his time in office, and encouraged Wilhelm's and Germany's involvement in what became the Moroccan Crisis (see **Diplomacy**).

Erich Ludendorff

April 9, 1865[35] – Venus at 24° Taurus, 41 days following greatest elongation as evening star, 7 days prior to retrograde station

German Quartermaster General, he was joint head of the German military with Paul von Hindenburg (who had natal Venus retrograde in Libra) during WWI. An early ally of Adolf Hitler – he participated in Hitler's famous Beer Hall Putsch of 1923 – he eventually broke with the future Führer for being too moderate. His theory of 'Total War' *(Der Totale Krieg)* argued that peace was merely an interval between wars.

Adolf Hitler

April 20, 1889[36] – Venus retrograde at 16° Taurus

If I need to explain who this man was, you probably have some other reading to do. I might as well warn you now, this jerk is going to keep showing up for the duration of this article. Hitler began and ended his life during this 140-day Venus period (see **Deaths**), and many other important turning points in his life also occurred during it (see **National Pride, Dissidents**).

Albert Speer

March 19, 1905[37] – Venus at 9° Taurus, 33 days following greatest elongation as evening star, 17 days prior to retrograde station

'The Nazi who said "sorry"', Speer was First Architect of the Third Reich and among Hitler's closest friends and confidants. Speer's design work was central to the impact of the massive Nazi rallies of the 1930s, and Hitler expressed personal warmth and affection for him. Speer had a lucky streak that saw him escape not only Nazi retribution after the attempt on Hitler's life in 1944, but also a death sentence at the Nuremburg trials.

DEATHS: Russia

Tsar Paul

March 24, 1801[38] – Venus at 18° Taurus, 4 days following greatest elongation as evening star, 43 days before retrograde station

The son of Catherine the Great, Paul reigned for only four years before he was assassinated in a military coup. His son, Alexander, who succeeded him to the throne, apparently knew about the plot to overthrow his father, but naively thought Paul would be allowed to live.

Tsarevitch Nicholas

April 24, 1865[39] – Venus retrograde at 24° Taurus

The oldest son of Tsar Alexander II and the heir to the Russian throne, Nicholas died of tuberculosis in Nice, France. On his deathbed he requested that his fiancée, Princess Dagmar of Denmark, marry his brother, the future Tsar Alexander III, instead.

Tsar Alexander II

March 13, 1881[40] – Venus at 7° Taurus, 20 days following greatest elongation as evening star, 29 days prior to the retrograde station

The reformer Tsar, Alexander II had freed the serfs in 1861, and was planning further major governmental reforms when he was assassinated by bomb-wielding nihilists in the streets of St. Petersburg. Alexander was also married during this 140-day Venus period (see **Royal Weddings**).

Grand Duke Sergei Alexandrovich

February 17, 1905[41] – Venus at 14° Aries, 3 days following greatest elongation as evening star, 47 days prior to retrograde station

The third member of the Russian Romanov family to be assassinated during this 140-day Venus period in just over 100 years, the Grand Duke was killed by a bomb-wielding member of the Social Revolutionary Party in the wake of the 1905 Russian Revolution. The 'Bloody Sunday' massacre – in which the military opened fire on a peaceful demonstration in the streets of St. Petersburg – had occurred barely a month earlier. As previously stated, Sergei began and ended his life during the same 140-day Venus period (see **Births**).

Mikhail Tukhachevsky

June 12, 1937[42] – Venus at 5° Taurus, 33 days following direct station, 15 days prior to greatest elongation as morning star

Soviet General and one-time commander-in-chief of the Red Army, Tukhachevsky was possibly the most prominent and conspicuous victim of Stalin's great purges of the 1930s. He was a fearless soldier who had escaped German prison camps at least four times during WWI, and Stalin regarded him as enough of a threat to plot his murder almost a decade in advance. Considering that war with Germany was only four years in the future, Stalin was lucky to have defeated Hitler without him.

Josef Stalin

March 5, 1953[43] – Venus at 26° Aries, 33 days following greatest elongation as evening star, 17 days prior to retrograde station

Stalin left this world during the same 140-day Venus period that took so many of his greatest nemeses, including Tukhachevsky, Hitler and Franklin Roosevelt. In fact, many great figures of World War II died during Venus retrograde phases, including Dwight Eisenhower, Charles de Gaulle and Queen Wilhelmina of the Netherlands. The exceptions were Winston Churchill and Canadian Prime Minister William Lyon Mackenzie King, both of whom were born with Venus retrograde.

DEATHS: Germany

Former Empress Augusta Viktoria

April 11, 1921[44] – Venus retrograde at 8° Taurus

Wife of the former Kaiser Wilhelm II, 'Dona' died while in exile with her husband in Doorn, Netherlands, where they escaped after his abdication at the end of WWI. He remarried a year-and-a-half later, on the date of the following Venus retrograde station (in Sagittarius) on November 5, 1922. Dona and Wilhelm were also married during this same Venus retrograde phase (see **Royal Weddings**).

Prince Heinrich of Prussia

April 20, 1929[45] – Venus retrograde at 29° Aries

Eight years after the death of his first wife, the former Kaiser Wilhelm II lost his brother Heinrich to lung cancer. One could speculate that if Heinrich had been Kaiser instead of his older brother, there might not have been any world wars.

Adolf Hitler

April 30, 1945[46] – Venus retrograde at 18° Aries

Yes, him again (see **Births**).

ROYAL WEDDINGS: Russia

Grand Duke Nicholas marries Charlotte of Prussia

July 1, 1817[47] – Venus at 6° Gemini, 30 days following direct station, 18 days preceding greatest elongation as morning star

The future Tsar Nicholas I, younger brother of Tsar Alexander I, was not in line for the throne when he married his bride, Princess Charlotte of Prussia, on her 19th birthday. His older brother, Constantine, would renounce his claim to royal succession in favor of marrying his second wife, a Polish countess, in 1822, three years before the Tsar's death. Nicholas' ascension to the crown following his brother's death in 1825 was complicated by the fact that Constantine's renouncement had never been made public, resulting in the Decembrist revolt of army officers loyal to him. Nicholas' first act as Tsar was to have them killed, beginning his thirty-year reign of intolerance towards political rebels throughout Europe.

Tsarevitch Alexander marries Marie of Hesse
April 28, 1841[48]– Venus retrograde at 2° Gemini
The son of Tsar Nicholas, the future Tsar Alexander II, married his wife, Princess Marie of Hesse, during the same Venus retrograde phase that his parents were married under and that he would eventually die under (see **Deaths**). Alexander insisted on marrying Marie, despite the fact that she was the product of an affair between her royal mother and a common man – even threatening to renounce the throne if necessary. Their marriage produced eight children, although Alexander also had three children with his mistress, Princess Catherine Dolgoruki, whom he married on July 6, 1880, a month after Marie's death and nine months before his own. It bears mentioning that Alexander's heir, the Tsarevitch Nicholas, was also supposed to get married during this same Venus retrograde phase, but died before it could happen (see **Deaths**).

ROYAL WEDDINGS: Germany

Prince Wilhelm marries Princess Augusta Viktoria
February 27, 1881[49] – Venus at 25° Aries, 6 days following greatest
elongation as evening star, 43 days prior to retrograde station
The wedding of the future Kaiser Wilhelm II joined the German royal houses of Hohenzollern and Holstein. Princess Augusta Viktoria, known as 'Dona', would also die during the same Venus retrograde phase as her wedding, forty years later (see **Deaths**).

Crown Prince Wilhelm marries Duchess Cecile
June 6, 1905[50] – Venus at 4° Taurus, 18 days following direct station,
30 days prior to greatest elongation as morning star
He was the eldest son of Wilhelm and Dona, the heir to the German throne, which he would abdicate alongside his father at the end of WWI in 1918. During the course of the marriage Wilhelm had affairs with several women, including the opera singer Geraldine Farrar and the dancer Mata Hari.

Princess Viktoria Luise marries Ernest Augustus

May 24, 1913[51]– Venus at 26° Aries, 8 days following direct station,
41 days prior to greatest elongation as morning star

The wedding of the Kaiser's youngest child and only daughter marked the last occasion that Wilhelm and his cousins, King George V and Tsar Nicholas II, were all in the same place at the same time. Just over a year before war would break out between their respective countries, Wilhelm was already deeply suspicious of the friendship between his two cousins, and did everything he could to keep them from being alone during the wedding party. Later, during the war, he would complain that they had been conspiring together even during this wedding celebration.

Adolf Hitler marries Eva Braun

April 29, 1945[52]– Venus retrograde at 18° Aries

This was not really a royal wedding in the typical sense, although Hitler was still Germany's Führer for the next day, until he and his new bride committed suicide together as Soviet troops advanced from a few hundred yards away (see **Deaths**).

NATIONAL PRIDE: Russia

Romanov Dynasty 300th Anniversary

March 6, 1913[53] – Venus at 29° Aries, 22 days following greatest
elongation as evening star, 28 days prior to retrograde station

Just eight years after the 1905 Russian Revolution, and four short years before he would be forced to abdicate, Tsar Nicholas II and his family embarked on a Russian tour to celebrate the tercentenary of the Romanov House. For the next ten weeks the Tsar's entourage was engaged in a long succession of formal receptions, opulent balls and festive carriage processions. With war in the Balkans already raging, the First World War that would lead to the fall of the Russian crown was less than a year-and-a-half away. But for a few short weeks the celebrations gave the impression that the Romanov dynasty would be around for at least another three hundred years.

Yuri Gagarin orbits the Earth

April 12, 1961[54] – Venus retrograde at 20° Aries

The last great achievement of the Soviet space plan until the Mir space station's launch twenty-five years later, Yuri Gagarin's *Vostok 1* capsule made its historic 108-minute flight around the Earth. As the first human being to orbit the planet, he later became an international hero. Gagarin himself was born on March 9, 1934, just eleven days after Venus stationed direct in Aquarius.

NATIONAL PRIDE: Germany

Crash of the Zeppelin Hindenburg
May 6, 1937[55] *– Venus retrograde at 19° Aries*
The pride of Nazi Germany, the airship Hindenburg famously exploded into flames as it was landing at Lakehurst Naval Air Station in New Jersey, killing 36 people. Commercial flights on airplanes were still two years away from happening, and the trans-Atlantic Zeppelin voyages were just beginning their second year as a business venture, but the tragedy cut the industry down instantly. Curiously, Herbert Morrison, the reporter whose play-by-play account of the fire became as iconic as the event itself ('Oh, the humanity!'), was born on May 14, 1905 and had natal Venus retrograde at 28° Aries.

ADMINISTRATION: Russia

Mikhail Gorbachev
March 11, 1985[56] *– Venus at 22° Aries, 48 days following greatest*
elongation as evening star, 2 days prior to retrograde station
Gorbachev was named the 6th General Secretary of the Soviet Union after the deaths of the previous two men to hold that post – Yuri Andropov, who held it for fifteen months before his death in February 1984, and Konstantin Chernenko, who held it for only thirteen months before he died on March 10, 1985. Just as the death of Josef Stalin during this same Venus retrograde phase opened the door to reform within the Soviet Union, Chernenko's death allowed another door to open. Gorbachev would be the last Soviet leader, the man who would eventually end the Soviet Union for good.

Boris Yeltsin wins referendum
April 25, 1993[57] *– Venus at 3° Aries, 3 days following direct station,*
47 days prior to greatest elongation as morning star
With a constitutional crisis brewing, the newly formed Russian Federation was at a crucial crossroads. Just over a year since the dissolution of the Soviet Union, Russian President Boris Yeltsin succeeding in receiving the confidence of the new Russian electorate in a four-question referendum, seeking to hold early elections that would allow the new government to introduce a new constitution. Despite winning the support of the Russian people, Yeltsin still had

remnants of the old regime in his way, and it would take an armed showdown the following October – in which almost 200 people died – before he could proceed with his mandate.

DIPLOMACY

Diet of Porvoo (Russia)
March 29, 1809[58] – Venus at 23° Taurus, 15 days following greatest elongation as evening star, 36 days prior to retrograde station
On March 13, 1809, King Gustav IV of Sweden, who had been blamed for his country's poor war performance against a Russian invasion of their Finnish territory the previous year, was arrested. Two weeks later, as Gustav agreed to sign his abdication, Tsar Alexander I came to Finland and pledged to preserve Finnish sovereignty as a new Grand Duchy of Russia.

Hünkâr Iskelesi Treaty (Russia)
July 8, 1833[59] – Venus at 1° Gemini, 30 days following direct station, 18 days prior to greatest elongation as morning star
The Ottoman Empire had been adversaries with Russia since the days of Catherine the Great, and they would be again in a few decades. But war with Egypt prompted the Ottomans to appeal to Tsar Nicholas I to come to their aid with troops. In return, Nicholas asked for and received exclusive rights to sail warships through the Dardanelle straits, which in turn enflamed British suspicions towards Russia's growing military influence.

London Straits Convention (Russia)
July 13, 1841[60] – Venus at 5° Gemini, 37 days following direct station, 11 days prior to greatest elongation as morning star
Eight years following the Treaty of Hünkâr Iskelesi, Russia tried to set European hostilities at ease. It signed the London Straits Convention, along with England, France, Austria and Prussia, which effectively closed the Dardanelles, Bosporus and the Sea of Marmara to all foreign warships, and ostensibly restored a balance among the European powers. In the end, it took just over twelve years before Russia came to blows with England and France over the region in the Crimean War of 1853–1856.

St. Petersburg Convention (Russia & Germany)
May 6, 1873[61] – Venus retrograde at 14° Taurus
In the wake of German unification at the end of the Franco-Prussian War of 1870, and the revolutionary Paris Commune that

followed in 1871, German Chancellor Otto von Bismarck rallied the conservative absolute monarchies of Russia and Austria to the cause of self-preservation. The first in a series of 1873 written agreements, the St. Petersburg Convention bonded Germany and Russia to a mutual promise to commit 200,000 troops to defend the other country should it be attacked by a third European power.

Schönbrunn Convention (Russia)
June 6, 1873[62] – Venus at 8° Taurus, 10 days following direct station, 38 days prior to greatest elongation as morning star
Austria was invited into the St. Petersburg alliance, but it declined due to the contentious matter of control over the Balkan region between it and Russia – a matter that would be central to the outbreak of WWI just over forty years later. Instead, the Schönbrunn Convention – signed between Russia and Austria just one month after the St. Petersburg Convention – allowed for the two nations to collaborate in military action should it ever become necessary.

Three Emperors League (Russia & Germany)
June 18, 1881[63] – Venus at 14° Taurus, 24 days following direct station, 24 days prior to greatest elongation as morning star
The Three Emperors League *(Dreikaiserbund)* of Germany, Russia and Austria, created out of the St. Petersburg and Schönbrunn Conventions of eight years earlier, was formalized in Berlin in 1881. Austria's suspicions about Russia's designs on the Balkans had hampered the agreement before it was even signed, and the agreement binding the league lapsed by 1887.

Kaiser Wilhelm II endorses Moroccan independence (Germany)
March 31, 1905[64] – Venus at 14° Taurus, 47 days following greatest elongation as evening star, 5 days prior to retrograde station
With an eye to disrupting the newly formed Entente Cordiale between England and France, the Kaiser, encouraged by Chancellor von Bülow (see **Births**), sailed to Morocco to announce in person Germany's support for Morocco's continued independence. The ploy backfired, however, when France was awarded a controlling influence in the region at the Algeciras Conference the following year, making the Kaiser and Germany look weak.

Yalta Conference (Russia)
February 4, 1945[65] – Venus at 2° Aries, 1 day following greatest elongation as evening star, 48 days prior to retrograde station
With Russian forces occupying much of Eastern Europe, and Allied

forces invading Germany from the west, Soviet leader Josef Stalin met with U.S. President Franklin Roosevelt and British Prime Minister Winston Churchill to discuss their respective agendas for Europe and the world following Hitler's now inevitable fall. Stalin agreed to join a new United Nations, provided the Soviet Union had a permanent place on the Security Council with veto powers. In return, he secured Soviet dominion over Poland and the rest of Eastern Europe.

Slovenian Summit (Russia)

June 16, 2001[66] – Venus at 9° Taurus, 57 days following direct station, 8 days following greatest elongation as morning star
This is one of only three entries in this chronology to fall just outside the 140-day period, by eight days. This summit brought together Russian Federation President Vladimir Putin and U.S. President George W. Bush for the first time. It was at this meeting that Bush – asked whether or not Americans could trust Putin – stated that he had looked into Putin's eyes and 'was able to get a sense of his soul'.

Reset Button (Russia)

March 6, 2009[67] – Venus station retrograde at 15° Aries
Newly inaugurated U.S. President Barack Obama's administration sought to repair relations with Russia following a rift between the two nations over Russia's invasion of Georgia the previous year. After Vice-President Joe Biden remarked that a 'reset' button was needed, Secretary of State Hillary Clinton presented Russian Foreign Minister Sergei Lavrov with a model button for the two of them to press together. Unfortunately, the Russian word printed on it, *peregruzka*, did not translate as 'reset', but rather as 'overcharged'.

London Meeting (Russia)

April 1, 2009[68] – Venus retrograde at 4° Aries
President Obama's first meeting with Russian President Dmitry Medvedev was held in London, and focused primarily on the subject of nuclear disarmament. Amicable and optimistic, the two men related easily to each other. However, new administrations proposing new policy were not likely to ease the suspicions of Russian Prime Minister Putin, the man really wielding power.

MILITARY

Tsushima (Russia)
May 27, 1905[69] – Venus at 29° Aries, 8 days following direct station,
40 days prior to greatest elongation as morning star
The Russo-Japanese War was the beginning of the end for the Russian Empire; its demoralizing failure helped spark the revolution of 1905 that would eventually carry over to the demise of the Romanov dynasty twelve years later. The Battle at the Tsushima Strait would become known as the greatest naval battle since Trafalgar a hundred years earlier. The Russian fleet – having sailed 20,000 miles in seven months from the Baltic Sea to the South China Sea – was ambushed and decimated by Japanese warships in a matter of hours.

Kronstadt (Russia)
March 7, 1921[70] – Venus at 0° Taurus, 25 days following greatest
elongation as evening star, 24 days prior to retrograde station
The Russian Revolution of 1917 had begun, in part, with an uprising of sailors based at the Kronstadt naval fortress in the Gulf of Finland. Four years later the same sailors – weary of the civil war, drought and famine that had plagued Russia since the Bolshevik takeover – issued a list of fifteen demands, including elections, freedom of speech and right of assembly. Red Army forces, led by Mikhail Tukhachevsky, rushed across the frozen waters to the fortress and took it over after twelve days of fighting, crushing the rebellion.

Guernica (Germany)
April 26, 1937[71]– Venus retrograde at 22° Aries
A precursor to WWII, the Spanish Civil War set left-wing republicans and anarchists against a right-wing military coup. German bombers, in support of the uprising, wiped out the northern town of Guernica, demonstrating Nazi Germany's renewed military might to the world.

Soviet troops enter Berlin (Russia & Germany)
April 22, 1945[72] – Venus retrograde at 21° Aries
Eight years to the week after the bombing of Guernica, the European part of WWII was drawing to a close. Soviet forces, led by Marshal Georgy Zhukov, entered the city of Berlin, as German officers fled to the west, preferring to be taken prisoner by Allied forces rather than take their chances with the Soviets. Hitler hung in for another eight days, hoping for a miracle, before finally taking the easy way out (see **Deaths**).

Sino-Soviet conflict over Zhanbao Island (Russia)

March 2, 1969[73] – Venus at 22° Aries, 35 days following greatest
elongation as evening star, 16 days prior to retrograde station
Nineteen years after the Sino-Soviet Treaty of Friendship and
Alliance (signed while Venus was retrograde in Aquarius on
February 14, 1950), mounting tensions between the two major
communist powers came to a head with a border conflict at Zhenbao
Island. Relations between Russia and China remained chillier than
the Cold War for the next two decades.

DISSIDENTS: Russia

3rd Congress of RSDP

May 8, 1905[74] – Venus retrograde at 0° Taurus
By the time the second congress of the Russian Social Democratic
Labour Party was held in Brussels and London in July–August
1903 (as Venus was about to go retrograde in TVirgo), the group
had been outlawed and many of its members were living in exile.
A dispute over membership led to a split in the party, factions that
came to be known as the Mensheviks and Bolsheviks, the latter led
by Vladimir Lenin. The third congress was again held in London,
this time in the wake of the 1905 Russian Revolution. Lenin's
Bolsheviks dominated the meeting, formalizing the split in the
party.

Battleship *Potemkin* mutiny

June 27, 1905[75] – Venus at 19° Taurus, 39 days following direct
station, 9 days prior to greatest elongation as morning star
With the Russo-Japanese War an obvious disaster, and the 1905
Russian Revolution in full swing, sailors aboard the Battleship
Potemkin of the Black Sea Fleet mutinied against their commanders.
The riot was apparently sparked by a minor incident – maggot-
infested meat brought aboard the torpedo boat *Ismail* the previous
day – but quickly escalated into a full-scale mutiny, with executions
and arrests of top officers. The rebellion was put down within
eleven days, but the incident remained an important symbolic
event for Russian revolutionaries, and served as the basis for Sergei
Eisenstein's landmark, semi-fictional propaganda film, *Potemkin*,
released in 1925.

Leon Trotsky exiled from Soviet Union

February 12, 1929[76] – Venus at 9° Aries, 5 days following greatest elongation as evening star, 45 days prior to retrograde station
Leon Trotsky, the founder and former leader of the Soviet Red Army, had been gradually ostracized by Josef Stalin and other Bolshevik rivals, until being exiled to Kazakhstan on January 31, 1928. A year later he was banished from the Soviet Union altogether and roughly forced onto a train bound for Constantinople, Turkey, where he lived for the next four years. After stints in France and Norway, Trotsky wound up in Mexico in 1937, where he was eventually murdered by a Stalinist agent on August 20, 1940, 33 days after Venus stationed direct in Gemini.

Anatoly Shcharansky arrested by KGB

March 15, 1977[77] – Venus station retrograde at 24° Aries
A Jewish-born founder of the 'Refusenik' movement, Shcharansky was denied an exit visa to Israel in 1973, on the grounds that he had been exposed to secrets pertaining to Soviet national security at an earlier time. After a few years as a highly visible dissident, he was arrested by the KGB on charges of spying and treason and sentenced to a Siberian labor camp, where he served for nine years before being the first prisoner to be released under the Gorbachev regime in February 1986.

DISSIDENTS: Germany

Dresden May Uprising

May 3, 1849[78] – Venus retrograde at 27° Taurus
In one of the last uprisings that had erupted in Europe over the previous year, Saxon liberals – demanding that King Frederick Augustus II accept a new constitution – came to blows with Saxon and Prussian militia. Among the protestors was composer Richard Wagner, who fled to Zürich to escape arrest.

Adolf Hitler moves to Munich

May 25, 1913[79] – Venus at 27° Aries, 9 days following direct station, 40 days prior to greatest elongation as morning star
An anonymous 24-year-old Austrian painter left his native homeland and moved to Germany. In less than fifteen months, WWI would break out and the young man would eagerly sign up with the Bavarian King's Own Infantry Regiment, with whom he would be awarded his first Iron Cross by the end of 1914. A soldier was born.

Hitler's first mass speech at Zirkus Krone

February 3, 1921[80] – Venus at 1° Aries, 7 days prior to greatest elongation as evening star, 57 days prior to retrograde station

This event and the next one both occur just outside the 140-day phase, but I include them here because they represent an important transition period in the career of Adolf Hitler. Hitler, now a decorated Corporal in the German army, was ordered to spy on the German Workers Party (DAP) and attended his first meeting on September 12, 1919, while transiting Venus was retrograde in Virgo. He soon left the army to join the party, and quickly became a prominent member. By January 1921 he was speaking to audiences of 2,000 people, although the DAP was still a marginal voice in the chaos of post-war Munich. However, with food riots erupting in Germany that winter, and the Allies now demanding 12 percent of German exports for the next forty-two years, he seized the opportunity to reach a much larger audience. On Wednesday, February 2, he booked the 9,000-seat capacity Zirkus Krone in Munich for a rally the following evening. Despite bad weather, and thanks to an aggressive promotion campaign, the hall was mostly filled, giving the rising star Hitler his biggest audience yet.

Hitler resigns from German Workers Party

July 11, 1921[81] – Venus at 3° Gemini, 58 days following direct station, 10 days following greatest elongation as morning star

Five months after his success at Zirkus Krone, Hitler was now the central figure of the DAP. However, when he left Munich for a fundraising trip to Berlin in June, party opponents took advantage of his absence and commenced negotiations with the rival German Socialist Party to organize a merger between the two. Upon Hitler's return in July, he tendered his resignation in protest. Realizing his departure would probably mean the end of the party, they asked him to return, which he did on the condition that he be named the new party chairman. By the end of the month, Hitler was known in the party by a new title: 'Führer'.[82]

References and Notes

All URLs were accessed in April 2012.

1. http://www.presidency.ucsb.edu/ws/index.php?pid=25800#axzz1shkRxgov

2. http://www.presidency.ucsb.edu/ws/index.php?pid=25801#axzz1shkRxgov

3. http://www.presidency.ucsb.edu/ws/index.php?pid=25803#axzz1shkRxgov

4. http://www.presidency.ucsb.edu/ws/index.php?pid=25805#axzz1shkRxgov

5. http://www.presidency.ucsb.edu/ws/index.php?pid=25807#axzz1shkRxgov

6. http://www.presidency.ucsb.edu/ws/index.php?pid=25813#axzz1shkRxgov

7. http://www.whitehouse.gov/about/presidents/williamhenryharrison/

8. http://www.presidency.ucsb.edu/ws/index.php?pid=25819#axzz1shkRxgov

9. http://www.whitehouse.gov/about/presidents/abrahamlincoln

10. http://www.presidency.ucsb.edu/ws/index.php?pid=25823#axzz1shkRxgov

11. http://www.whitehouse.gov/history/presidents/jg20.html

12. http://www.whitehouse.gov/history/presidents/jg20.html

13. http://www.presidency.ucsb.edu/ws/index.php?pid=25825#axzz1shkRxgov

14. http://www.presidency.ucsb.edu/ws/index.php?pid=25829#axzz1shkRxgov

15. http://www.presidency.ucsb.edu/ws/index.php?pid=25831#axzz1shkRxgov

16. http://www.presidency.ucsb.edu/ws/index.php?pid=25833#axzz1shkRxgov

17. http://www.presidency.ucsb.edu/ws/index.php?pid=21804#axzz1shkRxgov

18. http://www.presidency.ucsb.edu/ws/index.php?pid=21804#axzz1shkRxgov

19. http://www.presidency.ucsb.edu/ws/index.php?pid=15349#axzz1shkRxgov

20. http://www.presidency.ucsb.edu/ws/index.php?pid=9600#axzz1shkRxgov

21. http://www.presidency.ucsb.edu/ws/index. php?pid=8032#axzz1shkRxgov

22. http://www.presidency.ucsb.edu/ws/index. php?pid=1941#axzz1shkRxgov

23. http://www.presidency.ucsb.edu/ws/index. php?pid=6575#axzz1shkRxgov

24. http://www.presidency.ucsb.edu/ws/index. php?pid=46366#axzz1shkRxgov

25. http://www.presidency.ucsb.edu/ws/index. php?pid=25853#axzz1shkRxgov

26. http://www.presidency.ucsb.edu/ws/index. php?pid=44#axzz1shkRxgov

27. http://www.presidency.ucsb.edu/ws/index. php?pid=38688#axzz1shkRxgov

28. http://www.presidency.ucsb.edu/ws/index. php?pid=46366#axzz1shkRxgov

29. Sidney Harcave, *Count Sergei Witte and the Twilight of Imperial Russia: A Biography*, M. E. Sharpe, 2004, p. 3.

30. Christopher Warwick, *Ella: Princess, Saint and Martyr*, John Wiley, 2006, p. 85.

31. Dmytro Doroshenko, *History of Ukraine, 1917–1923, Volume 2*, Hetman Movement Leadership, 1973, p. 43.

32. Richard Abraham, *Alexander Kerensky*, Columbia University Press, 1990, p. 5.

33. http://www.astro.com/astro-databank/Tirpitz,_Alfred_von

34. Katharine A. Lerman, *The Chancellor as Courtier: Bernhard Von Bülow and the Governance of Germany, 1900–1909*, Cambridge University Press, 2003, p. 10.

35. Joseph A. Biesinger, *Germany*, Infobase Publishing, 2006, p. 539.

36. http://www.astro.com/astro-databank/Hitler,_Adolf

37. http://www.astro.com/astro-databank/Speer,_Albert

38. Henri Troyat, *Alexander of Russia: Napoleon's Conqueror*, Grove Press, 2003, pp. 52–57.

39. Edvard Radzinsky and Antonina Bouis, *Alexander II: The Last Great Tsar*, Simon and Schuster, 2006, pp. 166–167.

40. *Ibid.*, pp. 413–416.

41. *New York Times*, February 18, 1905, p. 2 (http://select.nytimes.com/gst/abstract.html?res=F00C1FFF345F13718DDDA10994DA405B858C F1D3).

42. Simon Sebag Montefiore, *Stalin: The Court of the Red Tsar,* Random House, 2005, p. 225.

43. http://news.bbc.co.uk/onthisday/hi/dates/stories/march/5/ newsid_2710000/2710127.stm

44. *Montreal Gazette,* April 12, 1921, p. 14 (http://news.google.com/news papers?id=wBMqAAAAIBAJ&sjid=v4EFAAAAIBAJ&pg=1881,16305 90&dq=princess+auguste+viktoria&hl=en).

45. *New York Times,* April 21, 1929, p. 27 (http://select.nytimes.com/gst/ abstract.html?res=F00C14F7345F1B7A93C3AB178FD85F4D8285F9).

46. http://news.bbc.co.uk/onthisday/hi/dates/stories/may/1/ newsid_3571000/3571497.stm

47. W. Bruce Lincoln, *The Romanovs: Autocrats of All the Russias,* Dial Press, 1981, p. 414.

48. *Ibid.,* p. 433.

49. John C.G. Rohl, Jeremy Gaines and Rebecca Wallach, *Young Wilhelm: The Kaiser's Early Life, 1859–1888,* Cambridge University Press, 1998, pp. 361–362.

50. Miranda Carter, *George, Nicholas and Wilhelm: Three Royal Cousins and the Road to World War I,* Random House, 2009, p. 274.

51. *Ibid.,* p. 346.

52. Karl Bahm, *Berlin 1945: The Final Reckoning,* Zenith Imprint, 2001, p. 150.

53. http://www.angelfire.com/pa/ImperialRussian/royalty/ russia/1913.html

54. http://www.incredible-adventures.com/yuriparty.html

55. http://www.airships.net/hindenburg/disaster

56. http://news.bbc.co.uk/onthisday/hi/dates/stories/march/11/ newsid_2538000/2538327.stm

57. *New York Times,* April 27, 1993 (http://www.nytimes. com/1993/04/27/opinion/a-resounding-yes-for-mr-yeltsin.html).

58. http://www.1809.fi/porvoon_valtiopaeivaet/en.html

59. Efraim Karsh and Inan Karsh, *Empires of the Sand: The Struggle for Mastery in the Middle East, 1789–1923,* Harvard University Press, 2001, p. 35.

60. Michael Graham Fry, Erik Goldstein and Richard Langhorne, *Guide to International Relations and Diplomacy,* Continuum International Publishing Group, 2004, p. 522.

61. Woodford McClellan, *Revolutionary Exiles: The Russians in the First International and the Paris Commune,* Psychology Press, 1979, p. 217.

62. John R. Deni, *Alliance Management and Maintenance: Restructuring NATO for the 21st Century*, Ashgate Publishing Ltd., 2007, pp. 12–13.

63. E. J. Feuchtwanger, *Bismarck*, Psychology Press, 2002, p. 215.

64. Carter, *George, Nicholas and Wilhelm*, p. 272.

65. Edward Reilly Stettinius, Jr., *Roosevelt and the Russians*, Kessinger Publishing, 2005, p. 99.

66. http://georgewbush-whitehouse.archives.gov/news/releases/2001/06/20010618.html

67. http://news.bbc.co.uk/2/hi/7930047.stm

68. http://www.guardian.co.uk/world/2009/apr/01/barack-obama-dmitri-medvedev-nuclear-disarmament

69. http://www.russojapanesewar.com/tsushima.html

70. Ida Mett, *The Kronstadt Uprising 1921*, Black Rose, Our Generation Press, 1973, p. 66.

71. Gijs van Hensbergen, *Guernica*, Bloomsbury Publishing, 2005, p. 3.

72. http://newspaperarchive.com/the-daily-huronite-and-plainsman/1945-04-22/

73. http://www.damanski-zhenbao.ru/chronicals_en.htm

74. Mark Aleksandrovich Aldanov, *Lenin*, E. P. Dutton & Company, 1922, p. 33.

75. Neal Bascomb, *Red Mutiny: Eleven Fateful Days on the Battleship Potemkin*, Houghton Mifflin Harcourt, 2007, p. 60.

76. http://www.marxists.org/archive/trotsky/1930/mylife/ch44.htm

77. http://news.google.com/newspapers?id=It0TAAAAIBAJ&sjid=mF0DAAAAIBAJ&pg=6566,23976&dq=shcharansky&hl=en

78. Frederic Ewen and Jeffrey L. Wollock, *A Half-Century of Greatness: The Creative Imagination of Europe, 1848–1884*, NYU Press, 2007, p. 302.

79. John Toland, *Adolf Hitler: The Definitive Biography*, Anchor, 1991, p. 50.

80. http://smoter.com/struggle.htm

81. *Ibid.*

82. http://smoter.com/defuhrer.htm

Tony Howard
A Personal Biography

All charts in this essay:
Placidus houses
+ Mean Node

I had my first astrology reading at 16 and have been hooked ever since. I graduated summa cum laude from the University of Colorado with a B.A. in History and Film. After successful careers in magazine publishing and somatic healing, I became a professional astrologer. I'd always planned on going into astrology as a retirement career, but my midlife transits led me to follow this dream sooner rather than later. My astrology mentor is Steven Forrest. Steven's teaching forms the basis of my work, which my clients experience profoundly. But as Mercury is the strongest planet in my chart, I love studying with many teachers. I have thoroughly enjoyed learning from Richard Tarnas, Caroline Casey, Demetra George, Erin Sullivan and Judith Hill and I feel blessed to be involved in such a rich and endlessly fascinating field, in which I'm always inspired. In 2009 I built FindAnAstrologer.com, the first interactive, searchable astrologer online database. I love doing interviews and have filmed and produced several video interviews with prominent astrologers, which I share on my website. I've also had two of my written interviews published in *The Mountain Astrologer*. In October 2011 I launched Raven Dreams Press, which edited and published Mark Jones's first astrology book, *Healing the Soul*. I like to stay busy, and in February 2012 I launched AstrologyUniversity.com, which will provide a unique online resource for the study of astrology, including online content and live workshops. I would like to thank all of my mentors past, present and future for lighting the way forward, and I would like to express humble gratitude that I am able to live a life doing what I love.

www.astroraven.com
tony@astroraven.com

Chapter Four

PLUTO IN LIBRA AND SCORPIO
Generations Transforming Relationship

TONY HOWARD

If we take even the most superficial look at the last 100 years in U.S. history without the use of astrology, we can see that each generation has its own lessons to learn and mistakes to make in a constantly renewing playing field of experience. Famously, each generation has a hard time relating to the motivations and expressions of the generations before and after. Each believes that its generation 'has it right' and loves to wax poetic about 'what is wrong with the young kids'. As one generation ages and comes into power, its collective ideals tend to clash with the younger generation who is just at the beginning of a life-long process of individuation. Cultural historians have done a fairly good job of identifying and labeling these generations, their goals and drives, but most have done so without the use of astrological knowledge. Astrology has the potential to create a bridge of understanding between these historically disparate factions. When we analyze the astrological evidence we are faced with a strong testimony that we are not meant to be learning the same lessons in the same ways or with the same timing.

Astrology shows us that there *are* some cycles of life, some transitions or key moments, that are universal, but there are some that are not. The transits of Saturn happen like clockwork for each person, marking time to the beat of a strict drummer. Each Saturn Return (when transiting Saturn returns to the same degree and sign at birth) marks a key stage of transition into a new cycle of life as part of what Steven Forrest calls the biopsychic script. But while these transits happen at the same age for each person on the planet, the signs and houses that are highlighted are unique to each individual. So while the timing of the cycle is universal, our personal experience of it is not.

Because the outer planets move slowly, they take many years to travel through the entire zodiac. So we can use an outer planet's transit through a sign as one marker identifying the unique traits of a group who carry that signature. However, things get even more interesting when we consider that there are some outer-planet transits that, while still considered part of the biopsychic script, do not happen at the same age for each generation. For instance, due to the widely elliptical orbit of Pluto, the timing of the roughly two-year period in which it transits in square to its natal position varies from generation to generation. For some, this powerfully transformative transit occurs in the mid 30s, while others won't experience Pluto square Pluto until much later in life.

Also due to its orbit, Pluto will spend a varying amount of time in each sign, with the most time spent in Taurus and the least in Scorpio. When we consider the meanings of the different timing of the transits in the biopsychic script, along with the sign changes of the outer planets and their timing variances, we have a much more complete picture of the drives, needs and unconscious motivations that each generation is wrestling with. Noting these differences can lead us into a more compassionate view of each person's experience. Astrology can help us accept that each generation has something unique and powerful to contribute to the evolution of the whole, and from that perspective we can start to honor the lessons and gifts that each of us carries, no matter how different our goals.

Here we'll look closely at the transit of Pluto through the signs of Libra and Scorpio in order to uncover the unique contributions these generations can offer the collective. Pluto provides insight into the deep unconscious motivations that drive us. In a generational context Pluto sheds light on the way each generation struggles with the most complex issues of its time. Symbolizing the archetypal underworld journey, Pluto's placement in our chart describes the potential for transformation that can be achieved through willingly undertaking the arduous voyage. The gifts we reap can include deeper awareness, reintegration of submerged or unconscious material and greater access to personal power. The journey is a perilous one, both figuratively and sometimes literally, but those who fare well carry unleashed energy into the larger culture, thereby transforming the collective.

Transforming Relationship

Perhaps the two most relationship-oriented signs of the zodiac are Libra and Scorpio. All signs tell us something about how we relate, but these two have a singular focus on it. Pluto transited Libra from 1971 to 1983/4, and Scorpio from 1983/4 to 1995. During this unique time, two consecutive generations were born to wrestle with the 'god of the underworld' on relationship issues.

It was no accident that Pluto's discovery occurred at the same time as the birth and spread of depth psychology, and the planet carries that association. But as the practice of psychology continues to evolve and shift, we're reminded that its genesis lay in the shocking, Plutonic announcement that we do indeed *have an unconscious*. Pluto transits demand that we take an unflinching look at what scares us and push the boundaries of our experience to claim the power that lies within. As the god of subterranean wealth, Pluto promises that we'll be granted riches – the natural gifts reclaimed from the unconscious – if we willingly agree to undertake the underworld journey. So, what are the specific gifts that these two generations might unearth?

Pluto in Libra (1971–1983/4)
Libra is the sign most aware of, and attuned to, the other. Seeking to understand the other's point of view, Libra appreciates that there are two sides to every story. Libra is concerned with tact and grace and the polite conventions that make everyone feel at ease. It seeks to maintain a feeling of serenity and will sacrifice authentic self-expression to do so. Libra prefers equilibrium and takes comfort in the middle path found between two extremes – although a Libran may need to experience extremes while finding that balance.

Pluto, on the other hand, expresses without tact and has no patience for social convention or niceties. Pluto blurts out the cold, hard truth, whether it's a convenient time to hear it or not. At its best Pluto offers penetrating insights that lead to growth – painful as that process may be. At its worst that same Plutonian truth may harm or wound. The Pluto in Libra generation has an innate desire to get to the bottom of things and speak its truth. But its members will be challenged to do so with tact, grace, courtesy and respect. These folks do not have an easy balancing act but they will leave the rest of us with a great gift: a transformation in the art of relating that leads us to a deeper, more honest experience of connection.

Where Pluto sits, so too does easy access to the shadow. These folks will have to wrestle with the shadow of Libran indecision. When they respond well to this challenge, they will dig deep into their inner resources, face some truly terrifying fears and push past these to make clear choices. If they respond poorly, they could find themselves paralyzed with the fear of making the 'wrong' choice, passively stuck in the limbo of uncertainty. They could fall into the trap of experiencing life as a spectator rather than as an active participant. Where Pluto sits, there is an ancient wound. Perhaps past-life decisions that played out negatively have left Pluto in Libra people with a crippling fear of inadequacy. Pluto has arrived to convince them to stare their fear in the face – to name it, own it and transform it.

Another Libran shadow is co-dependency. Libra seeks to know itself by knowing the other. Where we find Libra in the chart, the individual has reached a point in their evolutionary development where they can't move forward alone; they require outside input. A problem occurs if they grow fearful and begin to rely too heavily on others' opinions. They may then find it hard to do anything without getting everyone's feedback first. As part of this process, those with Pluto in Libra will face the perils associated with their impulse to maintain likeability. In trying to be liked by everyone, some will lose their inner compass.

What Pluto touches is intensified or amplified to titanic proportions. Some Pluto in Libra pop stars and actresses have achieved colossal success while raising likeability to an art form, with grace and beauty in tow. Unlike some Hollywood beauties from yesteryear, like Grace Kelly or Ingrid Bergman, whose elegance and style seemed otherworldly and unattainable, Pluto in Libra actresses like Gwyneth Paltrow, Liv Tyler and Kate Hudson share these qualities in a way that feels much more personable and approachable.[1] They portray characters that 'everyone likes', and carry themselves in a way that makes the average person feel comfortable approaching them without reservation.

As a culture we explore the issues signified by an outer-planet transit both while the planet is transiting a sign, and also through those who carry that generational signature and the imprints they leave on the culture. As Pluto transited Libra we were asked collectively to deeply contemplate our idealized images of the married couple – the romantic pairing or partnership – with our gaze skewed towards the ways in which our ideals have limited us. This process has been played out magnificently on the silver screen. Our cultural obsession with the romantic pairings of movie stars (both on-screen and off) has been fairly constant since the advent of film. But with the transit of Pluto in Libra, our obsessions with these images reached extremes, and the way in which this generation continues to explore them through art touches the deepest parts of all of us.

Four of the top eleven highest grossing Hollywood romance films of all time to date star Pluto in Libra actors.[2] For example, in James Cameron's *Titanic* Kate Winslet and Leonardo DiCaprio, both born with Pluto in Libra, captivated audiences worldwide with their portrayals in this intensely dramatic and tragic love story. The audience had such a resonance with the intensity of the relationship in this film that it became the biggest romance film of all time at the box office (and the highest grossing film until Cameron's *Avatar* overtook it). Where Pluto goes, success can reach, ahem, titanic proportions.[3] The film deftly portrays a storybook ideal of true love, and speaks to our cultural obsession with tragic love stories. Other clear Plutonian references in the film include the massive wealth represented, the ship's name, the loss of life and the plunging of the ship and its passengers into the ocean's depths. Adding the sign Libra, we see the grace and social customs of the upper class and the beauty and opulence of the ship. The Pluto in Libra archetypal field gives the film its real tension. Through Rose (Winslet) and Jack's (DiCaprio) romance, the film addresses the dark side of social stratification and aims to tell the truth about the confines of class and social mores.

The Pluto in Libra–style excavation of the tragic romance continues as we look at *Brokeback Mountain*, expertly acted by Heath Ledger and Jake Gyllenhaal, both born with Pluto in Libra.[4] Another of the all-time highest grossing romance films, *Brokeback Mountain* had a colossal effect on the American public. It championed issues of equality for gay men and women with a combination of Libran artistry and a hefty serving of Plutonian controversy by demanding that its audience have some hard-line Libran conversations about fairness and equality.[5] The film conveys its Plutonic truth in a way that commands respect and dignity (Libra) for its characters, while placing the love story between its leading men Ennis and Jack in the same canon of dramatic tragedy as *Titanic* and *Romeo and Juliet*. *Brokeback Mountain* is a taboo-breaking (Pluto) film in a world in which homosexuality is still a serious crime in most Middle Eastern nations and remains a taboo subject in many others.

Although I'm choosing to use the term 'gay' here for simplicity, the film stirred up a Pluto in Libra controversy around the labels used to identify the characters, who both maintain homosexual and heterosexual relationships in the film. Some gay rights activists have insisted on referring to the characters as gay, while others prefer to think of them as bisexual. Actor Gyllenhaal is quoted as saying, 'I approached the story believing that these are actually two straight guys who fall in love.'[6] Pluto in Libra is associated with the term 'politically correct', which entered our language in the early '70s as Pluto entered Libra.[7] The term has a long and varied history of usage, but here we can understand its goal as a specifically Libran one of selecting polite and respectful language to bring fairness and dignity to others. Pluto in Libra asks us to consider: for whom does the choice of words matter, and in what context? For Pluto there is not an easy answer, but Libra wants to grapple with the question.

The fact that the uncomfortable dialogue arose following *Brokeback Mountain* suggests that Pluto's work was successful.

The most quoted line from *Brokeback Mountain* is Jack's lament to Ennis, 'I wish I knew how to quit you.' This line speaks of the pathos and torment that can lurk beneath the surface (and above it) in the Pluto in Libra romance. Pluto in Libra lovers face the risk of staying in a relationship too long due to the fear of living without one. In order to 'keep it real' they have to learn to communicate with a high level of presence and honesty. Jack (Gyllenhaal) wrestles with his commitment to his feelings for Ennis (Ledger) and the restrictions this relationship has placed on his desire to express them freely.

Rather than remaining stifled by the social conventions of polite acquiescence, those with Pluto in Libra are asked to say what they really feel and listen as others do the same. In doing so they are able to set new standards for what constitutes harmonious communication. With the influence of Pluto they will feel compelled to shirk convention and get to the heart of the matter, but in a way that isn't alienating. With Ledger's character Ennis, this issue arises through the awareness of a Plutonian wound. Ennis is not a natural communicator. He doesn't know how to ask for what he wants and can't seem to say what he really feels. His character is shut down but teeming with Plutonian desire. Though he's a man of few words, his Plutonic intensity is unmistakable. Writer Luke Davies notes that Ledger's brilliance was his ability to portray a character 'so fundamentally shut down that he is like a bible of unrequited desires, stifled yearnings, lost potential'.[8] Ennis illustrates the enormity of the task that Pluto in Libra faces: it's much easier to talk about extreme honesty as an ideal than to practice it, especially after a lifetime of inexperience.

The transformation heralded by this generation's work within intimate partnerships will spill out into other kinds of relationship, too. We are likely to see this generation raise diplomacy, one of the highest expressions of the Libra archetype, to an art form. As these folks age and become leaders, we may see bridges that could never have existed before built between communities and countries. These folks are born negotiators and will be able to resolve situations of conflict in which a foundational appraisal of the cold hard facts is necessary in order to reach a compromise. They may be able to carry us into true bi-partisanship – to move beyond ideological polarizations such as Republican and Democrat. They will be able to mediate between groups in intensely polarized environments, build understanding and ultimately work together to achieve balance.

One technique this generation has that is especially synergistic with the archetypal field is Marshall Rosenburg's Non-Violent Dialog process. Created in 1972, just after Pluto entered Libra, this technique has now become well known around the world.[9] The main (Libran) components of the technique include empathy, active listening, mirroring conversation, checking in and asking for what one needs, as well as understanding the needs of the other as a gateway to healing conflict. Those with Pluto in Libra who actively use such techniques will likely expand and improve upon them, as well as become facilitators for sharing and disseminating this information further.

Pluto in Libra also speaks to the issue of gender equality. Two Pluto in Libra actresses, with starring roles in the hugely popular vampire-centric fantasies *Buffy the Vampire Slayer* and *Underworld*, made great strides towards leveling the gender playing field with their portrayals of strong female heroines. Historically, Hollywood has reserved the hero's journey for men. But Sarah Michelle Gellar and Kate Beckinsale gave us two of the first likeable, plausible and, most importantly, not laughable, ass-kicking female super-heroines on the screen.[10]

In the television series *Buffy the Vampire Slayer*, Sarah Michelle Gellar plays Buffy, a reluctant 'vampire slayer' who would rather pursue life as an 'average high school girl'. Throughout the series Buffy gradually comes to accept her destiny and claims her true strength and power, but in a markedly Libran fashion. Surrounded by friends who are always there to help her, she is the poster child for approaching problems the Libran way. Although she makes mistakes and sometimes struggles with making decisions, ultimately she accepts the assistance her friends offer and integrates their feedback. From there she takes her stand, facing literal underworld demons in the process.

Buffy is an easily likeable character. She carries herself with Libran grace and isn't without her fair share of beauty. But Pluto's influence sets the tone and, though the show is full of comedic moments, it has no fear of the dark. The show's writing itself represents a Libran balancing act between light and dark, as it plays with the concepts of good and evil and some characters switch sides from time to time. One of the more intriguing elements of the storyline is Buffy's Libran ability to bridge the distance between two 'natural' enemies: the slayers and the vampires. She achieves this via two heart-wrenching and complex romances with vampires who have turned away from the dark side, and thus she forms a bridge between the two warring factions.

Throughout the show, Buffy faces real danger and even a literal underworld journey, but survives (sort of) and returns to the world with a deeply sober new self. In the process she loses some part of herself, sacrificed to the underworld, but is reborn more whole, honest and powerful than ever. Pluto has made her an even greater force to be reckoned with.

The heroine of the film *Underworld* experiences another uniquely Pluto in Libra transformation. Kate Beckinsale dramatically plays Selene, a vampire whose life purpose is to slay werewolves, her natural enemy. Like Buffy she is a trained assassin, a killer (Pluto). She is loyal to her clan leader Vincent, who has 'raised her' as a daughter. While he sleeps she carries out Vincent's will by protecting the clan. During one of Vincent's sojourns Selene falls in love with a man who turns out to be a werewolf. In the process of coming to terms with her feelings and getting involved in this man's self-awakening, she ultimately fulfills her Pluto in Libra destiny: providing a bridge between the two warring communities and bringing werewolf and vampire into a mutually respectful, if tense, relationship. She accomplishes this with a heavy dose of Plutonian honesty mixed with Libran diplomacy and negotiation. But it turns out that Vincent hasn't been absolutely truthful with Selene about the history of the war between vampire and werewolf. Obsessed with discovering the truth (Pluto), Selene finally uncovers a tale of tragic love, torture and enslavement. With cunning and skill she uses the truth to heal the wounds between the two communities, fulfilling one of the highest promises of the Pluto in Libra archetype.

Unlike Buffy, whose story takes place in an 'average American town', *Underworld's* landscape is solely Pluto's domain. The sets are dark, gothic, rainy. There is a sense of tragic doom imprinted on every frame of the film. The characters are serious, intense and full of passion. But in the end, Libran goals of diplomatic resolution are achieved: the joining of two souls from opposite sides of the track in a love that, at its culmination, has moved far beyond a glamorized ideal to one that has been built on hard-won truth.

Finally we can't talk about the cultural bread trails being left behind by the Pluto in Libra generation without mentioning the colossal successes of Britney Spears, Justin Timberlake and Christina Aguilera, three megastars who got their auspicious starts as child performers and to date are three of the most successful pop stars ever.[11] The years between 1997 and 2001 were full of optimism and expansion. Pluto was already in Sagittarius and Uranus had moved into Aquarius, with Neptune following suit in 1998. The time was ripe for expansion and the internet took the world by storm. But in the pop world it was the Pluto in Libra generation who garnered the most fans. Pluto is associated with obsession, and when coupled with a teenage fan base, that obsession led to massive fame for the stars of the Pluto in Libra generation.

Timberlake's leap to fame began with him at the helm of one of the most successful boy bands of all time, 'N Sync. Later he rose to greater success as a solo recording artist and actor.[12] In another example of Pluto-style success, Spears has become the eighth-highest top-selling female artist in U.S. history.[13] In 2003 Spears held the Guinness World record for 'best-selling album by a teenage solo artist' with sales of over 13 million copies. Notably Pluto sits in Spears' 1st House, conjunct Saturn and square the nodal axis.[14] This prominent Pluto placement is representative of both her massive presence and success in her industry, as well as the constant drama that surrounds her as she struggles to heal karmic wounds related to her image. Pluto represents the impulse to strip away pretense.

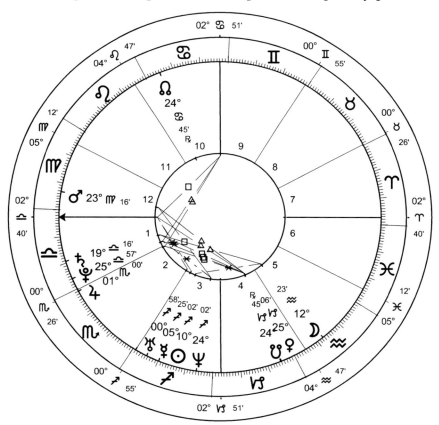

Britney Spears' Birth Chart

Spears famously struggled with the pressures of her public image and externalized that angst by deliberately shaving her head – a moment that one author suggests 'had little do with self-loathing, more a loathing against the public persona that had defined her until then'.[15]

Aguilera's album release *Stripped* also carries the Pluto signature. Fiercely defying cultural gender norms, Aguilera's in-your-face songs often defend a woman's right to free sexual expression without judgment. Both Spears and Aguilera have tested the limits of what had previously been acceptable sexual expression for a female pop star. And demonstrating how one Pluto generation's gains can influence the next generation, both artists are responsible for inspiring a feisty group of young Pluto in Scorpio females to claim their right to their sexuality. Aguilera and Spears addressed the issue in Libran ways – through their dress and appearance and with a focus on gender equality. For the Pluto in Scorpios that follow, we're likely to see an entirely different and more complex set of expressions.

Pluto in Scorpio (1983/4–1995)

Pluto has a highly elliptical orbit, so it spends varying amounts of time in each sign, with the longest part of its orbit spent in Taurus and the shortest in Scorpio. It has often been joked about in the astrological community that Pluto spends the least amount of time in Scorpio because that's all we can handle. And we all know how Taurus likes to take its time! In the sign of Scorpio, the lord of the underworld finds a willing companion, a kindred spirit. This means that the Plutonian archetype essentially has free reign to express to its fullest capacity. Dark intensity, uncovering truths, breaking taboos, pushing the boundaries of the acceptable, a comfort with the profane and an inability to be shocked by just about anything are all qualities found amongst the brave souls in the Pluto in Scorpio generation. Their passions run deep and they are completely unapologetic for them, as their poster child, Lady Gaga, proudly proclaims on her 2011 release, 'I was born this way, baby'. With an unwavering loyalty to the practice of profound honesty, this generation freely discusses topics that make other generations rather squeamish. The Pluto in Scorpio folks are proud that nothing shocks them, and they wear this quality as a badge of honor.

Scorpio is the sign most associated with sexuality, perhaps unfairly (something tells me that the other signs copulate as well). One reason Scorpio has this reputation as being the most sexual sign isn't necessarily because these individuals have more sex than the average person, but because they are less afraid to talk about it. Scorpio people are here to share intensity with other souls, to explore deep intimacy and to test the limits of their personal power. They do this in many ways, and sexuality is one of them.

Scorpio is deeply psychological. Scorpio's natural instinct for exploring twisted and unexplored internal terrain can take it into a labyrinth of psychological complexity. Scorpio loves a good mystery and because of this has excellent research and detective skills. Scorpio's tendency towards suspicion can lead it down dark hallways of obsessive thinking and this risks alienating others. At some point, when the time is right, Scorpio needs to learn to accept and trust, and also to let go.

Adding Pluto to the mix, we can say 'ditto'. But we're also considering the wound – the age-old Plutonian scars burned into the unconscious. The Pluto in Scorpio people wear these unconscious patterns emblazoned on their tattooed skin. This generation will offer up the human shadow for *all* of us to see. Its members won't be able to restrain themselves. They are here to explore the shadow more deeply than the rest of us. And for that reason they are likely to scare us, to challenge us and, at times, to make us wince.

Pluto is symbolic of material submerged in our unconscious. Pluto also simply alerts us to the fact that we have an unconscious. During a sensitive Pluto transit, unconscious material is thrust into our barely ready consciousness, and we are forced to respond, ready and willing or not. And yet Pluto doesn't represent everything the unconscious holds (there are other planetary bodies in the Kuiper Belt that may also relate to unconscious material). There is likely enough material to be harvested from our unconscious that it would take several lifetimes to do so.

All of this is interesting when we consider that Pluto and Scorpio are both secretive. The act of transformative revelation that Pluto symbolizes is dependent on the fact that until that moment, it has successfully kept that material under wraps. The Pluto/Scorpio signature is just as good at concealing as it is at uncovering. In relationship Scorpio loves to know your secrets but doesn't like to share its own. Pluto in Scorpio symbolizes the capacity to be secretive to a fault and obsess over privacy.

It's no accident that privacy issues became paramount with the phenomenally successful website Facebook, a creation that has completely transformed how we relate to one another. At first glance Facebook may appear to be a manifestation of Pluto in Libra. It has to do with the mask we present in social groups, our social interactions, and communicating, sharing, interacting and relating with 'friends'. But a quick look at founder Mark Zuckerberg's chart reveals a 0° Pluto in Scorpio.[16] When Facebook was launched in February 2004 to a very receptive and internet-savvy college-aged audience, the Pluto in Scorpio generation made up over half of the university population, with the eldest being 21 years old. If we think about this more deeply it makes perfect sense. Where better to spy on our friends than Facebook? As users we *control* what we want to reveal, and at the same time we can obsess as much as we want about what everyone else is doing. We can stalk, spy and research to our heart's content without ever revealing anything of ourselves. But who is the biggest spy of them all? Pluto in Scorpio Mark Zuckerberg, of course. Privacy concerns have plagued Facebook's users from the beginning. As Zuckerberg constantly tweaks the software – enticing us to share ever more personal information that can then be sold to hungry advertisers who are willing to pay top dollar for targeted marketing information – he has consistently faced the wrath of its users. Zuckerberg is constantly pushing the boundary of what feels comfortable to Facebook users. His obsession with digging into our private business has made him the youngest billionaire on the planet. If we had any doubt at all that Pluto is a lord of massive riches, doubt no more.

As the Pluto in Scorpio generation ages, we are likely to see it deeply concerned about privacy issues in all areas of life, including on the internet, as well those areas of life under the domain of our governments. In the U.S. it is possible that members of this generation will either have success restoring some of the civil liberties that were taken from us by the Bush administration, or perhaps they will further erode them. This ambiguity arises because of Pluto's complex relationship with totalitarianism. Pluto is associated with the fascism that arose at the time of its discovery in the 1930s. Pluto has the potential to express a diabolical need to control and dominate, and we may see this generation struggling with the desire to maintain its legal rights to privacy while also wanting to maintain the ability to pry into the business of others.

Pluto represents the cycle of death and rebirth, and is associated with the Hindu goddesses Kali and Shakti, who govern the powers of transformation, destruction and sexual creation. People in the Pluto in Scorpio generation will find themselves drawn to such images of power, ancient Tantric traditions, occult practices and mystery schools in an effort to tap into and expand their experience of personal power. But the pursuit of such elemental power is not child's play. In yoga, practitioners have sought to raise an elemental energy in the body known as 'kundalini'. In *The Stormy Search for the Self* Stanislav Grof attests to an experience that many seasoned kundalini yogis warn of. When this energy manifests, the potential for mental imbalance can arise as the result of either improperly raising the kundalini energy or by raising it before one is ready.[17] Grof notes the fine line that exists between the experience of raising this elemental energy and the symptoms of mental illness. It is therefore highly recommended that one only pursue such practices under the guidance of an expert teacher, with knowledge and direct experience of the practice. My point here is that the Pluto in Scorpio generation will learn firsthand that when playing with fire, it is easy to get burned. There will be casualties from this kind of exploration, as well as successful and positive transformations. The fires of Pluto are regenerative but they are also destructive – it is important to approach them with respect.

It is no accident that people report having had kundalini awakenings after near-death experiences.[18] Pluto relates to the death–rebirth cycle. The potential for greater power and regeneration lies in Plutonian transformation, but not without real danger. How many of us would willingly sign up to have a near-death experience, knowing that the possibility always exists that we might not make it back from the other side? The philosopher Nietzsche wisely reminds us, 'Only where there are tombs are there resurrections.'[19] Some Pluto in Scorpios will willingly plunge into this abyss without a second thought, for better or worse.

In Pluto we have the image of the phoenix, and the function of elemental fire as a destructive force. But it is also a fire that purifies and creates the balance needed for a rebirth into something profoundly more powerful than before. The poet Rumi offers us this:

> If your knowledge of fire has been
> Turned to certainty by words alone,
> Then seek to be cooked by the fire itself.
> Don't abide in borrowed certainty.
> There is no real certainty until you burn;
> If you wish for this, sit down in the fire.

Pluto represents some of our greatest fears. When we have a Plutonian conversation we can feel uncomfortable at the least. And one of the most frightening aspects of Pluto is its association with the energy we describe as evil. The Pluto in Scorpio generation is drawn to explore this concept in many ways. Some will be obsessed with images and stories of evil, as seen by this generation's interest in *Saw*, one of the most extreme horror movie franchises ever. At the time of its release *Saw* became the second most profitable horror film of all time.[20] In the films, part of a new subgenre aptly and Plutonically dubbed 'torture porn', the main character Jigsaw creates elaborate tests for people to pass, with life or death consequences. The story provides a vehicle for displaying humanity's most terrifying and horrible potentials for torture and abuse, all of which fall under Pluto's domain. And in a profane twist of Pluto's highest promise, Jigsaw believes that those who survive his methods will be stronger people for it.

It is possible that some souls in this generation will take a more direct route in their exploration of evil. What's important to consider here is that evil is just as much a part of God's universe as love and goodness. It exists for a reason that is challenging (if not impossible) for us to understand. Nietzsche explores the topic with intellectual rigor and offers helpful insight in his seminal work *Beyond Good and Evil*. But consider these words by the poet Rumi in *On Good and Evil*:

> To the one Love has instructed, things that seem opposite reveal their secret affinity and relation. Show me the evil in this universe in which no good at all is contained, or the good in which there is not the slightest touch of evil!... Show me good without evil, so I can agree that there is a God of Good and a God of Evil. You cannot – because good does not exist apart from evil. Knowing this does not bring any acceptance of evil – evil remains evil, to be fought and defeated. But knowing this lessens fear.[21]

Rumi reminds us here of the complexity and interrelationship of these polarities, while at the same time asserting their necessity and pointing to a way beyond the experience. With subjects like evil there are no pat answers, no *Chicken Soup* one-liners that can make us feel better or make us feel safe. Pluto asks us to face our fear, to stare evil in the eye and accept its presence. It does not ask us to participate in evil or to be evil – though a few always mistake Pluto's call and move in that direction. Perhaps in some way members of this generation will become our teachers. We will surely get a deeper experience of this profound subject through the spiritual work the Pluto in Scorpio generation undertakes.

Pluto is associated with birth and death – two seeming opposites. But the birthing process, though spiritually beautiful, is also dangerous, gory (think placentas, blood and mucus) and extremely painful. Pluto is also associated with the creative process that leads to birth: human sexuality. This generation's people will test the limits of human sexuality to experience their own power – both power over others and being overpowered by others. There is an attraction–compulsion process at the heart of the Pluto experience. These folks will experience power as a result of attracting others. They experience the flip side of that when they become overpowered by their attraction to others. When combined with their inability to be shocked by anything and their willingness to explore the taboo and speak freely about it, the members of this generation are poised to disturb us by pushing sexual limits, boundaries and norms.

As a performer with Pluto in Scorpio, Lady Gaga has already achieved colossal success and amassed much wealth mainly by expressing her creativity. A woman with a seemingly unlimited reserve of talent, she was initially given a record deal with the star factory Def Jam Recordings, from which she was dropped after three months. A blessing in disguise (though not for Def Jam), this experience caused her to fall back on her own resources, dig even deeper into her well of inspiration, and a year later Lady Gaga burst onto the music scene with a ferocious, volcanic energy that appeared as if it had been pent up for decades and finally unleashed. She developed an instant following with an almost cult-like devotion. With clear nods to the underworld, she calls her fans her 'little monsters', a reference to the title of her second release *The Fame Monster* and the tour for that release, 'The Monster Ball'.

Lady Gaga's work is always provocative and, at times, unapologetically sexual. She has appeared on talk shows dressed in an evening gown made of raw meat, which she wore as a statement about human rights.[22] More than one of her videos have irked the Catholic Church and it seems that each new work pushes boundaries just a little further than we're comfortable with. And yet she is also loveable, as millions of fans will attest. She speaks with grace and presence and has a sincerity that is visibly perceptible. And the prolific creativity expressed through her stage costumes and art direction is undeniable.

In one of the more memorable lines from her song 'Bad Romance', Gaga sings, 'I want your ugly, I want your disease. I want your everything as long as it's free. I want your love.' Pluto in Scorpio is unflinching. It desires to experience life with full intensity, fire and passion – or not at all. Gaga sums up the Pluto in Scorpio impulse as she explains these lyrics: 'What I'm really trying to say is I want the deepest, darkest, sickest parts of you that you are afraid to share with anyone because I love you that much.'[23] In the same song she illustrates the Pluto in Scorpio fascination with mystery and dark subject matter with a nod to director Alfred Hitchcock: 'I want your psycho, your vertigo shtick, want you in my rear window, baby, you're sick.' Other songs take on popular Scorpio subjects like betrayal, obsession, stalking and sex.

Those who write off Lady Gaga as a shallow flash-in-the-pan pop sensation who gets by on shock value alone might consider her far-reaching influence on her generation. More than just encouraging freedom of expression through fashion, she has dedicated heart-wrenching performances to teen victims of suicide, and her devoted fans love and support her advocacy of lesbian and gay rights. In 2011 she launched her own non-profit organization, The Born This Way Foundation, which focuses on youth empowerment and issues of self-confidence, well-being, anti-bullying, mentoring and career development.[24]

The Pluto in Scorpio generation will take its causes seriously and pursue them with unmatched ferocity and in-your-face gusto. Regarding her line of lipstick, whose proceeds will support HIV and AIDS prevention efforts, Gaga declares, 'I don't want Viva Glam to be just a lipstick you buy to help a cause. I want it to be a reminder when you go out at night to put a condom in your purse right next to your lipstick.'[25] Frank and unapologetic, Gaga is speaking of the reality of the consequences and dangers of sex.

Although Gaga may shock today's parents, she's right on target with her fans, a generation whose introduction to human sexuality could very well have included profane pornographic images easily found on the internet at an unimaginably early age. Once, a friend shared that her thirteen-year-old Pluto in Scorpio son asked her not *if* he could but *when* he could watch porn for the first time, while promising to not watch any 'rape, violence or bestiality'. Her teenage son had come to her with a full awareness of the dark potentials in human sexuality, stated his intentions clearly and instigated an uncomfortably honest conversation. We can't hide such dark truths from our Pluto in Scorpio children. They will (and do) discover them on their own. This generation's matter-of-fact approach will teach us much, even though the process may be unpleasant or unpalatable.

Transformation, Endings and New Beginnings
We've taken a brief look at some of the potentials for the Pluto in Libra and Scorpio generations. As these generations move through life our understanding of relationship and human intimacy will be

forever altered. As they heal some of their (previously) unconscious wounds, they will unleash a power and force that will guide us all towards new levels of self-empowerment. To some extent these will be lasting changes that echo down the generations, as did the cultural evolutions instigated by the 'Roaring Twenties' and Woodstock generations. Pluto warns of upheaval, death, decay and endings. But it also speaks of purification, elimination and the release of untapped potential. It's important that we learn to not fear Pluto's revelations, but to maintain a healthy respect for them. The poet Rumi warns, 'Most people guard against going into the fire, and so end up in it.' When we resist Pluto its fire burns us anyway. A wiser approach is to accept the process and take up Pluto's work willingly.

References and Notes

1. Grace Kelly (12 November 1929, 5:31 AM, Philadelphia, PA; Rodden rating: AA) was born with Venus in Libra in the 12th House (Placidus), 4° from the ascendant. In whole sign houses this is a 1st House Venus in Libra. Her Pluto is in Cancer in the 9th House (Placidus). Ingrid Bergman (29 August 1915, 3:30 AM, Stockholm, Sweden; Rodden AA) was born with Venus in Virgo (the perfection of beauty) in the 1st house (Placidus), 7° from the ascendant, conjunct the Sun in Virgo, and sextile (within 3°) her Pluto in Cancer in the 11th House (Placidus).

2. The four films are *Titanic, Pearl Harbor, Brokeback Mountain* and *The Notebook.* http://boxofficemojo.com/genres/ chart/?id=romanticdrama.htm (stats as of 29 December 2011).

3. I love the use of the word 'titanic' with Pluto, which I first encountered in Richard Tarnas's *Cosmos and Psyche,* Viking, 2006.

4. Jake Gyllenhaal birth data: 19 December 1980 at 20:08 (= 8:08 PM), Los Angeles, CA, USA; Rodden AA. Heath Ledger birth data: 4 April 1979 at 06:30 (= 06:30 AM), Perth, Australia. Rodden C. Source: AstroDatabank.

5. *Brokeback Mountain* predictably stirred up controversy, including one theater owner who refused to show the film due to its content, public backlash from right-wing pundits, and a claim that it was deliberately snubbed by the Academy Awards (http://www.boxofficemojo.com/ news/?id=1979). The film was nominated for more awards that year than any other and won several, but was passed up for Best Picture. Some critics accused the Academy of homophobia, and writer Michael Jensen made a strong case for unfair treatment by analyzing data from previous years' winners. He noted that up until the Oscars, *Brokeback*

Mountain had become 'the most honored movie in cinematic history', winning more Best Picture and Director awards than previous Oscar winners *Schindler's List* and *Titanic* combined. He also pointed out that no other film had previously won the Writer's Guild, Director's Guild and Producer's Guild awards and also failed to win the Academy Award for Best Picture, and that 'only four times in the previous twenty-five years had the Best Picture winner not also been the film with the most nominations.' He also noted that only once before had a film 'not even nominated for the Golden Globe's Best Picture *[Crash]* gone on to win the Academy Award'. Michael Jensen, 'The Brokeback Mountain Oscar Snub,' http://www.afterelton.com/archive/elton/movies/2006/3/snub.html

6. Benoit Denizet-Lewis, 'Jake Gyllenhaal Doesn't Want You to Know He's in Love,' http://www.details.com/celebrities-entertainment/cover-stars/200511/hollywood-actor-jake-gyllenhaal-talks-jarhead-and-brokeback-mountain. First published in *Details Magazine*.

7. http://en.wikipedia.org/wiki/Political_correctness

8. Luke Davies, 'Heath Ledger', 1979–2008, http://www.themonthly.com.au/monthly-essays-luke-davies-heath-ledger-1979-2008--821?page=0%2C2

9. Marshall Rosenburg, *A Manual for Responsible Thinking and Communicating*, St. Louis, Mo.: Community Psychological Consultants, 1972.

10. Sarah Michelle Gellar, 14 April 1977, New York, NY, no birth time. Kate Beckinsale, 26 July 1973, UK, no birth time. Both sources IMDB, http://www.imdb.com

11. According to his website, Timberlake's second album has sold over 9 million copies to date (http://www.justintimberlake.com/albums/futuresexlovesounds). In 2003 Spears held the Guinness World record for 'Best-selling album by a teenage solo artist', with sales of over 13 million copies (Claire Folkard, *Guinness World Records 2003*, Bantam Books, p. 288). Aguilera is Billboard's second top-selling singles artist of the 2000s behind Madonna: Billboard (2009): http://www.billboard.biz/bbbiz/charts/decadeendcharts/2009/singles-sales-artists

12. 'N Sync's second album became the fastest-selling album of all time with 2.4 million copies sold in its first week. 'Justin Timberlake', Wikipedia, 2011, Wikimedia Foundation, Inc., 1 December 2011, http://en.wikipedia.org/wiki/Justin_timberlake

13. Spears' success is another great example of Pluto obsession (here by Spears' fans) leading to massive fame (and wealth). Mitch Bainwol, 'RIAA – Gold & Platinum – May 3, 2010' (Recording Industry Association of America, 2010). Retrieved 3 May 2010. Notably, Pluto sits in Spears' 1st House, conjunct Saturn and square the nodal axis.

14. Britney Spears' birth data: 2 December 1981 at 01:30 (= 01:30 AM), McComb, MS, USA; Rodden rating A. Source: AstroDatabank.

15. Steve Dennis, *Britney: Inside the Dream*, London: HarperCollins Publishers, 2009.

16. No birth time is available yet for Zuckerberg. He was born 14 May 1984, in White Plains, NY. Source: Wikipedia and *The Mountain Astrologer*, http://mountainastrologer.com/tma/mark-zuckerberg-and-facebook. Facebook was launched on 4 February 2004. The launch time is unknown but is depicted around 10 PM in the film *The Social Network*.

17. Christina Grof and Stanislav Grof, *The Stormy Search for the Self*, New York: J. P. Tarcher/Perigee, 1992.

18. Yvonne Kason, *Farther Shores: Exploring How Near-death, Kundalini and Mystical Experiences Transform Ordinary Lives*, Toronto: HarperCollins, 2000.

19. Friedrich Nietzsche, *Thus Spoke Zarathustra*, New York: Modern Library, 1995.

20. Scott Foundas, 'Splattered: An Interview with James Wan,' Los Angeles: *LA Weekly*, 2007, http://www.laweekly.com/content/printVersion/61775/

21. Rumi, *Light Upon Light*, trans. Andrew Harvey, New York: Tarcher/Penguin, 1996, p. 142.

22. Ann Lee, 'Lady Gaga defends meat dress by claiming she's no "piece of meat"' (Metro.co.uk, 2010), http://www.metro.co.uk/music/840850-lady-gaga-defends-meat-dress-by-claiming-shes-no-piece-of-meat

23. Tamar Anitai, 'Lady Gaga On MTV's "It's On With Alexa Chung" – See the Photos and Watch the Interviews!' http://buzzworthy.mtv.com/2009/11/03/lady-gaga-on-mtvs-its-on-with-alexa-chung-see-the-photos-and-watch-the-interviews (MTV Buzzworthy Blog 2009).

24. Jocelyn Vena, 'Lady Gaga Launches *Born This Way* Foundation,' http://www.mtv.com/news/articles/1673633/lady-gaga-born-this-way-foundation.jhtml (MTV.com, 2011).

25. Ning Chao, 'Going Gaga,' http://www.marieclaire.com/celebrity-lifestyle/celebrities/lady-gaga-interview (*Marie Claire*, 2010).

Part II

Spiritual &
Evolutionary Journeys

Mark Jones
A Personal Biography

All charts in this essay:
Porphyry houses
+ True Node
Chiron

I am a Psychosynthesis Therapist in private practice in Bristol, England. I am a graduate of Noel Tyl's Masters Program in Astrological Counseling and a graduate of the Jeffrey Wolf Green School of Evolutionary Astrology. I have taught Evolutionary Astrology in the U.K. since 2003. I have been a professional therapist and astrologer for over a decade with more than six thousand hours of client work, readings and teaching. My publications include *Healing the Soul: Pluto, Uranus and the Lunar Nodes* (Raven Dreams Press, 2011), in which I outline an introduction to my core approach, and I have contributed chapters to *Insights into Evolutionary Astrology* (Llewellyn, 2010) on the Planetary Nodes, and to *Psychosynthesis: New Perspectives* (PS Avalon, 2009) on the fusion of astrology and therapy. I am a regular speaker and workshop leader at the NORWAC conference in Seattle and at various Evolutionary Astrology conferences. I teach workshops regularly in Minneapolis and the Seattle and Portland areas of the United States. My website www.plutoschool.com includes many resources for students, articles and talks that can be downloaded. It also offers information on the work I do: how to get a reading, undertake ongoing counseling work with the chart as a guide, and classes and workshops that I am giving. My work aims to integrate an in-depth approach to astrology (that includes prior-life and karmic perspectives) to the therapeutic model of healing, so that the astrology can add an extra level of understanding to why certain circumstances occur in people's lives, just as the therapeutic element can provide the possibility of integrating what the chart analysis reveals. I place this fusion of astrology and psychotherapy within the context of the Perennial Philosophy, the great spiritual teachings of the ages exemplified for me in the lives of the Buddha and Christ.

www.plutoschool.com
markjones@plutoschool.com

Chapter Five

THE DEVIL IN THE DETAIL
The Pluto in Virgo Generation

MARK JONES

In order to understand the Pluto in Virgo generation we need to understand both the nature of Pluto and the nature of Virgo. The view of Pluto I use here has been explained at length in my book *Healing the Soul: Pluto, Uranus and the Lunar Nodes*,[1] yet can be referred to in brief as the deep structure of the Self – the core unconscious security patterns that predominate within the Self. The Self is a notoriously complex thing to define. Ken Wilber, in his *Integral Psychology*, uses the phrase 'the archeology of the Self' to denote the complex layers of potential meaning. The deep Self that is referred to through the archetype of Pluto can be likened to the soul, as it is both beyond our conscious ego sense yet it retains an individuality that may be surrendered as we approach the realm of spirit. In Wilber's words:

> Not yet infinite and all-embracing, no longer merely personal and mortal, the soul is the great intermediate conveyor between the pure Spirit and the individual self.[2]

This individuality (soul) contains psychological complexes and attachments from prior lives, from *Bardo* (states between lives) and early uterine (womb) states to all the underlying material from the formation of our individuality in childhood in this lifetime. Soul is therefore a significator of depth, individual depth at a level beyond the Moon (the ego) and yet an intermediary to Neptune (spirit, the collective consciousness).

To understand the Virgo archetype at this level of depth (enhanced by Pluto), we can explore multiple approaches – one being the view of the archetypes as an expression of the development of the Self, both in psychological principle and as a temporal event in the progression of the human life from infancy to old age.

Aries to Leo: the Formation of the Individual Self

The self starts out relatively undifferentiated from its environment. That is, it cannot easily tell where its body stops and the physical environment begins... Somewhere during the first year, the infant learns that if it bites a blanket, it does not hurt, but if it bites its thumb, it hurts: there is a difference between body and matter. The infant differentiates its body from the environment, and thus its identity switches from fusion with the material world to an identity with the emotional–feeling body... As the conceptual mind begins to emerge and develop (especially around 3 to 6 years), the child eventually differentiates the conceptual mind and the emotional body...[3]

Here Wilber denotes the three earliest stages that are symbolized by the first three signs/archetypes: Aries (instinctual body/environment), Taurus (feeling body, internal needs) and Gemini (the development of conceptual mind and language). These three bodies (physical, emotional and mental) in their earliest formation coalesce into an overall personality that Wilber calls the 'rule/role mind' that can be seen in the Moon, Cancer and the 4th House: the formation of the ego, or conditioned Self through the experiences of the early childhood, parental and societal structures. From this nascent ego sense and through conditioned belonging develops what Wilber calls the 'self-reflexive ego',[4] the self-awareness and personal creative peak that we link in astrology with the sign of Leo. In the Leo archetype, the ego birthed from the home-life in Cancer becomes a creative force for the good of the individual, a necessarily selfish (full of self) phase of individual development.

Virgo
We can see the progression from Aries to Leo as a developmental process of the individual self. In following on from Leo, Virgo can be seen as an archetype in transition, as a bridge between the individual identity in Leo and the birth of the social self in Libra.

In order to make this transition developmentally the Self must learn to upend the pyramid of the self-expression achieved within the Leo archetype and humble the self through the recognition that it is just one of many; this is the necessary adjustment in order to be able to meet other people as equals in the archetype of Libra that follows.

Virgo is found 150° from Aries, the Ascendant/starting position of the natural (or archetypal) zodiac. The 150° aspect – the quincunx, or inconjunct – is one of crisis. Virgo has a relationship to crisis because all that the Self has achieved must now be humbled before the other. In regard to the collective need, the Virgo archetype represents a potentially profound crisis on an individual level; a crisis of the personal will.

This crisis is exacerbated when Pluto is in Virgo because, as the ruler of Scorpio, Pluto is also inconjunct the Ascendant within the natural zodiac. With two inconjuncts that are sextile each other, we have an archetypal Yod formation (Virgo and Scorpio applying to Aries/the Ascendant of the archetypal zodiac) that is echoed in the Pluto in Virgo generation. This magnifies a sense of crisis and speaks of a need to humble the personal self before larger forces: in Virgo, the sublimation of the personal will to the other, and, in Pluto/Scorpio, the sublimation of the social will to transpersonal forces.

Suggestions as to the Nature of any Potential Crisis: Pluto in Virgo through the Houses
(Note the word 'potential'. Here I am looking to find what may be blocking someone's self-expression and happiness, not to dream up new burdens.)

Pluto in Virgo in the 1st House
Potential crisis as to how to achieve personal freedom to understand one's needs on an instinctual level. The crisis occurs through past restrictions of this freedom and resulting internal messages of 'not being good enough'. There's the potential for relationship crisis, as relating – while being desired to promote freedom – is subconsciously feared as a restriction to that same need.

Pluto in Virgo in the 2nd House
Potential crisis as to the nature of the personal needs which, for various reasons, one has felt the need to deny or restrict in a fundamental way. There may be subconscious fears around the capacity to survive (materially and emotionally). The issue could be exacerbated by a denial of being stuck through subconscious anxiety about the capacity to overcome limitation.

Pluto in Virgo in the 3rd House
Potential crisis in the formation of the mind through the reception of persecutory messages from others, or from some fundamental insecurity in the formation of the conceptual faculties. Crisis may arise through over-identification with the mind – needing to know why everything happens the way it does – and through the lack of validation from others as to one's personal viewpoint.

Pluto in Virgo in the 4th House
Potential crisis in the early home life through the failure of one or both parents to understand the child or to validate the child's existence in some fundamental way. There is radical insecurity within the ego; fears of abandonment underlie a core crisis in establishing a foundation of self-acceptance.

Pluto in Virgo in the 5th House
Potential crisis in knowing how to manifest the creative will and the sense of self-destiny. There may be memories of restrictions on this capacity in the past, and subconscious doubts or fears about one's capacity to achieve one's goals. A lack of positive feedback contributes to an ongoing struggle to accept the limitations of one's actual achievements versus one's desired ones.

Pluto in Virgo in the 6th House
Potential crisis in the humiliation of the personal will in the face of the other. The need for self-analysis and an understanding of one's personal egocentricity reaches crisis proportions and contributes to a potential failure of will, denial of self, profound self-doubt or punitive patterns of thinking.

Pluto in Virgo in the 7th House
Potential crisis through persecutory messages from others, or through feelings of not being good enough for other people. These co-exist with a powerful need to be with others and, in the extreme, profound fears around being alone.

Pluto in Virgo in the 8th House
Potential crisis through powerlessness. The goal of radically transforming pre-existing self-limitations produces frustration to the extent that there's an identification with the old self as the basis of one's security. Crisis develops as fear and resistance meet the need for depth contact with oneself and others.

Pluto in Virgo in the 9th House
Potential crisis as to the meaning of life. There is a fundamental need to understand feelings of alienation and core aloneness, and to participate and relate to the cosmos in its living mystery. Crisis occurs when one can find no sense of higher meaning, or if one fails to share or understand the meaning that has been intuited.

Pluto in Virgo in the 10th House
Potential crisis as to the nature of past or present judgments. Persecutory anxiety: the feeling of being put down can lead to a psychology of defeatism. Constantly keeping busy can manifest as a denial of the Self. There is a struggle to achieve the standing or role in the world that one feels one needs or deserves – and how this relates to powerful subconscious fears of being criticized or attacked.

Pluto in Virgo in the 11th House
Potential crisis as to the meaning of past experience and conditioning patterns: one needs to re-contextualize the past, which frequently includes traumatic memories that have threatened the validity of the Self.

Pluto in Virgo in the 12th House
Potential crisis of meaning; cyclic experiences of meaninglessness and despair. There may be a struggle to orientate a realistic assessment of one's personal self in the greater context of the collective experience or the spiritual realms.

The Collective Context
The crisis of the personal will (Leo) in the face of the other (Libra) is a potential issue for every member of the Pluto in Virgo generation (born between 1956 and 1972). Before analyzing the signature of a generation, there are two possible ways of approaching an understanding of the core issues that these millions of individuals share:

1. Groups of individuals incarnate at specific times for specific evolutionary reasons/concerns.
2. The particular cultural and historical issues that each generation faces shapes that generation in some indelible fashion.

We could describe the difference between these two, not mutually exclusive, approaches as the difference between the inner causes (evolutionary pressures that appear to bring people into being at a certain time) and the outer causes (historical circumstances that shape the individual) that operate on the individual and collective levels.

We could say that historical circumstances influence this generation on the level of what to do (right work, right relationship to the environment) and how to be (crisis of confidence, the humiliation of the self) and that these influences have their own inner origin when examined from a viewpoint that includes the nature of karma. Karma reveals a further dimension of meaning within the collective, i.e. that these people have a conscious or unconscious intention to incarnate within the given historical circumstances (that are promoting potential crisis) because of certain inner needs and intentions to evolve. People 'choose' (consciously or not) certain historical contexts in order to express their inner evolutionary intention.

To examine the historical circumstances that might precipitate a crisis in the personal will on a generational level for the Pluto in Virgo group, I will give a brief overview of the preceding generations.

The Pluto in Cancer and Pluto in Leo Generations
The Pluto in Cancer generation (1912–38/9), born during and in the aftermath of the First World War, the boom and bust of the '20s, and the resulting Great Depression, has personal and collective security as a primary motif. This would play out ultimately through two world wars, both of which in their differing ways had their origins in the issues of global empire building (Capricorn, the polar sign of Cancer) and the projection that territory equated directly with security (Cancer). This generation saw tens of millions lost to the first genuinely industrialized conflicts as a result of the shadow of humanity's inherently destructive side. The generation was witness to the capacity of people, when cornered by material and emotional restrictions, to project the cause of this blame onto the 'other' (Libra, as seen through the insecurity of Cancer, a natural square), which led to consequences of unbelievable proportions.

The Pluto in Leo generation (1938–56/7) represents the generation of baby boomers born into the aftermath of a world devastated by the Second World War, the Holocaust and the first use of atomic weaponry. This was a generation whose creative vision and new energy rebuilt the world from the rubble of Europe, North Africa and parts of Asia. This was a necessary counter to the destructive side of the fight for security (the Pluto in Cancer generation) and it saw the birth of a new vibrancy in popular culture (rock 'n' roll, the explosion of cinema) and the optimism of an upwardly mobile populace that sought to break the confines of pre-existing gender and socio-sexual role identification, which had been so rigid in the preceding generation.

The Shadow of the Lion

The creative energy of the Pluto in Leo generation casts alongside its brilliance a long and powerful shadow. One is of narcissism, the kind of creative identification with the Self that finds it hard to see beyond the value of the Self and look towards others. One reason for this is expressed in the tension between the Pluto in Cancer parents, devastated by conflict and material struggle, and the new potential of the Pluto in Leo generation. This is an aspect that Jungian analyst Nathan Schwartz-Salant sees at the root of a complex:

> It has been suggested that idealization plays a crucial role in the formation of the narcissistic person... According to this theory, the child has been the target of lofty and grandiose parenting ideals. Through largely unconscious communications from parental figures he or she has been given the 'charge' to fulfill unlived ambitions, which are actually the archaic forms of parental failures of individuation. It is clear that if the child is treated as 'special', difficulties will arise from so concentrated a form of attention, since the basic requirement is to overachieve. But the matter is far worse. The narcissistic person has simultaneously been given a completely opposite message – namely, the devastating message of envy. The message is transmitted as follows: 'You are wonderful and I hate you for it. You have it all, and since I don't, I despise you for what I do not have.' Here, having 'it all' refers to more consciously idealized qualities espoused by the parents.[5]

This is a developmental issue that, under certain conditions, has the potential to be expressed in *every* generation, but I see this complex enacted most clearly between the Pluto in Cancer parents (the recipients of so much anxiety and loss) and their Pluto in Leo children (with their great future potential). The failure of one generation to individuate will seed deep unconscious wounds in the next: one of the causes of the Leo shadow of narcissism is the subconscious envy of the prior generation.

Another cause of narcissistic ownership is an inherent issue in the development of the Self: the subtle issue of authorship. Spiritual teachers of the quality of Nisargadatta Maharaj, David R. Hawkins, Eckhart, Rumi[6] and many others have said that it may appear as though we are the author of our actions, but in truth the Self is a construct or a small expression of the wave that is on the surface of a huge ocean. It is not the personal Self that is creative or beautiful, it is the ocean of spirit of which we are but a single wave.

Shadows of the Self

In the Pluto in Leo generation the narcissistic celebration of Self and focus on the cult of celebrity have seen the abandonment of limits on colonization and the misappropriation of resources. And through a lack of thought for all forms of life, there has been a degradation of cultural and biological environments. Whereas members of the Pluto in Leo generation expressed their creativity in the mainstream and without thought of limited resources, the following generation is preoccupied with the issue of *lack* in the world.

The Pluto in Virgo generation awoke to a world under the shadow of the mushroom cloud and the endless passive-aggressive conflict that was the Cold War. That inauspicious start, allied to an increasing recognition of the planet-wide loss of bio-diversity and non-renewable resources, added to an innate feeling that the generation was here to perform a clean-up operation.

Within this generation some are too paralyzed by nihilism or their relative insignificance to start the clean-up of both the Self and the environment. Denial becomes the classic Virgo defence for some, a stance that protects the narcissistic wound of the shadow of the un-tempered Leo Self within. The Pluto in Virgo generation is left with a choice between serving the best of the creative outpouring of the preceding generation and the avoidance of its grandiosity and selfish appropriation of resources.

The Pluto in Virgo Problem

The challenges for this generation are to find ways of expressing the creative urge of the Self and unleashing its creative power into the culture at large. The excesses of the preceding generation – the unbridled expansion, aggressive tapping of resources, the rock star clichés and the theory that social reality is constructed by individual 'giants' or political reality by one elite club – all seem anathema to the Virgo generation.

Even finding suitable work becomes terribly complex in a culture where commercial realities have overridden the genuine creative expression of the masses, as evidenced by the disappointment of graduates when faced with a production line, and the denigration of the old-style humanities and concept of an 'overall education'. The attainment of the right job is nevertheless a fundamental, moral imperative for this generation. Not all may follow the Pluto in Virgo need to purify the social, ecological and moral concerns of the workplace, but that does not make these concerns any less important for their generation as a whole.

Within this there is the developmental problem of the Self. The Pluto in Virgo individual has a desire to examine, explore and remove any excessive egocentricity (the Leo shadow) from the psyche. This intentional re-evaluation of the Self can lead to problems: instead of merely curbing the egocentric tendencies, the individual can experience a lacerating critique of its own being, leading into a vortex of negativity, inactivity or self-destruction.

To explore the deeper context of the origin of these kinds of inner states, we need to understand certain historical currents which have shaped the development of our culture and filled the storehouses of the collective unconscious.

The Astrological Age of Pisces and Sub-Age of Virgo

A further way of exploring the astrological archetypes developmentally is through the lens of the astrological ages. Each age is around 2,160 years in duration and is linked to the phenomenon of the precession of the equinoxes. We can identify a sub-age halfway through, which belongs to the sign's polar opposite.

This developmental system explores a cyclic relationship to history through the position of the spring equinox, in Pisces at the time of Christ. Through the polarity of the archetypes we can identify a Virgo sub-age that starts around 1100 AD, which coincides with the building of the great cathedrals and the flowering of the medieval imagination and the 'religions of the Book'.

The Problem of Lack

Within the Western tradition, for the first time in history the presence or divinity of life is seen as absolutely transcendent of the creation, and this creates a problem of lack: the individual is not inherently divine, is not inherently saved. In fact the individual is guilty until proven innocent because of carrying the ancestral sin of the first humans. This is a world where the idea of sin predominates every activity. Later reformers such as Calvin found devilishness in the most innocent and joyful of activities.[7]

This endless quest for salvation then builds ever-increasing circles of misdemeanours and sins, which we then ironically need saving from. The obsession with purity sees us finding dirt wherever we look. This is an issue that Marion Woodman in *Addiction to Perfection* has detailed movingly when writing of the feminine psyche and the nature of self-esteem, eating disorders and body image, which I believe reveals the subconscious legacy of these teachings.[8]

The Fallen Self

Due to the evolutionary intention to purify the Self of excessive egocentricity and narcissistic delusion, members of the Pluto in Virgo generation become particularly sensitive to the underlying message of internalized guilt and 'inner lack' that so permeated the Christian origins of our culture.

The message of Original Sin, of the incompleteness of humankind's existential/spiritual state held separate from a purely transcendent divinity, saturated the collective unconscious during the Christian era. Those within the Pluto in Virgo generation or with a Virgo/6th House archetype emphasized in their chart are simply more prone to the impact of this message, as it forms a (un) natural alliance with the internal need to denigrate the value of the Self.

If the myth of the Pluto in Leo generation is that of the hero's journey of never-ending progress towards the creative fulcrum of the Self, the Pluto in Virgo generation inherits a strong suspicion of the assumptions contained within this myth. The belief that all is onward and upward – that every generation earns more than its parents, that acquisition of value is an endlessly increasing spiral, that there are endless resources – is a fantasy. We may note with some humour, in a study reported by clinical psychologist Richard Bentall, that depressed people frequently score more accurately in some self-reality testing![9]

The Lonely Crowd

> The reigning economic system is founded on isolation; at the same time it is a circular process designed to produce isolation. Isolation underpins technology, and technology isolates in its turn.[10]

> What we call 'normal' is a product of repression...[11]

The problem of existential and emotional isolation within the image of the collective is one of the critical paradoxes of modernity and the industrialized world. It presents a challenge to the Pluto in Virgo generation for a number of reasons. For some the conscious or unconscious message of inner lack, loss of Self or existential or inherited guilt (i.e. Original Sin as mediated through the culture) is so severe that they are paralyzed into nihilism, masking the loss of Self in addiction or extreme denial of their inability to act. For others, although they wish to overcome their isolation and serve their community, they find in place of their will and capacity to act that they have erected a series of rationalizations. This is another manifestation of a problematic loss of Self.

Others harbour profound feelings of not being good enough, of not deserving success or happiness. This constellates as a form of psychological masochism as I have seen in my counselling practice, where good people treat themselves worse than they would treat any other living creature. Another approach is through workaholism or extreme achievement, which in its hub of activity masks any internal feelings of lack. Others struggle to cope with anything more than a servile role or a 'McJob' in order to minimize the stress on their already-sensitized system.

There is potential within the Pluto in Virgo generation to see through the loneliness and narcissism of the quest for money and success. These individuated people are naturally suspicious of success (personal, social or environmental) 'at all costs', which is the prevailing attitude of much of the 'casino economics' of the modern world order.[12] The creative and highly functional Pluto in Virgo wishes to work with others to improve the overall standard of life for everyone. This is an important quality and one that is emphasized within a variety of alternative social and economic models, such as the growing transition town movement, or in collective approaches to creative self-expression (rather than the solo quest of the Pluto in Leo heroic figurehead).

The Power of the Internal Voice
The Virgo side to Mercury is the *internal* voice, while in Gemini it is external. A common issue that I have found within the Pluto in Virgo generation is a sensitivity to messages from others that imply some sort of value statement about the Self. These are then internalized and termed 'introjects' (literally Latin for 'thrown inside') by psychologists.[13]

Introjects can involve internalizing direct or indirect messages about the Self – i.e. what someone has said to us ('you are worthless') or what has been implied by word or action (in mistreating me consistently for no reason, it must be because I am worthless). Introjects occur most deeply when they are formed in early childhood and can involve a complete internalization of the parental figure. If that parental image includes judgmental, dissociative or abusive behaviour in its expression, then the individual can internalize profound shame or inner lack. Such introjects can create a barrier to forming healthy relationships and block the goals of the Libra archetype that follows on from Virgo.

Just as the Pluto in Leo generation has bought into its own myth, the Pluto in Virgo generation is proving susceptible to believing the negative myths that others have offered it. This is a result of natural needs for self-criticism and self-analysis (to promote growth) that become detached from all reason. Pluto in Virgo suggests deep mental processes, incredible capacity for self-analysis and rigorous self-examination – when the tendency towards excessive self-purgation or negativity is transcended. This generation has a fluid sense of Self (Mercury – the quick-moving, ever-changing archetypal expression) and a capacity to sense the multiple selves that constitute identity – and not be so trapped in just one fixed and unbending nature.

Uranus Conjunct Pluto in Virgo

The Uranus–Pluto conjunction in Virgo (1962–68) represents what I have called a trauma signature.[14] Every person born with this aspect manifests a subtle body trauma linked to the individual and collective issues already raised. This subtle, mental body trauma (a far or deep memory existing in the unconscious) has psychological and emotional consequences (Pluto) and is often experienced as a core betrayal of the Self (Uranus–Pluto in Virgo).

The nature of this betrayal is seen in the house position of the conjunction and through an analysis of the nodal axis, as I have written elsewhere.[15] This analysis becomes crucial in liberating the brilliance of this generation from persecutory messages of the past, including fearful memories of having been abused by authority or significant others.

I have found this kind of anxiety to have a virus-like structure that can infect every area of a person's life. In the extreme the Pluto in Virgo generation (certainly those with Uranus–Pluto conjoined) is capable of a self-lacerating cycle of thought. For example, a client of mine with this signature recently recognized that she had been anxious and depressed due to denying her relationship with a deeper Self that had been built in the past. Even though she had this insight, the virus of anxiety descended and she beat herself up for not having the insight sooner and for letting herself down. The positive insight is co-opted by the virus to prove that the Self, once again, is unworthy. This process belies an inner perfectionism, or static perfect standard, which the person is unable to ever completely live up to. This has echoes of the perfectionism of the figure of Christ or the distant God. In the modern psyche this creates compulsive feelings of failure despite external, positive events and successes.

With the Uranus–Pluto trauma signature we see that complexes of persecution have their origins in prior-life memories: being persecuted by tyrannical political systems, inquisitions or various 'witch' trials in literal form (in the medieval period) and symbolic form in more modern contexts (a distinction made by Arthur Miller in the play *The Crucible*).

The post-traumatic anti-authoritarianism present within the psyche of the Uranus–Pluto generation can be seen in the radical movements of the 1960s, which occurred during this conjunction, and in the punk ethos of the late '70s: the extreme actions and violence of the rejection of authority are reactions to past mistreatments by authority figures, as well as a core ambivalence about the Self.

Neptune in Pisces

From 2003 to 2011 Uranus transited Pisces and now Neptune is in Pisces from 2011 to 2025. As it travels through Pisces Neptune will oppose the Pluto placements of the Pluto in Virgo generation. The importance of the opposition point of Pluto is that it represents the evolutionary intention of the core Self. Pluto symbolizes the way in which the nature of the deep Self is seeking to evolve. The sign opposite to the Pluto placement, in this case Pisces, represents the polarity that must be embraced for the deep Self to find fulfillment. Just as we can see individuals moving from the South Node (past) to their future potential in the North Node, we can see people evolve from their deepest past identification (Pluto) to the polarity point directly opposite Pluto. Uranus created an awakening potential for this generation as it reached mid-life and now Neptune's very long transit will offer a powerful healing opportunity for this generation's sense of internal crisis.

This healing potential is revealed through the symbolism of Pisces: love, forgiveness and a profound self-acceptance on all levels, which becomes the ultimate antidote to anxiety. Within that acceptance there is nothing wrong, no mistake. In this way the profound experience of 'not being good enough' is understood as a form of inverse narcissism, a hangover from the preceding archetype of Leo. Seeing the Self as especially bad is just as delusional as seeing it as especially good. Such acceptance to my mind has a spiritual core yet it has an emotional and existential reality for all people, whether or not they have a spiritual perspective. Everyone can understand forgiveness towards the Self if offered a safe space from which to recover from the rollercoaster of anxiety and shame.

Einstein, when asked what he believed was the most important question in life, famously answered, 'Is the universe a friendly place?' This question holds the key to whether it is possible for the individual to accept his or her life. The transit of Neptune in Pisces offers the chance to realize this potential, as it refers on an ultimate level (Neptune transit) to the universal energy field, the flow of life from which anyone can find personal enrichment if one is able to surrender to life. This transit also includes the potential shadow side of escaping into fantasy, addiction or an identification with confusing or restrictive mass ideologies. If we move beyond shadow, if we encounter real presence with an open mind, then we can open to an energy field in which forgiveness and self-acceptance unite into a natural state. Andrew Harvey describes this experience as something that many people have when they meet the Dalai Lama:

> Everyone must begin from where he or she is. I've seen many atheists fall silent in the presence of the Dalai Lama... you find people giving up their fear in Christ's presence simply because he was so full of love. As always, hope lies in the truth that we all have the Buddha nature working in us to bring us to the recognition of our divinity, regardless of how long it takes. That is why the mystics never give up. They know that the secret order of the universe is on their side. However appalling the suffering of the world is, its ultimate nature is... love–knowledge–joy.[16]

The Sacred Feminine

A shadow side to the Virgo archetype of the harvest maiden is the denigration of the feminine within Western culture and religion over the last millennia. For example, the foundation of Western democracy in the Greco-Roman times held profound shadows of slavery and feminine disempowerment.

Such repression has produced the view that nature, the body, sexuality and the emotions are part of a corrupt or 'fallen' nature that the true seeker overcomes through intense striving. This has seen huge splits occurring within communal life, where masses of people have rejected conventional forms of religion or official governance because of the implicit or explicit rejection of life as it is actually lived within those forms. The sad truth is that the narrow-mindedness and distortion of much conventional religious or spiritual dogma have alienated many people from the nature of their true Self altogether.

The healing potential of Neptune in Pisces on a spiritual level is found in an understanding of the divine feminine (Sophia, the Shekinah, the Dakinis) experienced in the love of the Earth, our bodies and an emotional connection to each other and the planet, rather than in escapist flights away via transcendent religion, the religion of science, the glorification of the intellect or of power over others.

The transit of Neptune in Pisces as it opposes the Pluto placements of this generation represents an opportunity for a healing of what has been repressed individually and collectively. Many of the achievements of modernity, while impressive, contain a shadow of rejection of our embodied experience in this world ('something is better than this Earth, some virtual world will be more fulfilling'). For those attuned to this potential, this transit indicates a powerful opportunity to embrace this world for what it is: innately beautiful and meaningful. The mystical potential of this insight is stated in the Buddhist Heart Sutra, where the usually contrasted states of *samsara* (the world of continuous desire and, therefore, suffering) and *nirvana* (literally 'no wind', no desire, and a resulting peace) are seen in a moment of fusion as one and the same thing.[17] In mystical Christianity the same insight is expressed as the Kingdom of Heaven being in the *here and now* to the awakened heart, instead of in a distant hereafter. To touch upon this truth even for a moment is to transform one's sense of the joy in being alive.

Transitional Archetype, Transitional Culture

Not all individuals with Pluto in Virgo are in crisis personally, but I am a psychotherapist and astrologer who spends much time with people who are, and I have developed specialized skills for analyzing and working with these crises. However, whether or not the individual is in crisis, it is obvious that the concept of crisis has a global economic, ecological and political relevance at this juncture in history. Mass species extinction, the non-sustainability of most of our methods of energy generation, global temperature anomalies, the crisis of the marine environments (from agricultural pollution and non-biodegradable waste), and the separation between actual and imagined resources that forms the driving force of the world's economy are just some of the core issues facing the world at this time. One of the more sober assessments of our current crisis characterizes the nature of the times as the Long Descent of Civilization.[18]

The Pluto in Virgo generation, the youngest currently at forty and the oldest in their early fifties, is reaching the point where its members must be elders and mentors to the next generations. The later generations have grown up in a multimedia world in which the idea of a general education or the classical humanities (or even reading at all) is no longer deemed so pertinent. With Virgo, a Mercury-ruled sign, there is a need to preserve certain standards of knowledge that can be passed on, and this is part of the work of this generation. Others will actively seek cooperative work structures to build a more sustainable future. With transiting Pluto in Capricorn in trine to this generation's Pluto, the cooperative potential of preserving knowledge and creating healthier forms of governance could re-orientate structures of power in the world that have become too punitive and restrictive towards the populace.

Hakim Bay, the radical Sufi-influenced cultural critic, argues for the formation of *Temporary Autonomous Zones*,[19] places where the prevailing cultural hegemonies can be overcome by playful and cooperative loving revolutionaries. The idea would be that one would create temporary safe zones – spaces as diverse as a communal allotment or an astrological consulting room – in which individuals can express their needs freely. All individuals can feel judged and criticized, but this generation requires extra support to achieve healthy self-expression because of its extreme sensitivity and tendency to internalize negative messages. Freedom from internal criticism ensures that the autonomous nature of the psyche – the true life potential within the individual – can be validated. The Pluto in Virgo group needs to find, create and maintain these spaces in order to liberate the potential at the very heart of this generation: to serve others and to serve life.

References

1. Mark Jones, *Healing the Soul: Pluto, Uranus and the Lunar Nodes*, Raven Dreams Press, 2011.

2. Ken Wilber, *Integral Psychology*, Shambhala, 2000, p. 106.

3. *Ibid.*, p. 93.

4. *Ibid.*, p. 96.

5. Nathan Schwartz-Salant, *Borderline Personality: Healing and Vision*, Chiron Publications, 2007, pp. 55–56.

6. *I Am That: Talks with Sri Nisargadatta Maharaj*, Chetana Publications, 1974. David R. Hawkins, *The Eye of the I: From Which Nothing Is Hidden*, Veritas Publications, 2001. *Meister Eckhart, from Whom God Hid Nothing* (selected writings), Shambhala, 2005. *Rumi: Bridge to the Soul*, trans. Coleman Barks, HarperCollins, 2007.

7. Colin Wilson, *A Criminal History of Mankind*, Granada, 1984, p. 376.

8. Marion Woodman, *Addiction to Perfection: The Still Unravished Bride*, Inner City Books, 1982.

9. Richard P. Bentall, *Madness Explained: Psychosis and Human Nature*, Penguin Books, 2003, 'depressive realism hypothesis', p. 244.

10. Guy Debord, *The Society of the Spectacle*, Zone Books, 1995, p. 22.

11. R. D. Laing, *The Politics of Experience and the Bird of Paradise*, Penguin Books, 1967, p. 23.

12. Radio interview with Morris Berman, cultural historian and social critic.

13. From http://www.integrativetherapy.com/en/articles.php?id=35

14. Mark Jones, *Healing the Soul: Pluto, Uranus and the Lunar Nodes*, pp. 190–209. *How To Identify and Heal Trauma* mp3, www.plutoschool.com

15. Jones, *Healing the Soul*.

16. Andrew Harvey and Mark Matousek, *Dialogues With a Modern Mystic*, Quest Books, 1996, p. 240.

17. My recollection of the heart sutra is from a reading I gave hosting the Maitreya Project Heart Shrine Relic Tour. The line 'samsara is nirvana, nirvana is samsara' is one of the great statements of the mystical paradox of immanence and transcendence combined that has ever been made.

18. Greer, *Long Descent*.

19. http://www.autistici.org/2000-maniax/texts/taz.pdf

Maurice Fernandez
A Personal Biography

I enrolled in an astrology course around the time of my first nodal return, oblivious then that astrology would rapidly take over my life completely. I was living in Israel and was privileged to have found a teacher who combined a psychological and spiritual perspective on astrology; to this day, that is my primary orientation. She introduced me to the work of Jeffrey Wolf Green, who became my main teacher during the '90s and provided a vast, deep and new dimension to the template of my astrological study. Around the same time, I began to practice kundalini yoga and this sacred practice has had a direct impact on the way I practice astrology. The meaningful impact of yoga on my development inspired me to teach astrology in more holistic ways, unifying body, mind and emotions with spirit. A whole body of knowledge emerged gradually, the content of which I teach in my educational program and is published in my books *Neptune, the 12th House and Pisces* (2004) and *Astrology and the Evolution of Consciousness, Volume One* (2009). Today I organize journeys to powerful sites where participants study astrology with an emphasis on health consciousness and a community experience, honoring wildlife and nature, with an astrologically timed ceremony, yoga and meditation. I organized a conference, The River of Stars, in Hawaii in 2011, the first of its kind to incorporate the holistic principles described above. Having relocated to the United States in 2003, I moved to the Big Island of Hawaii in 2010. Looking to the future, I strive to solidify my commitment to help humanity reconnect with the earth and to the stars.

Aloha, Uhane Nui

Chapter Six

AN ASTROLOGICAL AND SPIRITUAL PERSPECTIVE ON MENTAL HEALTH

MAURICE FERNANDEZ

Addressing the subject of mental disorders is an extremely delicate matter, first and foremost because there is controversy about what the term 'mental health' actually means and includes. We live in an era where mental health is an industry and many people, including young children, are readily medicated to remedy behavioral patterns deemed extreme or dysfunctional. While some may find genuine relief through these treatments, others see their creativity and spirit dulled very early on and, particularly in the case of younger people, to the point of completely reconditioning and restricting their self-image and sense of self. Our psychiatrists and psychologists manage to help a considerable amount of people in distress, both the patients and their family members, but we also find that a significant portion of patients are not treated adequately or, in other cases, may suffer more from the side effects of conventional treatments than from the supposed ailment itself.

The purpose of this essay is to consider how astrology can provide an additional perspective on mental health, since human development and evolution can be correlated directly with planetary cycles. I have to emphasize that I do not have formal training as a psychiatrist or psychologist and I have not conducted an academic study on the subject per se. My point of view is purely astrological, from the viewpoint of the evolution of consciousness, based on my own research and direct experience through consultations with thousands of clients, many of whom have dealt personally with mental health issues, or have had someone close to them affected. I have found astrology a very helpful tool to understand the human condition. When we better understand the 'why' of a particular behavior, we can evaluate and choose more appropriate therapeutic approaches.

I'm a firm believer that mental disorders are not the mere result of possible chemical imbalances, but rather that these existing imbalances originate from earlier environmental, emotional, mental or spiritual misalignments. But the subject of mental health is so vast that only a fraction of it can be addressed through this essay.

I shall be touching only on some aspects of mental health, yet I do hope the content provides readers with enough inspiration to pursue their own research and expand on these observations. I will add that while I write about my observations, I do not claim them to be original; many of these ideas may have been contemplated earlier by people using other terms and forms. Moreover, readers are invited to practically implement the correlations offered and assess their value through their own experience, rather than taking any of the following content for granted.

The Context of a Challenging Existence

We live an extremely complex existence charged with recurrent challenges that test our capacity on every level, be it physical, psychological or spiritual. At a very basic level no one is born with an instruction manual and life gives us complex messages about ways to survive and establish consistent well-being. If there were a clear-cut, one-dimensional formula that would describe ten reliable steps to health and happiness, we would not need to discuss mental health problems; life would be managed easily.

Personally, I would define 'living well' as five fundamental experiences of being: *health, love, joy, creative inspiration* and *productivity.* We may not have all five elements at all times, but straying from them for too long is a sign that our lives may not function optimally. In further extremes we may live in dysfunction when, instead of sustaining or increasing the quality of our life, we move into decline and a deepening unhappiness.

Our references to living well are subject to constant redefinition – one day we learn that fighting for what is right is necessary for survival, and another day we learn that letting go will give us true peace of mind. As life circumstances prompt us in opposite directions, we end up alternating back and forth, in this case between extreme defense mode and trust. Fluctuating between opposite approaches is part of life's drama, and finding balance in the midst of these extremes is a constant work in progress. As we attempt to decode what can provide us with dependable happiness, we endure episodes of difficulty, pain and trauma. These existential challenges take their toll on our mental resources. To our advantage, nature has it that with a decent support system in our childhood, we usually develop the resources and the capacity to address life's complex challenges without pathologically breaking down mentally. We develop *psychological and spiritual immune systems* that help us to ward off mental ailments or recover from them fairly well. Notwithstanding, high stress levels are common currency in the general experience of life and evidently some people slip between the cracks.

We possess different centers of function in our consciousness. Each of these centers is responsible for particular processes, ranging from primal survival needs to higher spiritual alignment. In the course of this study I shall concentrate on our psychological and spiritual centers, both of which, I believe, have a crucial role in our mental health. These two centers interrelate and affect one another closely. To define them briefly, the *psychological center* controls our mind and emotions, which serve as mechanisms to absorb, process and integrate life experiences so that we may function, develop and grow. Astrologically I associate our psychological center primarily with the Moon, Mercury and Pluto. On the other hand the *spiritual center* controls our navigation in life; it is our compass for existential well-being. The spiritual center regulates our sense of peace and trust, as we endeavor to discover meaning and inspiration in life. Peace and trust are founded on the realization that greater forces are at play in life and that these forces are essentially trustworthy. Accordingly the spiritual center is responsible for a healthy relationship between humans and existence, or humans and nature. Astrologically I associate the spiritual center with Jupiter, Uranus and Neptune.

It is important to note that when I make astrological associations, I refer to the archetype as a whole rather than the planet alone: for example, when referring to Neptune's influence, I also naturally include its respective sign (Pisces) and house (12th House) as factors of influence.

When we are weak *psychologically*, we are vulnerable to 'emotional indigestion', during which we fail to process and classify an experience, and run the risk of compromising our development. For example, a shock in our lives may be difficult to adjust to and, even if life appears to go on externally, we freeze on an internal level. If this internal blockage persists, our development can become seriously obstructed. When we are weak *spiritually*, we are vulnerable to existential insecurities: we doubt existence, see nature as a daunting force, become more confused and disoriented. Gradually we become consumed by fear, our faith in life and ourselves decreases and we stop believing that 'everything will be all right'. If this state of being persists it can cascade to overwhelm, cover and shut down other functions (such as the psychological or physical centers).

While the psychological and spiritual centers closely affect one another, they each pertain to a different dimension of existence.

The psychological center pertains to *the dimension of time and space,* while the spiritual center is linked to the dimension *beyond* time and space and, for lack of a better reference, I will refer to it as *the dimension of timelessness.* As individuals we live simultaneously between these two dimensions and it is my observation that our mental health depends on transitioning smoothly back and forth from one dimension to the other; time and space and timelessness are essential dimensions of experience in our lives.

Two Dimensions of Existence:
Time and Space Along with Timelessness
We all are well aware of time and space. As the Earth rotates around the Sun (which itself rotates around other spatial centers), we measure time through hours, days, nights, etc. Time is completely interdependent on the location (space) of our experience (daytime in the United States is night in Europe), and so space defines time and vice versa. Each time, each space captures a very particular experience of life: we work, eat or rest in separate moments, and so in time and space we experience existence in *fragments.* Like a movie comprising multiple frames to create a continuum, our life is a sequential collection of multiple 'time and space' experiences. As we proceed through time and space, we go through *motion* and absorb, digest, grow and create life; at some point we reach our maximum capacity and begin to physically, mentally and emotionally exhaust our resources – and eventually we pass away.

On the other hand the dimension of timelessness is not always as obvious as time and space, but equally relevant nonetheless. Timelessness relates to *all* the elements of our lives which are not bound to the wheel of time and space. In some ways timelessness includes all times and all spaces at once. It is the sum of all life fragments. Through timelessness we tap into inspiration and concepts such as love or justice. These are concepts that remain our references throughout the twists and turns of life; they are undying, they do not grow or change – *love and justice, in their essence, are not subject to evolution, but they do inspire evolution.* We experience the dimension of timelessness through our spiritual center and it serves as our reference when we proceed with life. For example, we may go through a phase where we feel loveless in our time and space experience, but we can still tap into the immutable and timeless quality of love, and remain inspired. *Through the dimension of timelessness we receive inspiration on how to proceed within time and space.*

We can perhaps better understand the intricate interdependence between the psychological and spiritual centers by exploring our approach to death. Life prompts us to fight death but simultaneously accept it; this is one of the greatest existential paradoxes and it is no surprise that it leaves many people confused. From the perspective of the psychological center, our instinct is to fight death and control it in order to live longer and with quality; we learn to take better care of ourselves so that we may gain more time and space, and push death further away. From the spiritual center perspective we realize death is a larger force that is absolute. Sooner or later it will win 'the battle' – we will die. Despite our possibly having spiritual beliefs about reincarnation, the fact remains that death is a completely overpowering experience that ruptures us forever from life as we know it; it is a generally irreversible change which is in most cases imposed on us. Even great spiritual masters suffer grief from loss, humbly so. The great spiritual challenge is not so much to develop intricate theories about the afterlife that may bring more clarity about death, but rather to accept that we cannot change the fact that we will die – peace is found in accepting the limits of our potency. Our relationship with death is an important indicator of how well our psychological and spiritual centers balance one another: such balance can be measured by how well we manage to alternate between control and surrender.

Timelessness brings us what is *greater than us, eternal, still, neutral and whole,* whereas time-and-space brings us what is *finite, in motion, evolving and individualized (in fragment).* While timelessness appears more appealing in its higher essence, the benefit of living in time and space is that we are allowed to experience life in a gradual fashion and expand our consciousness progressively. If we lived in timelessness only, we would experience everything, simultaneously, at all times; we would be overwhelmed by the totality of all and likely disintegrate as a result. (To further expand on the qualities and influences of timelessness and time and space, you can refer to the 2012 edition of my book, *Neptune, the 12th House and Pisces.*)

Let us use the table below to gain more clarity on the different attributes of each dimension:

Time and Space	Timelessness
Psychological center	Spiritual center
Emotions and mind	Spirit
Motion, change, evolution	Stillness, immutability
Fragments	Whole

Individuality	Oneness
Boundaries	Infinite
Relative	Absolute
Absorb, integrate, classify, grow	Inspire, gain direction, harmonize
Control and function	Receptivity, surrender and trust
Skills and creativity	Inner strength, immunity
Details, personal	General, impersonal
Giving	Receiving
What I can create	What existed before me
Stimulation	Peace

Mental Health and the Bridge between Dimensions

Reiterating my earlier statement, I strongly believe that balance and a fluent interplay between our psychological and spiritual centers (or in other words, between time and space and timelessness) are key factors in our mental health. However, as described previously, it is obvious that these two dimensions are very opposite in their essence; integrating them and coordinating balance between them is a work in progress.

The psychological center is balanced by the spiritual center when the latter provides context for our life by taking us outside our personal reality to gain greater perspective on life and accept what is yet unknown. On the other hand the spiritual center is balanced by the psychological center when the latter facilitates the integration of larger concepts into our personal life so that we may implement our inspiration practically – this provides us with a greater sense of existential security.

In circumstances when the flow between these two centers is severely compromised, mental disorders can emerge. In this essay I shall explore the dynamics of some of the main mental health disorders from this perspective, and I'll offer general guidelines and insights.

When an imbalance exists between the psychological and spiritual centers, I have observed that one center begins to overwhelm and 'dominate' the other. The domineering center becomes in various ways overactive and excessive, usually as a way to compensate for the lack of balance. In some disorders the psychological center is the one that becomes 'overactive' while the spiritual center is weakened and neutralized, and in other disorders the roles are reversed. Sometimes both centers are very strong and active, but without balancing one another; this in turn causes each center to operate in extreme form.

A variety of life circumstances can trigger such an imbalance. A trauma may shock the system in early life, or even later in life, and engender a whole spectrum of posttraumatic stress symptoms; when these are severe and/or untreated, mental health can be chronically compromised. In other circumstances a shocking trauma with similar effects may in fact have taken place *in a past life*. In this case the baby is born already marked by mental health vulnerabilities or full-blown disorders. Growing up, he or she may be exposed to additional experiences that aggravate or appease the initial condition.

Overactive Psychological Center Disorders:
Anxiety Disorders, Obsessive-Compulsive Disorder, Hysteria (Histrionic personality disorder), Depression, Paranoid Schizophrenia

When the spiritual center is weakened and not productively operational, I have observed that a person can develop behavioral patterns that reflect existential insecurities, where confidence in the flow of life is compromised. The person might compensate for that with an overactive psychological center. The experience of timelessness may be flawed and dysfunctional in this case.

A common symptom for this condition is the loss of existential trust that throws the person completely upon him- or herself: nothing outside the person's personal immediate reality is reliable anymore. There is *no trust in anything that cannot be personally controlled*. Life, the universe, nature or, on some occasions, other people are perceived as intimidating or threatening factors. More often than not, *fear of death* consumes the person, whether the fear is conscious or unconscious. This fear is a strong indication that the person is in deep conflict with existence. With a compromised spiritual system, he or she lacks inner peace.

As the spiritual center is weak, it is common for optimism to fade because the essence of one's relationship with life is damaged. At a core level *one does not trust life or nature*. There is no faith in tomorrow, nor is there a belief that existing problems can be managed successfully by other forces, such as society or nature. The person relies only on him- or herself to be able to secure positive circumstances, but sometimes even faith in oneself is compromised. Naturally a compromised spiritual center engenders anxiety, the form and intensity of which varies from case to case.

As the psychological center overcompensates for the 'damaged' spiritual center, the need for control quickly becomes excessive. This approach is futile and does not bring back well-being or a sense of security, but for the person it seems to be the only way to react to the loss of trust. Anxiety can engender *anxiety disorders, Obsessive-Compulsive Disorder, hysteria (Histrionic personality disorder) and panic attacks*, among other conditions.

With an increasing need for control, there is a simultaneous and immense difficulty in letting go. When expressed physically, there may be the habit of repeating rituals over and over or phenomena such as compulsive hoarding. When expressed emotionally and intellectually, this dynamic may take the form of stalking ex-lovers or arguing one's point of view in relentless ways. Such people do not accept any other way but their own because trust is fundamentally lacking, and 'letting go' is interpreted as putting themselves in danger.

Individuals suffering from these conditions may surely have a spiritual consciousness or tremendous inspiration, but it fails to be integrated psychologically; the psychological and spiritual centers are not cooperating. For example, these individuals may be visionaries or pioneers in their field, but the fractured trust in life shows that, at a core level, the spiritual wound is festering and there is a split between the two dimensions of being – time and space versus timelessness.

Astrologically, when the psychological center is over-compensating for the compromised spiritual center we commonly see a strong presence of the archetypes of *Cancer, Virgo and/or Scorpio* (with their respective houses and rulers) in the natal chart. Generally these three archetypes (alone or in combination) describe a strong desire to establish security and foster development through personal control. Great attention is invested into internal processes and personal experiences, and great emphasis is put on the details of practical and/or emotional experiences. The person feels everything strongly and is compelled to regulate most aspects of his or her existence with much attention. When these dynamics are expressed in healthy proportions, we can identify a very nurturing, attentive, skillful and emotionally intelligent personality. But when out of balance, this dynamic escalates to excessive attachments, a consuming attention to detail, dramatization of danger and compulsions.

More specific chart signatures include having the Sun, Moon, Mars and/or Ascendant involved with the Cancer, Virgo and Scorpio archetypes by sign, house (4, 6, 8) or aspects to the angles (from rulers Pluto, the Moon or Mercury). Additional astrological factors that indicate the potential for these conditions commonly involve a very potent Mars position in the chart – for example, Mars conjunct or square the angles, or Mars locking into the nodal axis.

While the above signatures describe the *potential* for an overactive psychological center, we must also address astrological factors that affect the spiritual center, namely the archetypes of Sagittarius, Aquarius and Pisces (including their respective planets and houses). The wound to the spiritual center can show in various ways. A couple of possibilities include having Pluto, which can describe severe trauma through loss, or Mars, which can describe violence, shock or hurt, tied to these archetypes in challenging ways: for example, Pluto or Mars in the 12th, 11th or 9th House making angular aspects to other planets; or Pluto or Mars challenging Jupiter, Uranus or Neptune.

List of Chart Signatures

- The prominence of Cancer, Virgo or Scorpio archetypes (including emphasis on the 4th, 6th or 8th House, and/or a prominent Moon, Mercury and Pluto aspecting the angles or the nodal axis).
- The Sun, Moon, Mars, South Node or Ascendant associated with the Cancer, Virgo or Scorpio archetypes by sign, house or aspect to the rulers.
- Tight aspects between Moon, Mercury and/or Pluto.
- Mars tightly aspecting the angles or the nodal axis.
- Mars and/or Pluto in tight association with the Sagittarius, Aquarius or Pisces archetypes (including being positioned in the 9th, 11th or 12th House, or in tight aspect to the respective rulers).

These are not the only signatures to potentially engender an overactive psychological center, but they do play a strong role in this dynamic and must be seriously considered. The more these configurations repeat in a chart, the greater the potential for stress levels to increase in association with the issues described, and consequently the greater the vulnerability to lose balance between the centers in the ways described.

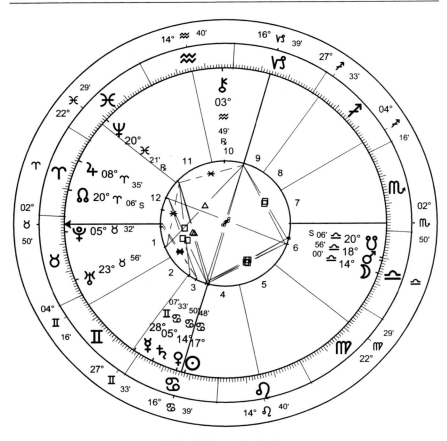

Nikola Tesla's Birth Chart

Example Chart: Nikola Tesla (July 10, 1856 at midnight (of the 9/10), Smiljan, Croatia), Koch house system. RR: B.
Condition: **Obsessive-Compulsive Disorder**

Short biographical references (from Wikipedia, AstroDatabank):

> *Serbian-American inventor and engineer who was a master of electricity at a time when it was changing American life. He is the unsung creator of the electric age, without whom our radio, auto ignition, telephone, alternating current power generation and transmission, radio and television would all have been impossible.*
>
> *Tesla may have suffered from obsessive–compulsive disorder, and had many unusual quirks and phobias. He did things in threes, and was adamant about staying in a hotel room with*

a number divisible by three. Tesla was physically revolted by jewelry, notably pearl earrings. He was fastidious about cleanliness and hygiene, and was by all accounts mysophobic (germ phobia).

He never married, and cited on at least one occasion that marriage wasn't good for inventors. He was driven by compulsions and had a progressive germ phobia, washing his hands frequently and avoiding shaking hands and measuring the volume of his food before he ate it. He liked a fresh tablecloth with every meal. Always a fastidious dresser, he wore new gloves weekly and a new tie daily. He maintained the same weight through his lifetime – 142 lbs – and always slept two hours a night.

...he openly expressed his disgust for overweight people, once firing a secretary because of her weight. He was quick to criticize others' clothing as well, on several occasions directing a subordinate to go home and change her dress.

Nikola Tesla's astrological signatures for Obsessive-Compulsive Disorder Tendencies:

An Overactive Psychological Center:

- Sun in Cancer and in the 4th House conjunct the IC.
- Moon in the 6th House, square the MC/IC axis.
- Moon conjunct Mars and the South Node in the 6th House.
- Pluto on the Ascendant.
- Potent Mars (conjunct the nodal axis and the Moon).
- Mars in the 6th House.

Compromised Spiritual Center:

- Jupiter in the 12th House square Saturn.
- Neptune in Pisces in the 11th House and Uranus in the 1st House in a Yod formation with the South Node and Mars in the 6th House as the apex.

Nikola Tesla is a good example to illustrate the dynamics described. The strong chart emphasis on the sign of Cancer, the 6th House and Pluto reflects the archetypal predominance of the signs of

Cancer, Virgo and Scorpio, which are associated with an overactive psychological center that, in his case, triggered obsessive-compulsive tendencies. It is not clear if he was officially diagnosed during his lifetime, but accounts of his behavior depict clear symptoms of the condition.

In his chart the Mars–Moon–South Node conjunction in the 6th House reflects an acute emotional intensity and relentless need for control. This triple conjunction is the apex of a Yod linked to Neptune (in Pisces in the 11th House) and Uranus (in Taurus in the 1st House) through two quincunxes (I use an orb of up to 5° for Yod configurations). This suggests that his spiritual center was very strong, and we surely know how inspired a person he was. Nonetheless, because Neptune and Uranus are conditioned by the quincunxes to the Yod apex configuration in the 6th House, we can see the struggle between his spiritual and psychological centers – a pressure to integrate his spirit through his mind and emotions. On the one hand, he tapped into higher worlds of infinite wisdom but, on an intimate level, he was overwhelmed by existential insecurities and shattered trust. He stayed away from people, especially women, and feared germ contamination. While he was raised in a family with three sisters, the Moon–Mars conjunction suggests adversity or even abuse from female figures that possibly contributed to his problems around trust.

He clearly was immensely creative and apparently his excessive attachment to detail, which was intrinsic to his obsessive behavior, also contributed to his genius.

From Wikipedia:

> *Tesla was stricken with illness time and time again. He suffered a peculiar affliction in which blinding flashes of light would appear before his eyes, often accompanied by visions. Much of the time the visions were linked to a word or idea he might have come across, at other times they would provide the solution to a particular problem he had been encountering; just by hearing the name of an item, he would be able to envision it in realistic detail. Modern-day synesthetes report similar symptoms. Tesla would visualize an invention in his mind with extreme precision, including all dimensions, before moving to the construction stage; a technique sometimes known as picture thinking. He typically did not make drawings by hand, instead just conceiving all ideas with his mind.*

Contemplating Ways to Balance an Overactive Psychological Center

Besides Obsessive–Compulsive Disorder, there are other symptomatic variations of an overactive psychological center that can result in other forms of mental health disorders. We cannot examine the full spectrum of these conditions in detail within the scope of this essay. However, I have observed that an important step in addressing an overactive psychological center is to find ways to heal the person's relationship with life and nature; this would allow for *greater tolerance for what cannot be controlled* and a chance to regain a sense of existential peace. Accepting the consequences of not having complete control may help with the acceptance of death. Strategies to heal these matters vary from case to case, depending on the initial trauma that caused the problem. For some people, I could see that activating their physical body, particularly by sweating or developing spinal flexibility (through modalities such as Yoga), would promote better hormonal distribution and a pacification of the excessive mental and emotional energy charge. For others, it may be that developing a broader spiritual approach towards life provides better acceptance and management of existential pain.

Overall, combining chart analysis with reliable conventional and alternative therapeutic treatment may offer a person a holistic platform to address existing imbalances.

Overactive Spiritual Center Disorders:
Bipolarity, Attention Deficit Hyperactivity Disorder (ADHD), the Autism Spectrum, Addiction Disorders

When the psychological center is weakened and not productively operational, I have observed that a person can develop behavioral patterns that reflect a disassociation from life's practical reality. This can lead to severe adaptation and isolation problems. This dynamic is commonly compensated through an overactive spiritual center.

With an overactive spiritual center the person taps into the unlimited potential of life where opportunity, spiritual ideals, freedom of spirit and reservoirs of ageless truths are accessible. Inevitably this is a very enriching and uplifting state of being that keeps the person in high spirits. Yet, since the psychological center is compromised, little is substantially processed within time and space. The timeless experience is not well adapted to everyday reality. Already, in normal circumstances, the dimension of time and space is evidently a more narrow dimension of being, compared to the vastness of timelessness; but when the spiritual center is overactive, this sense of narrowness is amplified many times over. Consequently the person experiences tremendous frustration when having to be in the time and space dimension. As a result, a recurrent reflex is to 'flee' time and space and to linger in timelessness for as long as possible. Such a position can render the person restless, scattered, disengaged, neglectful, naïvely optimistic and trusting, euphoric or excessive.

Integration within the realm of time and space is fundamentally compromised when the psychological center is wounded or underdeveloped and, as a result, *the person fails to synchronize with the rhythm of the world.* Being out of sync causes increasing dissociative tendencies and awkwardness. In these cases everyday life details are often overlooked, and consequently, (self) maintenance and attention to survival needs are neglected (to varying degrees of severity). Compensating through an overactive spiritual center keeps one within the realm of timelessness, where infinite potentials and larger ideas are more appealing than the 'trivialities' of everyday management. In the timeless realm there is a sense of eternity and vastness that provides one with a *seeming sense of freedom*; it becomes a private world where codes of behavior and communication are completely unchecked. Yet, when having to leave this universe of ideals to reengage within the sequence of everyday life (the time and space dimension), it may require a monumental effort that is often experienced as a recurring shock. For example, the person expresses acute frustration when projected back into everyday life because this is experienced as extremely limiting or dull. Sometimes this frustration can manifest physically, with the body feeling caged. It is as if the 'free genie' is forced back into its narrow bottle.

The absence of boundaries within timelessness engenders different forms of excesses, from inexhaustible energy levels to incessant discourses, a lack of focus, larger-than-life ambitions and/or an over-dramatization of one's personal life purpose. Along with that, communication with the environment is commonly poor, sometimes to the point of being dysfunctional. This can occur for two reasons. First, the person is out of sync with people, rendering personal expression awkward. Second, the person is commonly under the impression that everyone else thinks the same way as he or she does, thus no real effort is invested to properly explain internal realities. Accordingly, poor critical thinking inhibits self-adjustment opportunities.

The sum of these circumstances usually leaves the person in an isolated bubble. Mental health disorders that may emerge from such an imbalance are *bipolarity, ADHD, addiction disorders* and *autism spectrum,* among others. While autism is considered a neuro-developmental disorder rather than a mental illness, I would personally still associate it with the described imbalance.

Numerous individuals suffering from bipolarity or autism spectrum possess exceptional capacities, sometimes to the point of sheer genius, and this reflects their connection with the greater dimension of timelessness. Examples include the capacity to compute complex equations with relative ease and speed, or to demonstrate courage and extraordinary vision, or again, to manifest immense creativity. Some individuals also develop extrasensory capacity such as sharpened sight and smell, or an aptitude for inter-species communication. Tapping into timeless reality with greater intensity enhances the potential to access uncharted territory and more ethereal realms. In some ways these individuals venture farther into spaces where the average human does not commonly go. Yet, as previously described, the price to pay for possible genius can be heavy. In addition to neglect and excess, and given that their processing and integrating mechanism is weakened, these individuals can easily overwhelm their nervous system and shut down because they become unbearably sensitive to their environment.

Importantly, roaming the realm of timelessness without adequate references renders these individuals vulnerable to delusions because Truth and self-indulgent wishful thinking intermingle without critical thinking. The person is inclined to get carried away and lose track of common sense. In critical cases he or she can develop *messianic complexes* or *compulsive lying*. With an overcompensating spiritual center, the line between genius, madness and fantasy is thin.

Some individuals with these disorders may possess deep emotional intelligence and also be conscious of their condition, but because their psychological center is compromised, time and space remain a burden difficult to bear. They can feel like caged animals who may have made peace with their enclosure, but still think of ways to escape.

Astrologically, when the spiritual center is overactively compensating for a compromised psychological center, we commonly see an emphasis on the archetypes of *Sagittarius, Aquarius and/or Pisces*. For example, the respective planets Neptune, Uranus and/or Jupiter may be in aspect to one another, or conjunct or square the chart angles or the nodal axis. Along those lines, the Sun, Moon, Mercury, Mars, the Ascendant or the South Node may have tight associations with the Sagittarius, Aquarius and/ or Pisces archetype – whether positioned in these signs or in the respective 9th, 11th or 12th House, or in aspect to Jupiter, Uranus or Neptune.

In addition to the above signatures, the Sun, Moon, Mars, Mercury and Ascendant in the sign of Libra or its respective 7th House and, to a lesser extent, in tight aspect to Venus, can further accentuate extreme imbalance and increase the odds for dissociative tendencies. The Libra signature would only be relevant if added to the ones described in the previous paragraph.

When the above signatures are expressed in a healthy way, the person can possess a broad perspective on life that inspires vision, faith or higher wisdom. This could enable him or her to integrate larger collective or spiritual dynamics into practical realities, and foster development on a personal and collective level. There is generally a healthy trust in life that engenders a better, more positive flow with circumstances without needing constant control over processes. Yet, when out of balance, these signatures translate into excesses, escapism, naïve idealism or, in further extremes, delusions and/or dissociative behavior.

While the above signatures describe the potential for an overactive spiritual center, we must also address astrological factors that describe a compromised or underdeveloped psychological center. Among others, these signatures include Moon and/or Mercury in tight aspect to Pluto and/or Mars, as well as Mars in aspect to Pluto. This can be exacerbated if the above factors are also involved with the Pisces, Aquarius and/or Sagittarius archetypes by sign, house or aspect to their respective rulers.

List of Chart Signatures

- The prominence of Sagittarius, Aquarius or Pisces archetypes (including an emphasis on the 9th, 11th or 12th House, and/ or a prominent Jupiter, Uranus and Neptune aspecting the angles or the nodal axis).
- The Sun, Moon, Mars, Ascendant, Mercury and/or South Node associated with the Sagittarius, Aquarius or Pisces archetypes by sign, house or aspect to their respective rulers.
- Tight aspects between Jupiter, Uranus and/or Neptune.
- The Sun, Moon, Mars and/or Ascendant in Libra, the 7th House, or in tight aspect to Venus.
- Tight aspects between Pluto or Mars with Jupiter, Uranus

and/or Neptune (accentuated if positioned in the 9th, 11th or 12th House, or in the signs of Sagittarius, Aquarius and/or Pisces.

• Mars, Saturn and/or Pluto in tight association with the Moon, Mercury, the angles or the nodal axis.

The more the configurations above repeat in a chart, the greater the potential for stress levels to increase and engender the disorders of an overactive spiritual center, and consequently the greater the vulnerability to lose balance between the centers.

Example Chart: Virginia Woolf (January 25, 1882 at 12:15pm in London, UK), Koch house system, RR: A.
Condition: **Bipolar Disorder**

Short biographical references (excerpts from About.com):

> *Adeline Virginia Stephen was born in London into a family of intellectual accomplishment and psychiatric disturbance. Although she received no formal schooling, exposure to her father's vast library, coupled with an innate ability to craft language and a vast energy, fueled Virginia's ambition to write from an early age.*
>
> *Virginia finished her first novel,* The Voyage Out, *in 1913 but did not see it published until two years later as a result of a severe breakdown which she would describe in letters and fiction the rest of her life. 'I married, and then my brains went up in a shower of fireworks. As an experience, madness is terrific... and not to be sniffed at, and in its lava I still find most of the things I write about. It shoots out of one everything shaped, final, not in mere driblets as sanity does.'*
>
> *In 1912, she married Leonard Woolf, and the couple came to be considered part of the 'Bloomsbury Group'. This circle of avant-garde writers, artists and philosophers was known for challenging artistic, sexual and moral norms of the late Victorian era and documenting – in flagrant detail-- their often homosexual affairs with one another in prolific diaries and letters.*
>
> *Woolf continued to suffer mood swings and breakdowns throughout her life. Her last novel,* Between the Acts, *was almost completed when she committed suicide at the age of 59 by walking into the River Ouse with a large rock in*

> her pocket. An androgynous modernist casualty of manic
> depressive psychosis.

Virginia Woolf's astrological signatures for Bipolar Disorder:

An Overactive Spiritual Center:

- Jupiter and Neptune conjunct, both trine Uranus.
- Jupiter and Neptune in the 12th House, both square Mercury in Aquarius (and Uranus is quincunx Mercury).
- The Moon in the 11th House.
- The Sun in Aquarius in the 9th House.
- The South Node in the 12th House.

Compromised Psychological Center:

- The Moon semi-sextile Pluto and Pluto tightly semi-sextile Mars.[1]
- The Moon in the 11th house, and Pluto in the 12th House.
- Mercury square Pluto.
- Saturn square the Sun and angles (and in this case, the MC/IC axis).

With an abundant 12th, 11th and 9th House archetypal emphasis, Virginia Woolf's chart describes a strong association with the spiritual center. Her inspired writings and avant-garde lifestyle reveal her inclination to transcend time and space conventions and conditions: she aspired to live and love with a free spirit.

Multiple psychological shocks in her early life – notably the loss of her mother and sister during her teenage years and the loss of her father when she was 22, along with reports of having been sexually abused in her youth – account for her wounded psychological center. The Moon to Pluto to Mars semi-sextile connection, along with the prominent Saturn square Sun/MC/IC, describes the emotional shocks that obstructed a smooth psychological development.

Because the chart shows such a strong emphasis on the 9th, 11th and 12th Houses, the tendency for her was to compensate for the psychological–spiritual imbalance by creating an overactive spiritual center. She experienced euphoric psychotic episodes that fed her artistic work, but this vast world of timelessness failed to be integrated emotionally and she suffered radical emotional breakdowns and depressive extremes when having to cope with

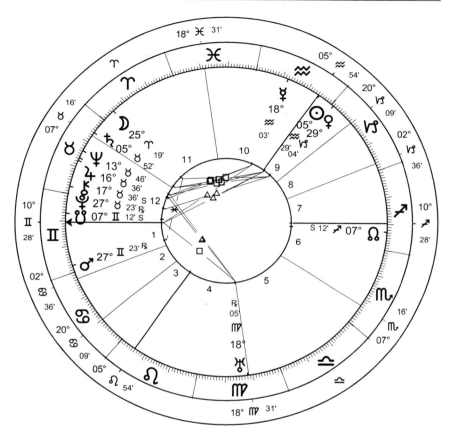

Virginia Woolf's Birth Chart

the time and space dimension. This dynamic took its toll: tragically, she felt overpowered by her illness and ended her life.

Contemplating Suggestions to Balance an Overactive Spiritual Center

Once again, only general suggestions are offered to balance an overactive spiritual center, as a more detailed approach would require a much more elaborate study. Notwithstanding, I have observed that in the case of bipolar disorder we can often detect earlier emotional trauma through which the person felt completely overpowered and/or humiliated. This can be a sudden loss, a severe violation or recurrent endurance of abuse. To compensate for a sense of helplessness or powerlessness, the person overactivates his or her spiritual center, because it can provide a sense of invincibility and even immortality.

It is my observation that making peace with the time and space dimension requires the acceptance of personal imperfections and limitations. Ways to address the trauma of having been victimized earlier in life must be pursued without succumbing to the temptation to escape or *compensate through a demonstration of invincibility*. For example, learning martial arts can be a way to address one's memory of victimization and helplessness, because it teaches one to be strong without abusing this power. Along with strengthening one's body and psyche, it is important to learn to ask for help, so that vulnerability is not experienced as dangerous anymore. Accordingly I find that establishing a solid support system is essential.

A Note about the Rise of ADHD Diagnosis in the Past Decades
According to a new 2011 US Government study, one child in ten is diagnosed with Attention Deficit Hyperactivity Disorder (www. cdc.gov/). Whether the statistical rise is the result of more cases, better diagnosis or simply more rigid standards of behavior is still to be determined, but it remains the case that more children today are medicated for this condition.

Astrologically we cannot overlook the fact that the children in question were born under the generational influence of the conjunction or mutual reception between Uranus and Neptune – both planets representing the spiritual center. Between 1990 and 1998 the two planets were within a five-degree orb of conjunction. From 1998 until 2003 both planets were travelling together in the sign of Aquarius – a sign also related to the spiritual center – and in 2003 when Uranus moved into Pisces, they both were in mutual reception and in signs associated with the spiritual center. This occurred until 2010, when Uranus moved into Aries. Individuals born between 1990 and 2010 are, according to these chart factors, inclined to have a strongly active spiritual center. While the majority of this generation manifests related qualities in balanced ways, we can also correlate this signature with a stronger prevalence of ADHD diagnosis in the past two decades. New Age movements labeled this generation the Indigo (or Crystal) Children, explaining that their potential for more intuitive and conceptual thinking will result in less conformist behavior (source: www.allaboutindigos. com). In more extreme cases less conformity means flawed adaptation to time and space, which can escalate into more dramatic hyperactivity, disorientation and lack of focus.

To enhance better adaptation and reduce the potential for scattering and restlessness, it is often suggested to people who suffer from ADHD to cultivate a stronger connection to their body as a means for grounding their energy (for example, exercise and a healthy diet that limits sugar intake have often proven helpful). For some, integrating within time and space requires a retraining of the brain in such a way that greater attention is given to detail. This basically entails practicing 'detail work' over time.

From a psychological point of view I have contemplated that short attention span may result from deep emotional insecurities associated with self-image problems; the person fears 'missing something' when being too focused on one matter. The vastness of opportunities symbolized by the expansive qualities of Uranus–Neptune can make one feel very small and insignificant on an intimate level and, as a result, prompt a need to 'be everywhere', 'experience everything' or 'have it all' in order to feel worthy. It seems that nothing is ever enough – beginning with oneself – and, as a result, one can unconsciously develop (or be born with) a scattered mind.

Ultimately the individual can learn that boundaries do not necessarily mean 'imprisonment'. It is misleading to fear that being in the time and space dimension will prevent him or her from experiencing the freedom intrinsic to timelessness; it is important to balance boundaries with risk and exploration so that these fears of losing freedom are mitigated.

Conclusions

I hope that the observations made through this essay – describing possible consequences caused by imbalances between the psychological and spiritual centers – can help us gain a better perspective on a variety of mental health conditions. However, it is important not to approach this study in a one-dimensional 'cookbook' way, but to understand that there are sometimes more intricate overlapping tendencies. For example, in the case of autism spectrum we may detect symptoms that are associated with both overactive psychological and spiritual centers. Autistic individuals with an overactive spiritual center may exhibit a neglect of personal care and hygiene, deficient communication and a withdrawal into the abstract dimension of timelessness. However, autism also comprises symptoms that reflect an overactive psychological center, where compulsive repetitive rituals or obsession for particular ordering of objects is exhibited.

There are many variables and mitigating factors that bring more complexity to a 'well-defined' theory. The birth chart can provide clues about these variables, but even astrology has its limitations because it cannot measure the extent of free will. Two people with the identical chart may respond differently when confronted with the same life circumstances. Therefore, one must not use the principles described in this study rigidly, but rather understand the *essence* of the paradigm and use it as a foundation from where symptoms and causes can be identified.

Accepting the limitations of astrology also implies that when we identify planetary signatures in a chart that suggest a potential for a particular disorder, there is no guarantee that the disorder will manifest in actual reality. The chart shows a potential, not a final outcome. A person may manage to express chart challenges in a healthy way and avoid extreme circumstances. As astrological counselors, we must avoid projecting definite scenarios onto our clients. Our role is to discuss placements, configurations and dynamics while guiding clients to an optimal expression of their chart's potential.

Notes

1. The semi-sextile is a very potent aspect when exact or tight and *bridges* the themes of the planets involved. In this case, the Moon in Aries in the 11th House (a potent, personal, emotional response) to Pluto in Taurus in the 12th House (a vulnerability to existential trauma that challenges a general sense of trust); and Pluto in Taurus to Mars in Gemini in the 1st House (a strong defense mechanism expressed through intellectual outlets).

Eric Meyers
A Personal Biography

All charts in this essay: Porphyry houses + True Node, Chiron

One day in my mid-twenties I had that indescribable moment of insight which changed the trajectory of my life. I left mainstream academia and the 'official' accounts of truth, and set out to discover my own. I journeyed to Boulder, Colorado, to receive training as a counselor at Naropa University. My opened mind easily held vacancy for astrology's arrival. I soon found Steven Forrest's astrology, which was meaningful, colorful, and fun. My apprenticeship with him overlapped with graduate school, and I sought ways to bring astrology to counseling. At my Saturn return I developed my soul intention to be a writer. I sank my teeth into the larger questions to develop my thinking and discovered a new world inside. Just as I had questioned academia, I brought this inquisitive approach to astrology. I held the possibility that our collective body of knowledge, and the paradigms which stem from it, must continually evolve. I found that my mind became sharper when connected to my heart, so I learned to find validation of ideas through emotional resonance. As my thirties played out, my quest arrived at another turning point. Through the teachings of various Nondual spiritual teachers and my own experiences and contemplation, I had the realization that the egoic self is ultimately a made-up story, perhaps even a dream. However, it appeared that astrology was preoccupied with it! Now at 40, I'm living what I understand to be my life's cause. My vision is an astrology that centers around Spirit, not ego – to see the Sun as our source energy which we can only *borrow*, never own. I invite you to consider the ideas which follow, but ask you to bring them into your heart. It is there that we may renew and refresh astrology for the next generation.

www.soulvisionconsulting.com
eric@soulvisionconsulting.com

Chapter Seven

THE PLANETS AND AWAKENING

ERIC MEYERS

In my new book, *The Astrology of Awakening: Eclipse of the Ego*, I argue that the mindset which primarily drives astrological inquiry and discourse is motivated by self-gain. Most of us would like greater self-knowledge, to have an inside peek into what's going to happen, or to know if 'the stars' will be kind. These needs are understandable, but they place several demands on astrology. It postulates that astrology is focused strictly on *personal* information, that it can reveal specifics, and that the universe doles out rewards and punishments. This perspective may compromise what astrology is capable of, while also keeping us orbiting around the ego instead of moving beyond it.

In this essay, I'll explore the idea that astrology can be used to clarify a path of awakening, which moves beyond a personal orientation and towards soul realization. Instead of astrology being able to provide us with specifics about what will happen, it is the chart owner who has control over the manifestation of the chart. The astrology chart is analogous to a car, while the chart owner is the driver – and we can all learn to drive competently or not.

The ability to drive capably results from the development of awareness. There is a wide spectrum of consciousness, from the darkness of being unconscious to the vibrancy of spiritual awakening. Our position on this range is the determining factor for whether our life turns out to run smoothly or not (what the ego often defines as 'good' or 'bad').

The focus here is specifically on the planets, how each of them can be either in service to the ego and its hunger for self-gain, or in partnership with soul realization. I believe the planets are energy for us to utilize as we learn spiritual lessons. Planets are not forces that deliver our fate. When we change the focus of our astrological inquiry and discourse, we can have a renewed sense of partnering with the universe to co-create a more awakened civilization.

The Sun and Moon: A Spiritual View

The Sun: awareness, vitality, soul realization, radiance, energy
The Moon: unconscious, instinct, ego, heart foundation, basic humanness

The shift in consciousness from the ego to the soul can be understood in how we view the Sun and Moon. The ego tends to look at life in terms of its own experience. Since gender and parental influences play such a large role in one's development and identity, it's natural to see the Sun, which radiates energy out, as masculine, and the Moon, which is thought of as a receptive energy, as feminine.

This is certainly one way to see it, but is it the only way? The amazing developments in the twentieth century teach us that there is no objective reality – everything is relative to the consciousness of the observer. There are many ways to approach life, many possible meanings. We can look at the Sun and Moon through the lens of gender, and we might also look at them through the lens of developing consciousness. There might be additional lenses too, but the focus here will be on how the Sun and Moon relate to the process of spiritual awakening.

The Sun's light is paired with awareness, while the Moon exists in the darkness of unconsciousness. The Moon is classically considered a 'luminary', but this designation belies our understanding that the Moon only reflects the light of the Sun. The Sun's light (and heat) promotes growth and sustains life – the Sun signifies being present and vital in the moment, awake. In contrast, very little grows where it is dark and cold. The various degrees of illumination of the Moon are analogous to the varying degrees of awareness we might have of our 'well' of accumulated experiences that are held in the unconscious.

From our vantage point on Earth, the Sun and Moon appear to be equal in size. This goes along with the truth that the masculine and feminine represent complementary and equal energies. However, astronomical reality provides a reason to have another view. We know the Moon reflects the light of the Sun. Would that suggest that the feminine is a reflection of the masculine? A transpersonal view suggests that the human condition (Moon) is a reflection of Spirit (Sun). Adopting this view, we can learn to see life anew and connect our energy with a broader reality.

Another example of inequality is found in the fact that 64 million Moons would fit inside the Sun. From the spiritual lens, the enormous difference in size illustrates how the Sun pertains to our 'bigger self', our soul connection to the radiance of Spirit, while the

Moon goes with our smaller, egoic self which operates from instinct and ego.

There is an evolutionary movement from resolving the past (Moon) to the realization of the present (Sun), but this doesn't mean that the Sun is better or more important than the Moon. We are growing from the *unconsciousness in the Moon* to awakening and honoring the sacred marriage *by fully being in both worlds*. Though the Moon 'holds' our lunacy or madness – the regressive parts of our nature, it's also full of beauty. Instead of any negative judgments about the Moon, it's more gentle and accurate to see it as a *less conscious* version of ourself. There is nothing wrong with being four years old, and our inner child remains with us too. The point is to move beyond the limitations of being like a four-year-old. We assist the Moon in *maturing*, so Moon seeds can sprout into Sun flowers. Plants continually need water – the Moon (seed) requires love (water), not abandonment.

We see that the light of Spirit (Sun) does not need individual human consciousness (Moon) for its existence; rather, individuals are enveloped in the broader spiritual sustenance of the Sun. Sri Ramana Maharshi says, 'The body cannot exist without the Self [his term for Spirit], whereas the Self can exist without the body.'[1] In our spiritual growth we integrate the broader awareness and presence of the Sun into the vehicle of the separate self (Moon). The Sun and Moon are in a sacred marriage to bridge the metaphysical (Sun) with the physical (Moon).

The Moon is associated with our humanness, the requirement to eat, sleep, exercise and perform all bodily functions. The Moon is our well of emotion, urges, attachments and memories that are unconscious, which become activated in various ways. In our vulnerable position, our reaction to life is extremely subjective and changeable, all stemming from the past, which colors our experience of the present. Many spiritual teachers call this state of subjectivity the *ego dream*, which is continually projected upon the world.

Most of us exist in this dreamlike state and spend our lifetime seeing to our personal needs for maintenance and contentment. From this perspective of *separation consciousness*, there is little (or no) awareness that our energy is connected to everything. Broader transpersonal issues are not relevant for our base level of functioning, and certainly do not appear to be urgent, so the focus remains on more mundane matters.

The Moon stores our experience in the unconscious; we hold on to the energy which impacts us most strongly. There are many degrees of awareness in understanding why we hold on to what is past. All of us are unresolved about various experiences and we hold on to the memory. The Moon ideally wants love and security, which is not usually available in our most trying moments. Eventually we might find self-love and acceptance, to make peace with the past and let it go. We can release the impact of the past by moving the energy through emotional catharsis, breath work, exercise or any other means to free what has been pent up. When we empty the proverbial cup, we naturally open to the dynamism and possibilities of the present.

Releasing the past allows us to become more informed by the solar field of creativity surrounding us. Some who have awakened describe heightened intuition and the emergence of creative impulse. We are then able to serve as channels or vessels for Spirit. Some teachers call this process of self-realization 'spiritual awakening' or 'enlightenment', though the vocabulary is unimportant. The point is to wake up from the dream of existing only in separation consciousness and our egoic reaction to life.

The only thing which prevents greater illumination is the contraction of the separate self due to any unfinished processing of the past. Without resolution, the Sun serves as a projector of our unconsciousness. This is helpful as it brings these contents to light. We can either awaken to the reality that we are in contact with ourselves *through* the world, or we can renew familiar defense strategies to deflect this reality and thereby stay only in the reactivity of ego (the Moon).

As we evolve, we gradually increase our awareness, like a seed (Moon) maturing into a flower (Sun). Our individual Sun placement has the potential to shine brighter as we expand our ability to be aware and present. Like a light connected to a dimmer switch, we have the capacity to increase our wattage. Eckhart Tolle says that awakening is a 'state of connectedness with something immeasurable and indestructible, something that, almost paradoxically, is essentially you and yet is much greater than you'.[2] When we become less attached to the personal story, we can view ourselves more objectively – like watching characters in a movie. Then, life becomes an interesting series of learning experiences instead of being driven by the urgency to survive. Ultimately we identify with nature itself – just as astrology illustrates that we are connected to the broader universe. Then, we are able to bridge the metaphysical with the physical to serve evolution most effectively.

The process of awakening can be resisted by the ego because it sees little benefit in releasing control. As increased awareness shifts our identity, the ego might become threatened by such a prospect.

Ultimately the ego can learn that it too is a radiant part of Spirit. Those who awaken learn to forge a partnership between self and Spirit. We find that the ego, the body and everything to do with being a separate self enable Spirit to be active in the world. The only difficulty is when we *over-identify* with separation consciousness.

We can view the process of awakening on a continuum from darkness to light.

Dark/Unconscious —————————— *Bright/Conscious*

Everybody is in a different place in this process. Babies and children tend to be less conscious than adults simply because we all start out in complete unconsciousness. In fact, as adults, we do not have any conscious memories of our first couple years of life. The same is true in terms of spiritual development. Most of us fall somewhere in the middle of the range of consciousness. We exist in the familiar confines of ego and separation consciousness while we also have moments of experiencing Oneness. We like to believe that all people are equal and this is true at an absolute level. However, there are various levels of spiritual growth at the relative level.

The astrology we've inherited does not include the important variable of the development of one's awareness. There is a focus on the perceived merits of various chart factors rather than the consciousness of the chart's owner, which is what brings the chart to life. The focus is on the 'car' to the exclusion of the 'driver'. This has influenced our perspectives on the Sun and Moon, and everything else too. Instead of seeing the Moon and Sun in terms of awakening, we tend to see them only in terms of gender, which keeps an orientation on dualistic separation. In this essay we will explore each of the major planets and how they might function for the ego in separation consciousness, and how they can be used in an *awakened way* to assist in the fuller realization of Oneness.

Mercury: A Spiritual Nerve Ending

Mercury: intellect, relative understandings, egoic brain, rational function

For many, the mind is the centerpiece of personal identity. This is captured by the famous phrase from Descartes, 'I think therefore I am.' With this mentality, the broader awareness which sustains us (Sun) is obscured by the mind, and therefore we cannot identify as a part of Spirit. As Mercury is always near the Sun, our awareness tends to go along with mental commentary. Spiritual growth involves taming the mind in order to more fully embody soul. If we fail to do this, then the tiny sidekick (Mercury) becomes a hero, promoted by the Sun's largesse.

In our egoic development it becomes greatly advantageous for us to use the mind to achieve a sense of order (a prime concern of the ego). We have named and categorized everything according to our limited ideas and frameworks. The mind has projected itself on the world and we have believed it all to be true! Who says a stone should be called a stone? Certainly there is nothing wrong with categorizing our surroundings, but few stop to realize how relative this all is. We like to think we have it all figured out. The ego thinks, 'The confusing world around me has order – therefore, my life is in order.'

Mercury is the personal mind in the relative world, where there is simply no objective truth. We see this in any polarity: science/religion, Democrats/Republicans, or opposing countries fighting a war. In all of their subjective minds they are all right, which is true from their respective viewpoints. However, it's never true in an absolute sense. Many spiritual teachers advocate forms of 'inquiry' into our thought patterns to discover that they are relative in nature. We can never know anything to be *absolutely* true, though the ego tends to object to such a notion.

Understanding Mercury's subjective and relative nature allows us to move beyond it. By so doing, we can use the mind for contemplative, intuitive or psychic reasons. With greater awakening and soul realization, Mercury plays a different role. Its closeness to the Sun is ideal for framing our thoughts as intentions, like sending little messages into the broader matrix of our interconnectedness. On the other side of the coin, if our thinking patterns are egoic and negative, that too radiates out and shapes our reality accordingly.

Mercury is a marvelous *tool* for us to use in the relative world. Spirit teaches us through the tool of Mercury and our part of the bargain is to learn how to listen. However, it is often the case that individuals like to claim ownership of ideas, which opens the possibility of distortion. When we identify as vessels of Spirit, we allow information to move through us and we give it form. It turns out that our thoughts are not just our own, they are part Spirit too; the individual brain (Mercury) is like a nerve ending of a larger brain (Uranus). When we release our preoccupation with thinking, we make room for true understanding.

Venus: Spirit's Paintbrush

Venus: physical senses, connection to environment, social self, aesthetics, 'sacred mirrors'

The earth side of Venus, associated with Taurus, involves physical beauty and worth, including anything of value. The separate self wants to be comfortable and have suitable clothes, shelter and money. With the ego involved, these 'wants' turn into 'needs'. Then, we might turn into 'users' of nature if we believe survival is at stake. We may equate having material possessions with happiness, so accumulation has a relationship with self-worth. At the extreme, we create a materialistic culture where the amount of money is the means to evaluate success.

The air side of Venus (Libra) includes social and conceptual realms. This is the energy of attraction, connection and relation to the external environment. Through air Venus we learn to adjust to culture and society. However, when the ego runs the show we *use* others to attain popularity, status or social security. We might use the law to unnecessarily sue others or employ other tactics for social strategizing in the name of 'fairness'. Instead of justice for the collective, we see only what is in our self-interest.

In mythology, Venus emerges from the severed genitals of Uranus. This is symbolic that beauty takes form in the manifest world from the broader transpersonal intelligence. Venus brings Uranus through the Saturnian gate which separates the visible world from the metaphysical. Like a scientist, we might analyze the physical world as having various properties and conditions, or we can see all color and aesthetics as the 'paintbrush' of Spirit.

Nature has an aesthetic precision which is unparalleled and miraculous. There are patterns in nature which are anything but coincidental; chief among them is what is termed the 'golden ratio'. This simple mathematical ratio permeates nature in countless forms, including seashells, fruits, plants, a developing fetus, crystals, musical patterns, numerical sequences, brain waves, and in scores of other ways. The planet Venus forms a conjunction with the Sun roughly every 1.6 years and completes a series of five conjunctions every eight years. A five-pointed star (or pentagram) is drawn in the sky, which has been called 'The Venus Star'. The mathematical relationships of the star's segments reveal the golden ratio. As discussed in Arielle Guttman's *Venus Star Rising*,[3] we each have a relationship to the Venus Star pattern which forms in the sky. The

Venus Star reveals another layer of Venus (arts, civilization, culture) pertinent for our collective evolution.

Venus can invite us out of separation consciousness and into broader connectivity. At a transpersonal level, the conceptual side of Venus may bring a more mindful and conscious form of civility and interdependence to our customs and laws. How can we live together in greater harmony? Whereas the ego looks at others and thinks, 'What can you do for me?', the soul learns of itself *through* others. Just as Venus reflects the Earth as its sister (or twin) planet,[4] other people teach us who we are by being 'sacred mirrors'. At this more awakened level, we are all one. The greeting *namaste* is the acknowledgement of Spirit in each other.

Another spiritual purpose of Venus (its earth side) is to become poised, peaceful and natural; being adept at using the body as a vehicle for spiritual evolution. We have the potential to give Spirit the arms and legs necessary to mold our surroundings to reflect its impulses. Our identification with the body may become so strong that it seems ridiculous and implausible to suggest that it's not *really* ours. The transpersonal reality is that the body is just energy borrowed from Spirit that we get the chance to be in a relationship with. Through this understanding we can use the body to bridge the metaphysical and the physical, heaven and earth.

Mars: The Spiritual Warrior

Mars: action, libido, karma creator, desire, self-orientation

Mars gets us out of bed to tackle life, take risks and develop courage. Necessarily selfish with its allegiance to instinct and the satisfaction of primal urges, Mars is raw and untamed. The ego is deeply in touch with the drama of staying alive, the necessity to fight or flee. It often takes years of cultivating awareness to behave *consciously* instead of subtly acting from the necessity to survive.

In order for us to cultivate habits of behavior consistent with a broader soul realization, we must bring presence and awareness (Sun) to the unconsciousness (Moon) of our underlying needs. If we don't engage the awakening process, behavior doesn't stem from choice, only from the illusion of it. Most people have little idea that their behavior is governed by deeply ingrained patterns. Here's the paradox of Mars: we experience personal free will, but we are truly free only when the ego becomes awake. Then, our liberated behavior is informed by soul realization, so it turns out not to be personal at all.

The cost of remaining unconscious is high. It is through the action of Mars that karma is created. When we behave in accordance with soul, there is no karmic residue because we are behaving as instruments for Spirit. Sri Ramana Maharshi says, 'Work performed with attachment is a shackle, whereas work performed with detachment does not affect the doer. After realization there is no karma.'[5]

Behaving from the dictates of ego creates issues to resolve. Whether in this life or another, we must venture through the karmic patterns we have created. When we become aware of the merry-go-round we've been on, Mars is the energy which arouses us to make changes. By accepting the past, we take responsibility for our karmic situation and move forward assertively. Martial energy becomes our ally as we learn to behave as a spiritual warrior.

How do we know if our actions are free of the continual recreating of karmic dramas? Awakened teachers describe a condition where spiritual creativity is an emergent process, and the role of the individual is to partner with this creativity. Ideally the fire of our Sun (connected to Source) becomes channeled in a certain direction through Mars. We understand, cooperate and enhance what the energy is informing us to do. We feel spiritual impulses emerge, which are generally directed towards meaningful (fire) projects or 'connecting'. In contrast, when the ego is in control, our action tends to be tethered to emotional attachments and preferences. The awakened Mars is a fearless spiritual warrior blazing with fire, yet completely unattached to outcomes.

Jupiter: The Spiritual Quest

Jupiter: soul purpose, sense of mission, belief systems, moral considerations, meaning

Jupiter is called the 'Greater Benefic' and we can add '...to the ego' to more accurately describe what this means. Jupiter has the potential to bolster our egoic self-interests, but is seduced by the notion that having more (money, status, popularity, adventure, etc.) is always preferable to less. In the grips of ego, we may choose unwise, even immoral, courses of action to attend to this grandiose priority. The many moons orbiting Jupiter can be indicative of having others serve 'the king'. Jupiter/Zeus is famous for his many infidelities, and his relationship with his wife Juno/Hera is analogous to the historical imbalance between the masculine and the feminine. Jupiter can be emblematic of the dictatorial tendencies of Patriarchy.

Jupiter has societal influence. With healthy ego functioning, we are fueled by a spiritual mission. The unhealthy Jupiter may wish to set up a culture and society based on bounty, greed and blind faith. Jupiter enjoys having philosophical consensus (all the moons obeying its declarations). When it functions darkly, it rewards conformity, puffs up the ego and limits progress. At the extreme, Jupiter might see one particular way of living as 'the best' and see everything else as a threat. Poorly managed, Jupiter is the mindset and justification for launching wars, sending planes into skyscrapers or destroying our planet for self-interest.

Ideally Jupiter invites the self to extend outwards. 'How can I best serve the world?' is one healthy expression. If we stay within the grips of ego, Jupiter's energy is distorted into 'how can the world best serve me?' Instead of rising to meet a life calling, the egoic Jupiter calls on the world to be benevolent. There is entitlement and expectation, backed by a belief system designed to affirm one's specialness or deservedness to receive reward.

These belief systems are broader than religious views, but religion is a main area where such ideology plays out. Most religions strengthen the ego with doctrine that promises some sort of salvation, the confirmation that the individual is living the 'right' path, and membership into acceptable communal circles that provide social reinforcement and cohesiveness. Also, social religious activities are fertile fields for mate selection and business connecting – two areas of prime concern for the ego's survival. It serves the ego to affiliate with like-minded people; this is all made possible by conforming to a particular ideology.

The more awakened response is for Jupiter's expansiveness to move us away from self-preoccupation. If we don't continue to venture outside the personal, we might be at risk of destroying the world. The frenzy for *more* eventually gobbles up all available resources and results in a titanic clash of interests. The choice is to either come together (Oneness) or be torn apart.

Ideally Jupiter gives us inspiration, a taste for adventure and peak experiences. The great stories and fables about 'the quest' tend to end with something beyond the personal. Jupiter invites us to seek, though it doesn't tell us that the ego may not ultimately 'like' what it finds. However, the spiritual quest is a noble process to embrace.

Philosophy, religion and higher education (Jupiter) may inform our quest for what lies beyond the ego. It is helpful (perhaps necessary) to have the dominant organizational structures (Saturn) support, rather than inhibit, this movement. Too often churches, educational systems or prevailing paradigms are entrenched in their own tradition and preservation. When there is institutional openness, then Jupiter may fill our structures with a more informed approach. Operating within the orbit of Saturn, Jupiter brings broader understandings into comprehension and usefulness.

Saturn: The Gate of Manifestation

Saturn: structures, mundane reality, preservation, maturation, functionality, social organization

The ego has a complicated relationship with Saturn. On one hand, they get along great. Through Saturn, the ego strategizes with Jupiter and becomes concretized into society. Any policy driven by ego takes form in the world through our institutions, organized religions and social systems. We can create an infrastructure in our favor! Since men have largely controlled the levers of power and authority, Saturn does correlate strongly with Patriarchy.

Perhaps the only constant is change, and astrology reveals this vividly. The planets move into new signs and make an assortment of aspects to each other, all of which are designed to spur evolution. The outer planets are concerned with change and transformation and can puncture or even destroy what has become outdated and in need of transformation. Saturn is located *within* this reality. To be an instrument of progress it must cooperate, yield control and flow with evolution. If it chooses to deny the reality of constant change, then Saturn becomes a barrier, continually watching over the integrity of its walls in a defensive stance. It spends its time securing any leaks and warding off any threats. What the ego had wanted to erect eventually turns into burdens to maintain. This is partly why Saturn is malefic *to the ego* – reality can be harsh.

The ego tends to resist maturation (Saturn) because evolution turns out to be threatening to it. Beyond Saturn is the non-attachment and self-transcendence of the transpersonal planets. The ego must accept its limitations and trust there is something beyond it. Lao Tzu said, 'When I let go of what I am, I become what I might be.' Most people have been unable to do this, so the transpersonal territory remains out of reach, and Saturn is blamed for being the jailor that keeps us contracted. Most do not fully accept reality (our karmic predicament, the fact we're going to die or that we can't possibly attain eternal happiness in an uncertain world) and Saturn receives the projection of being malefic.

Those who take responsibility for the conditions of their lives and accept the limitations of being incarnate are able to forge an effective partnership with Saturn. With a healthy ego structure that is durable but not overly attached, we can learn our lessons, attain wisdom and evolve into elders. This energy allows us to *amount* to something and, if we do it right, we outgrow the need to take credit for it. We can have a relationship with Saturn that is as beautiful as that planet itself.

We can grow to see how futile the act of preservation is in a setup designed for continual change and evolution. This takes humility, maturity and perspective – the gifts of Saturn. We may well find that feverishly trying to meet egoic needs can paradoxically lead to non-attachment. After reaching the supposed pinnacle of success (making several million, gaining enormous popularity and reward, etc.), now what? We might see how hollow the whole game is if it's not being informed by broader spiritual nourishment. This is captured in the famous story of the Buddha who leaves a life of riches and splendor to discover Spirit.

Saturn requires that we live in the manifest world, and we can sculpt a contribution to society that serves more than our self-interests. Then we can feel honored and humbled to use our Spirit-given gifts to benefit evolution. Saturn serves as a gate for Spirit to become manifest. We are blessed to have a viable, functional container to play out this evolutionary project and make the most of our time here – for ourselves and others.

Uranus: The Matrix

Uranus: interconnectedness, deconditioning, beyond the known, liberation, synchronicity

Uranus is often classified as a 'generational' planet and it does have that side to it. However, every individual has a personal relationship with phenomena that have been disruptive, sometimes traumatic, 'out of bounds' and difficult to integrate. Uranus invites further steps, breakthrough and individuation – to go where the ego has not fully gone before. We throw off the shackles of prior conditioning to be true to our soul intentions, instead of jockeying to get ego needs met.

Self-alignment is a prime area for the ego to get passionate and revved up about. With Uranus, we may intuit what we need to do in order to be completely true to the self on a soul level, only to have the ego pursue these aims in self-serving ways. Broader awareness becomes distorted and reduced to 'justified' selfishness, even grandiosity. Taking pleasure in being ornery, counter-cultural or rebellious is not awakened – quite the opposite. In the throes of ego, revolutionary tendencies might stem from a need to prove something, get back at someone or sometimes just to cause mayhem. Many fictional villains such as Harry Potter's Voldemort or Batman's Joker portray this vividly. Villains tend to be eccentric geniuses who have some condition that makes them unacceptable (Uranus) to others.

Uranus is a sparkling and busy energy which potentially ushers in the future to benefit all. However, the ego might use its access to this brilliance for personal gain. Another possibility is that a person may choose not to accept responsibility for original ideas and refuse to contribute. A Uranian may shun society and be a lone wolf. Instead of selfless service, there is a rejection of evolution.

In contrast to the egoic version of Uranus as seen with villains, superheroes often portray the egoless version. They usually hide their personal identity and refuse to take any personal credit for assisting the world. They have access to attributes that go beyond what is 'normal' in the everyday (Saturn) world, and they use their supernatural powers consciously. The awakened Uranus is willing to put the self on the line (even die) as there is no investment in personal outcomes, just service to evolution.

Uranus invites us to transcend the ego, to feel interconnected to life around us. Deepak Chopra says, 'The tree is my lungs; the earth is my body; the waters are my circulation.' The ego no longer has an identity confined in the parameters of the body–emotion–mind system. It learns to participate in an interconnected web (or matrix) that holds all experience.

Every individual is like a nerve ending of a colossal mind. The matrix holds endless ideas and possibilities circulating within its neural framework. All of creation begins with the spark of ideas. The matrix serves as a behind-the-scenes coordinator of our growth. Everything has some kind of purpose and potentially catalyzes greater integration – whatever is occurring in our lives is exactly what we need. We can see the universe as doing things *for* us, not *to* us. We can trust and align with this intelligence and cooperate with our necessary spiritual lessons.

The matrix is a colossal mirror for the self because it reflects back exactly who we are. Lessons are sometimes presented in the most unlikely packages and disguises. When we believe that the world out there is separate from the self, there is no way to recognize how entangled we are with nature. There is confusion and a tendency to feel alienated and disconnected, to see the world as devoid of meaning. At the transpersonal level everything is pro-growth – no matter how difficult, perplexing and camouflaged it may appear. When we see something in negative terms, we are just not understanding or perceiving its purpose.

Everything turns out to be the self – and paradoxically, nothing is *really* ours. We have a synchronous relationship with the world: the outer world is a reflection of the inner. The universe echoes back our consciousness because it *is* our consciousness. Synchronicities may invite thrilling expansion or may welcome you into the repressed urges, the buried pain, the memories you wish you had never gathered. Unconscious material is hidden for a reason! Synchronicities are about awakening to it all.

Karma is the basic idea that what we put out comes back to us – often in mysterious and perplexing ways that transcend time, space and the immediate reality – and perhaps even in the present lifetime. We reap and sow in an endless exchange. The matrix delivers our consciousness back to us and it's also available for us to use skillfully through clear intentions. The universe meets us where we are right now, so be careful what you wish for – or be conscious what you wish for – because the universe is also in harmony with what's unconscious.

Neptune: The Dream Space

Neptune: releasing attachments, unconditional love, egoic surrender, visioning, intuition

As the dreamer can easily get lost in the dream, the ego's relationship with Neptune can be most challenging. Neptune's selflessness can turn into identity confusion, victim and martyr issues or the many avenues of escapism. The ego might use Neptune as the rationale to destructively disobey laws of order and rationality. Lost in Neptune's trance, the ego might ask why one reality is preferred to another. This could lead to despair, even suicide.

Perhaps the greatest ego trap with Neptune is mistaking Neptune energy for enlightenment. One of the main teachings from awakened figures is that awakening is not about having positive or peak experiences. It's about presence and awareness, being clear and attuned to life. Many seekers are interested in experiencing ongoing bliss, which may stem from a need to cleanse ego suffering. There is nothing wrong with feeling 'good', but having this as a requirement keeps us imprisoned in ego.

One criticism of the New Age movement is that its culture can be syrupy and loving to the point of lacking authenticity and ignoring the shadow. This has been termed the 'spiritual bypass' because of the avoidance of encountering conflict. The ego adopts a Neptunian orientation and enjoys the interpersonal, sometimes professional, rewards this bestows. At the extreme, the ego can have a messianic complex: everyone should feel the benefits of being in *my* presence.

Ultimately Neptune is about releasing attachments through the awareness that the physical world is an illusion, so there is no need to get too caught up in it. Neptune lifts us out of ourselves to remember that we are spiritual beings having temporary human experiences; we can 'be in the world but not of it'. Neptune energy infuses a vision. Any spiritual practice, from lucid dreaming to chanting to meditation to prayer, is part of its scope. Contemplation can remind us that the ego is a tool, and assist us in loosening our identification with it. When we are able to tame the separate self, we open the channels of intuition which connect us with Neptune's dream space.

The dream space is where the dreamer (Moon) enters a formless, invisible, interactive field of timeless possibilities – another way to see the apparently empty space all around. We learn that we co-create everything that happens. With Neptune everything is possible. However, the multiple dimensions of Neptune must pass through Saturn's gate, which always entails some kind of negotiation. Much has been said in recent years about 'creating your reality', and many see this as quixotic. What is often left out of this discussion is that we are co-creating *with Spirit*; it's not a blank and open canvas for us to use. Only those things which are consistent with reality in the Saturnian realm come into being. A frail 63-year-old woman is not going to manifest a career in the National Basketball Association, no matter how much meditation on this goal she performs.

In order for the ego to awaken it must release control and trust life. This is made increasingly possible by having compassion for the self, the dreamer and everything that we've previously dreamed up. This doesn't mean that we must *like* what we've created, for like or dislike belong to the ego. Instead, we must *love* our dreaming, in all of its perplexing unconscious corridors and entrapments. If not, we stay unresolved and defended, trapped in the endless machinations of ego.

Astrology (Uranus) provides the technology to navigate in dreamland (Neptune). When we use astrology as a tool for awakening, we have a map – a guide that takes us through the organization of the dream. We can understand our attunement to the dream space, as revealed in the natal chart, and learn to partner with it. We can also navigate current events consciously and maximize our ability to co-create with Spirit as we go.

Pluto: The Claiming of Power

Pluto: the shadow, interpersonal impact, power, annihilation, transformation

The resistance to addressing the underlying issues at the core of our attachments has the potential to enlarge the shadow. Pluto involves the material we keep off limits. Our issues fester unconsciously and compromise our sense of well-being in a variety of physical or psychological ways. Or, these issues might reach some crisis point and explode into the world. The ego does not want our shadow material to come to light – a draining strategy that makes life difficult in the short term, and there is no prospect of this strategy being successful in the long term, either.

Keeping the shadow at arm's length, we unconsciously act it out. With an understanding of reincarnation, this may conceivably play out for eternity; perhaps that's what 'hell' is. Plutonian reams include sexuality, power, painful emotional exchanges with others, fears, unprocessed hurt, grief, anger or anything at all that has been received and interpreted as abusive. If we don't confront these issues, we remain unwise, unbalanced and ineffective – until we are ready to meet Pluto. We often become the very thing that we have objection to: being emotionally difficult to deal with, unable to perform sexually or show up in relationship. It turns out that we *are* Pluto and have been all along. This is not to suggest that we have been 'bad', it's to say that we've all been *unconscious*. We didn't know what we were doing in these realms and faced some tough lessons. As we mature, we may accept our prior unconsciousness and shadowy behaviors as part of our ego's curriculum. In fact, we can even learn to love them.

Until we are able to integrate Pluto into the light of our soul, the egoic version controls life on the Earth. Pluto puts the 'maniac' into 'egomaniac'. All the dictators, power-grabbers, manipulators, criminals, the insane and deranged – every pathological and abusive behavior we see stems from here. It's not always so dark or dramatic either. There is also the emotionally absent parent, garden-variety neurotic or run-of-the-mill porn addict. However, no matter how anyone manifests the darker side of Pluto, it is possible to recognize this shadow material, to integrate it, and learn to love the self more authentically.

Unhealed, the egoic Pluto will annihilate us all. One individual's unconscious wounding may not destroy the planet, but the collectively repressed Pluto ultimately will through some form of catastrophe. We might ruin the planet, engage in nuclear war or create hell on Earth in some other way. If we fail to grow, Pluto becomes a collective self-destruct mechanism. If we perish through our unconscious ways, we'll be recycled like the proverbial phoenix rising from the ashes. The alternative is spiritual awakening, which is not something optional, luxurious or for a select few. It's a necessity.

We must *honor* the shadow and cultivate the deep wisdom in it. We must partner with the anger, pain, sadness or fear in order to transform it. What is usually needed is some form of a deep dive into the unconscious to tap into it. This can be catalyzed by a number of therapeutic techniques and modalities. Gaining in popularity are shamanic practices such as ayahuasca and other plant medicines to facilitate this. We need to purge and release what we've been holding on to – a process not so different from defecating after holding it in. Yes, Pluto is our 'crap' and we need to release it. Ultimately we find that our crap is fertilizer; our greatest wounds become our power. We then venture forth courageously in support of healthy and bold action in the world.

As we become the awakened Pluto, we direct evolution. We become empowered to embrace all of life. We maintain our connection to personal will, but it becomes informed by transpersonal will (Pluto). Whereas the egoic version wants to control the world for personal gain, the transpersonal Pluto takes control for completely selfless reasons. We fiercely 'become the change we wish to see in the world', and we might even end up dying for it.

The awakened Pluto has psychic dimensions. As we see with shamans, sorcerers or some alchemists, there's the ability to move between worlds, to radically transform between energy and matter. A popular depiction of this is found in *Journey to Ixtlan* and the other Carlos Castaneda books. Such abilities are present in many cultures, though the individuals who are adept at this tend not to advertise. This ability is often held in secrecy (Pluto) and requires a dedication to spiritual development.

Pluto is our connection to the *evolutionary intelligence* that permeates the cosmos. This intelligence is aware that a virus, earthquake or famine can have enormous evolutionary importance for the survival of the collective. Pluto is relentless but it has a profound evolutionary reason for every transformation it activates. Pluto's truth is often difficult to swallow – this is why it's often feared and demonized. For evolution to continue, we must be fearless and be willing to become the demon, which turns out to be powerful beauty in disguise.

Our Choice

We are at a pivotal moment in history: the fabled year of 2012, the purported end of the Mayan Calendar, a growing awareness that we can operate differently on Mother Earth. All of this can be found in today's dominant astrological configuration: the Uranus–Pluto square. We are presented with the challenge of awakening (Uranus) into a new way of being (Aries), but we must be fearless (Pluto) in transforming what has become outdated (Capricorn).

We have inherited an astrology that is centered around ego, as that is the usual understanding of the Sun. Now, more people have awakened to the reality that we are enveloped in the radiance of Spirit, our source energy. We can update our paradigm to see the Moon and Sun as a partnership in consciously reconnecting with Spirit, to bridge the physical (Moon) with the metaphysical (Sun) and bring spiritual creativity to manifestation.

In our process of spiritual development, we can choose to use planetary energy to serve the self, or to create a more conscious existence on this planet. We are awakening to find that we do not *only* exist in separation consciousness. Our astrology can similarly evolve to reflect our interconnectedness with all of life. It is my most sincere hope that we choose to do this. *Namaste.*

References and Notes

1. Godman, David, ed. *Be As You Are: The Teachings of Sri Ramana Maharshi.* Penguin. 1992.
2. Tolle, Eckhart. *The Power of Now.* New World Library. Lovato, CA. 1999.
3. Guttman, Ariel. *Venus Star Rising.* Sophia Venus Productions. Santa Fe, NM. 2010.
4. Venus is known at the Earth's sister planet due to its comparable size and closeness. The analogy is that other people teach us who we are by being 'sacred mirrors'.
5. Godman, David, ed. *Be As You Are: The Teachings of Sri Ramana Maharshi.* Penguin. 1992.

Part III

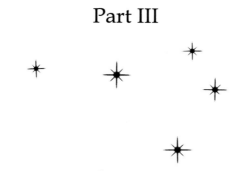

Techniques:
Modern & Traditional Tools

Moses Siregar III
A Personal Biography

No free will about it, I was born into astrology. My mother, an astrology student since before I was born, had me reading Liz Greene's children's book, *Looking at Astrology*, when I was in the first grade – something I had completely forgotten until I found the book in my early 20s and discovered that the Sun signs of the kids in my first-grade class were scribbled on its pages. Turns out, the kid who had convinced me that he controlled an underground lair full of beautiful women was a Libra. Smooth, that one was. During my first nodal return in Scorpio in 1994 I found myself (once again, with gratitude to Mom) at the Metropolitan Atlanta Astrological Society. That night I heard David Railey lecturing about the Moon's nodes and Steffan Vanel lecturing about Liz Greene's psychological astrology; over the next few years I would attend many lectures at MAAS, including one by Dennis Harness, who stoked a flame in me that would turn into a great love of Vedic astrology. In those early years, I read Rudhyar, Greene, Forrest, Hickey and Arroyo. Now in 2012 I'm experiencing my second nodal return and I'm working on an astrology book of my own, a book on locational astrology. This topic has been the focus of my consulting work since 2003, and I've lectured on the subject at astrological groups around North America. Over the last decade I've spoken at UAC, ISAR and ACVA conferences; I became a co-founder and the first president of the Association for Young Astrologers: and I've organized The Blast Astrology Conference in Sedona, Arizona. I'm ISAR C.A.P. certified and a certified Astro*Carto*Grapher. I've been a mostly full-time consulting astrologer since 1994. I do my best to do no harm.

www.AstrologyForTheSoul.com • www.TheBlastAstrologyConference.com
Moses@AstrologyForTheSoul.com

Chapter Eight

A New Look at Locational Astrology & Astro*Carto*Graphy

Moses Siregar III

Locational astrology, or astro-locality, has become a popular branch of astrology frequently used to help individuals find their 'best places' on Earth. The late Jim Lewis and those who have followed in his footsteps deserve credit for the prominence of this new approach to astrology. Lewis of course called his approach Astro*Carto*Graphy, or A*C*G. Charles Harvey and Michael Harding, in their book *Working with Astrology*, called A*C*G one of the three most important modern advances in astrology – the other two being harmonics and midpoints.[1]

A Brief History of Locational Astrology and Astro*Carto*Graphy
Before Lewis, locational astrology was more commonly utilized for the purposes of mundane astrology rather than natal astrology. Earlier astrologers who correlated zodiacal qualities with places on earth include Manilius, Ptolemy, al-Biruni, Lilly, Raphael, Green, Sepharial, Carter, Johndro, and Wynn.[2]

Applying locational astrology techniques to individual nativities with an emphasis on angular planets at the moment of birth, which is what the term astrocartography (without asterisks) normally refers to, was perhaps initially developed by Cyril Fagan more than anyone else, even though Fagan didn't write a great deal about the subject or do much to popularize the idea (as Lewis certainly did).[3] Charles Jayne wrote in a 1985 article, 'As far as I have been able to determine, the Astro-Cartographic method was first developed by Cyril Fagan.'[4] In 1966, ten years before Lewis wrote his famous *Astro*Carto*Graphy* booklet, Fagan used the technique in his 'Solunars' column in the magazine *American Astrology*. In that article he looked at the chart of a woman born on June 29, 1940, at 9:15 am GMT, 31N35, 105W50. He wrote:

> With Uranus on the Ascendant in conjunction with Algol, it is not surprising that she mentally has been pushed to points of extreme desperation. A distant removal from her place of birth will displace the natal Uranus from this

dangerous position... Should this unhappy girl wish to remedy matters, she should remove sufficiently far away from her place of birth to put her Sun and Venus on the Midheaven; she will then know fame and happiness.

Fagan also explained why he would not recommend an angular Jupiter line for this woman, even though he would normally recommend that a person 'bring the benefics, principally the greater benefic Jupiter, onto an angle.' The reason he gave is that her Jupiter was closely conjoined with Saturn (among other reasons).

In Fagan's 1971 book, *Primer of Sidereal Astrology*, which he co-wrote with Brigadier R. C. Firebrace, there is an appendix about the 'Calculation of planets in mundo'. In his Solunar column Fagan also wrote about parans in the context of both natal and relocated locations.[5] Of course two of the key elements of Lewis's Astro*Carto*Graphy are drawing 'in mundo' maps[6] and using parans for relocation work.

Kenneth Irving wrote to me that Jim Lewis 'was certainly steeped in the hard-as-nails technical approach of Fagan & Bradley,' but says that Lewis was 'genuinely surprised' when Irving showed him examples of Donald A. Bradley's maps from *American Astrology*. He said that Jim Lewis 'sincerely didn't think anyone else had done this before him, and I had no reason to doubt him.' He also thought it was unlikely that Jim Lewis would have read the contents of any given past column written by Fagan or Bradley. Irving also said that 'Bradley *did* use the idea of locality in regard to birth charts extensively, but as far as I know never through the use of maps.' Jim Lewis gave particular credit to Donald A. Bradley, the only astrologer Lewis listed by name in the dedication of his 1976 booklet, *Astro*Carto*Graphy*.

Without a doubt one of Jim Lewis's most significant contributions was his popularization of *natal* astro-locality maps. Before Jim Lewis, astro-locality maps were employed in astrological literature as early as 1941 but only for mundane purposes, such as showing the angularity of planets at the moment of the winter solstice.[7]

I consider Jim Lewis a modern astrological giant for developing and promoting astrocartography, and I feel profoundly grateful for all that I have learned from his work. However, in this article I won't focus on the countless places where I agree with Lewis but instead on some major elements of Astro*Carto*Graphy that I want to examine critically. Because Astro*Carto*Graphy is such a pervasive influence on astrocartography, I believe that all astrologers interested in locational astrology should look deeply into A*C*G's origin and legacy.

Before I go further, a bit about myself. I have supported myself as an astrologer since 1994, and ever since the Jupiter–Uranus opposition in 2003 (a transit I remember because I also have Jupiter–Uranus opposed natally), I have made at least two-thirds of my living as a practicing locational astrologer. Because I review my clients' histories and look over all the previous locations where they have lived, I estimate that I've been able to ask questions about and confirm the results of well over 5,000 relocated charts, including techniques like parans and local space lines. I am only one astrologer, but I have done my best to test the popular theories of astro-locality, and in this essay I'll share some of the things I have learned.

To Map or Not to Map?

For me there's an ironic element in this quote from Jim Lewis at his 'Professional Training and Certification Seminar' in 1993:

> 25 years ago when I started doing astrology, Locational Astrology was hardly talked about at all. The only thing they did was if you were going to move to a new city they might relocate your chart to that city and read it as if you had been born there. But all of these new techniques like A*C*G, and local space and geodetics, nobody talked about because it simply did not exist, and that was only 25 years ago. Also, there were only about 10 books on astrology at that time – it was real easy to read them all.[8]

The ironic element for me is that the only technique mentioned above that focuses primarily on an astrological *chart* is the one that Jim Lewis seems to give the least weight to: the relocated chart. A*C*G, local space and geodetics are viewed as lines on geographical maps. These techniques also refer back to the natal chart but they can change the astrologer's focus from charts to maps, and I feel that the map-first mentality of locational astrology has led to some problems.

Astro-locality maps are invaluable tools. I use maps extensively as I look at A*C*G (including parans), local space and geodetics (from tropical and sidereal natal placements), as well as finer techniques like midpoints and aspects to angles. But I have found that far too many astrocartographers put the cart before the horse, the map before the chart, not only when it comes to analyzing astrocartography but also in that many astrologers skip over the fundamentals of interpreting astrological charts and rush over to fascination with shinier modern inventions, whether astrocartography or anything else (there are too many to name). I've been there too. I began as a modern, groovy psychological and spiritual astrologer, but the accuracy of my astrological work grew by leaps and bounds when I began to study more traditional astrology, particularly Vedic astrology in my case.

Too many astrology students and locational astrologers seem to have abandoned the gold mine that is the natal chart and the relocated chart *in combination*. Most, though certainly not all, of the information locational astrologers need can be found in those two places. I would never want to give up any of the astro-locality techniques that I use – such as the parans and *in mundo* positions of A*C*G and Cyclo*Carto*Graphy (C*C*G), local space and geodetics – but if forced to choose only one astro-locality tool, I would reluctantly give up everything else and focus on the natal and relocated charts in combination.

A*C*G and Fame

Lewis's work emphasized angular natal planetary lines and the fame that sometimes comes with those positions. He co-wrote with Ariel Guttman *The Astro*Carto*Graphy Book of Maps*. The subtitle of the book reads: 'The Astrology of Relocation: How 136 Famous People Found Their Place.' Although parans are also mentioned in these 136 case histories, the book is nearly 300 pages of examples of famous people doing famous things in places where they have angular planetary lines. Lewis's 1993 certification seminar shows this same emphasis on angular planetary lines.

So it's not surprising, because of Lewis's example, that astrologers tend to put such emphasis on *angular* planetary lines when studying and practicing locational astrology – even though most clients don't come asking where they can find fame. Most of my own clients just want to be happy, and I've found that living close to angular lines more often leads to unhappiness because the angular lines indicate places where one's life experience will be so *intense* – for better or for worse and usually some of both. More on that below.

Lewis cited the Gauquelin research in his 1993 certification seminar, and rightly pointed out that what Gauquelin discovered is that the natal chart's angles are powerful places for famous people:

Gauquelin... found out... if you were born in a place where Mars is in the Midheaven, you have a more chance than statistical average of becoming a more successful athlete. He took the charts of 50,000 French people and excerpted a couple thousand outstanding athletes and found that far more than statistically predictable, the outstanding athletes had Mars in the zone near the Midheaven in their charts... The Gauquelins have shown that it only works for eminent French athletes, for outstanding French athletes. It didn't work for the second string, little leaguer types. That's an important thing, angularity of a planet brings it into personal and collective attention.[9]

In Lewis's certification seminar he talks about a 'spectrum of health' for each planet. He asked his students to come up with examples for each planet when denied/repressed/projected, assimilated and famous. For instance, according to his examples, denied Neptune would be psi-cops and skeptics who appear on TV, assimilated Neptune would be 'alcoholics anonymous', and famous Neptune would be Gandhi, Timothy Leary and Bill Wilson (founder of Alcoholics Anonymous).[10] It's worth noting that Lewis routinely considered the highest potential for any planet to be the achievement of 'fame' connected with that planet, while his work in astrocartography focused on angular planets.

On the other hand, also in his 1993 certification seminar, Lewis said, 'That reminds me to remind you that the point in A*C*G is not to find someplace to go to become rich and famous... The point in the study of astrology is to become a whole person, a complete, entire person.'[11] Lewis had a clear interest in a psychological approach to A*C*G. But maybe because so much of his A*C*G literature and teaching was about angularity and fame, I believe that many people have acquired the wrong idea about astrocartography.

Most people are more interested in happiness than fame. They'd rather have money in the bank, good friends, satisfying relationships, a nice home and fulfilling work. Yet too many people seem to think locational astrology is about, above all else, moving to an angular planetary line, even though this is so often *not* a good recipe for happiness. People talk about what happened when they went to their Jupiter line, or Mars line, etc. They wonder which new angular line they *should* go live on. We think these lines are what locational astrology is all about, but that is a very dangerous misunderstanding.

Full Volume: The Price of Angularity

I have found that, as a general rule, living a comfortable distance from angular lines – rather than very close to such lines (I'll say that within 150 miles qualifies as 'very close', but that's a general guideline rather than a hard boundary) – is more often the best choice. This is because angular planetary lines, when we live very near to them, give us the full, intense force of any given planet's significations according to our unique natal charts – and most planets in our charts promise more than just lollipops and gumdrops.

Jim Lewis was well aware that the natal condition of a planet is important when analyzing A*C*G lines. He knew that not all Jupiter lines are created equal. But I can understand, when looking at the emphasis of his teachings, why so many people focus more on the generic positions, such as VE–ASC, SUN–DSC and so on. Because even though Lewis explained the more nuanced truth and the importance of seeing the planet's situation in the natal chart, he still focused his teachings and writings on the sheer power of angular planets in astrocartography.

I've learned that living on a major A*C*G line is like turning up the volume on that planet to '11'. In other words, it's asking that planet to become so emphasized in your life that you can never get away from its generic significations (Mars as Mars) and its specific natal significations (Mars in *your chart*). Most planets in any chart exist under a combination of easy and difficult conditions – mixed bags. Maybe your Mars is in Cancer (its fall or depression), but it's also in a trine to Jupiter in Scorpio (a mutual reception) and a tight square to Moon in Aries (a more complicated mutual reception because of the square), while ruling the 7th and the 12th Houses (the 12th being a relatively challenging house, with the 7th being for the most part an inherently positive house). Living on that Mars line would likely lead to a lot of intense experiences – sometimes very enjoyable, other times very unpleasant. This is not just because Mars can be considered a natural malefic – something we don't want to lose sight of – but also because of its specific placement in the above chart.

A Good Planet Is... Hard to Find

Ideally we could all live close to the angular lines of relatively pristine planets in our charts. A pristine planet is dignified by sign, ideally by rulership (i.e. Moon in Cancer), mutual reception or exaltation (Moon in Taurus), although exaltation is a more complicated condition which can also indicate some powerful challenges, such as when the exalted planet rules difficult houses in either tropical or sidereal astrology (those houses being primarily the 6th, 8th and 12th). A pristine planet should be well aspected and its aspects would ideally involve harmonious reception (e.g. Sun in Sagittarius trine Jupiter in Aries; Jupiter rules Sagittarius and the Sun is exalted in Aries). A pristine planet would rule over the more positive houses (such as the angles and the 5th and 9th – though different houses can be considered positive depending on the person's work and interests) while not ruling over the more difficult houses. A pristine planet sits in a positive house where it is also comfortable. A pristine planet would be disposited by similarly pristine planets, or at least by planets well positioned overall. Whether a pristine planet should be direct or retrograde is too complicated to sum up here – it's not a simple matter of saying that retrogrades are mostly bad (something that some traditional Western astrologers say) or that retrogrades are mostly good (something that many Vedic astrologers say). And when looking at what makes for a well-placed planet, there are too many possible considerations to mention. Different astrologers will focus on different conditions. Some may use midpoints, others may use the Vedic nakshatras, while others will use the Egyptian terms and so on.

Traditional astrology gets a bad rap from many astrologers who don't understand it. I love modern astrology, but I believe modern astrologers ought to be able to also use traditional concepts to become better at making predictions without losing the positive, humanistic and psychological spirit of modern astrology.

Locational astrologers need to be able to make predictions. We need to be able to say what we think it would be like for client A to live on her angular line B. But to make these kinds of predictions we need to be able to differentiate a complicated, difficult Jupiter line from a relatively straightforward, positive Jupiter line. Many concepts from traditional astrology help us to do this. Just as modern astrologers recognize the difficulty of a planet in a T-square with Saturn, Chiron or Pluto, traditional astrologers recognize the difficulty of a planet in its fall with a weak dispositor, who is involved with challenging reception (e.g. Sun in Gemini trine Jupiter in Libra), who rules difficult houses while also sitting in a difficult house. We don't need to judge any of these conditions as inherently good or bad; we just need to recognize challenges for being what they are, as well as for the opportunities they offer.

Close to the Edge? Or Far, Far Away?

Back to angularity in astrocartography. One of the reasons we tend to focus on the A*C*G lines is because when someone finds a great line – for his or her unique chart and his or her unique interests and goals – the results can be spectacularly good. Living on a line *that works well for you* can be profoundly life-affirming because it can give you much stronger connections with other people in that place. A good angular line can in fact give us a certain amount of fame, even if just locally. The way this usually manifests is that we're more socially or professionally connected, or both, in such places. We're not just in the background there; we're front and center in the flow of life. Having the volume turned up to '11' can be great when you really love the song you're listening to (i.e. when you work well with the planet in question) and when you want to be more prominent or more connected to whatever is happening locally, or perhaps even nationally or internationally.

The problem is that few planets in any given chart work very well at full volume. And in many charts – perhaps as many as half the charts I see in my work – there may not be a single planet that I can recommend turning up to '11'. In other words, with roughly half the clients I work with, no planet comes even close to being in relatively pristine condition. For example, in charts where hard aspects predominate, it's often difficult to recommend any major lines because if Mars squares your Moon then that aspect will be profoundly felt and experienced whether the person lives on a Mars line *or* a Moon line. And if nearly all of one's planets are in difficult squares, oppositions or quincunxes then it will be hard to find a comfortable place close to a major A*C*G line.

When someone lives on the line of a planet whose condition is mixed (some nice stuff, some major challenges), all of those conditions will manifest in that place. It's like asking the planet to hit you with its best shot. It's almost like having a continual transit from that planet. How many people would like to have a major Saturn transit every single day? Or a major Jupiter or Venus transit, for that matter – sometimes you have to be careful what you wish for.

On the one hand, these conditions will manifest according to the nature of the line in question. For example, living just east of a difficult Mars–ASC line will put Mars in the 12th House of the relocated chart, so its story will play out in a noticeably 12th-House way. Living just to the west of a Mars–ASC line will put Mars in the 1st House of the relocated chart, so in that case the effects will be felt most strongly in the 1st House.

But on the other hand, living close to *any* major Mars line – no matter which angle – will activate the natal story of Mars, including its aspects and whichever houses Mars rules natally and whichever houses it resides in natally.[12] All of the planet's natal conditions will manifest in such a place, including reception if there is any, essential dignity or lack thereof, declination, connections with fixed stars, important midpoints, nakshatras and other Vedic considerations such as shad bala, terms/bounds, sect and any other factor one can study and use.

Another consideration is that some people are more likely than others to enjoy the intensity of angular lines. For example, a younger person wanting to experience all that life has to offer, including its lessons, may want to live near his or her major A*C*G lines. Living near a major line likely means greater successes and greater failures, though the balance of success and failure will depend on the unique natal planet in question. On major lines we are likely to have more significant relationships with more people, so living on major lines usually leads to more significant friendships; however, the individual situation has to be taken into consideration – living on the line of a planet ruling one's natal 12th may symbolize a good deal of isolation and hardships instead.

Meanwhile, those who would rather live in relative seclusion and privacy, or who simply don't mind being in the background socially, ought to give serious consideration to *not* living near a major A*C*G line. For example, an older person looking to retire in a place that will be mellow for her, who isn't concerned about having a great deal of social prominence, should probably avoid her major A*C*G lines unless maybe she has one of those pristine planets in her natal chart and can find those lines somewhere on habitable land (i.e. not out to sea or in the middle of a war zone).

In my experience it's more common to find people who say that they cannot live comfortably on their angular lines. Many people come to me, I think, because the major line they are living on is too intense. In some cases these people have been told by Astro*Carto*Graphers to go and live on these major lines. They may enjoy the positive things that the major line seems to give them, but they also find that the problems that come with those major lines are too much to handle on a daily basis.

Living on a major line is *intense*, though it can be a very good kind of intense in the case of a well-placed natal planet; but in most cases it's intense in both positive and negative ways. Living far from major lines is *mellow* but that can also indicate a place that is boring or unfulfilling, as well as lacking in social connections. Let's think then… how can we get the best of both scenarios? The energy, activity and connections of a major line as well as the sustainable mellowness of a place with no major lines?

Often the best solution is to live a moderate distance from a major line. That way, you can experience some of the positive intensity of a major line without too much of the negative intensity. And you can have the more mellow experience of not living terribly close to a major line, but without the boredom or sense that 'nothing is happening' that can prevail when living too far from angular planetary lines.

How Far Is Too Far, and How Close Is Too Close?

Now you might be wondering, then how far away should you be? First, let me restate that if you do have a planet in relatively pristine condition in your chart, it may be worth trying to live very close to that line. If you're in the half of the population[13] that has at least one of these very well-placed planets in your natal chart, you might still have only one or two such planets (and having four such planets is probably the most I've ever seen – one or two is much more common according to my way of assessing things). Then you have to hope you can find a livable place near one of these lines, in a country where you want to live, with weather you like, where you can find a good job and on an angle where you'd like to have that planet.

One more caveat before getting into distance and orbs. The emphasis on astro-maps has taken the attention of many astrologers away from relocated natal charts. I think this is really tragic, and for more than one reason. For example, you may have one of the nicest Venus placements in creation, but it might also be the case that when you get that Venus on your ASC, you end up with every other planet in your relocated chart in either the 12th, 8th or 6th House: that's almost certainly not good. Venus would still give you her wonderful results, but the rest of the relocated chart would most likely drag you down.

Now the orbs. First, the bad news. Orbs are always debatable and astrologers rarely agree on them. For example, Jim Lewis said that individual parans have an orb of influence up to 1.5–2 degrees of latitude on either side of the line,[14] but most practicing locational astrologers I've spoken with use a smaller orb, often 1 degree on either side, which is the orb I used for many years.[15] In recent years, based on client histories, I've started to look only at ½ of a degree of latitude as my orb for a strong paran, although I still find that there is some influence up to a full degree of latitude away.

Lewis put his emphasis on maps rather than charts, so he measured orbs in inches on his maps as well as in miles. He said: 'On the A*C*G map, the official version, the orb is about 3/8 of an inch either side of the line and that equates to about 700–800 miles either side of the line; that's a huge orb, like 1,500 miles with the line in the center of it. However, I assure you that the lines are not nearly as strong if you're at the edge than if you're right under the line.'[16]

Although he taught that *in mundo* mapping and mapping according to zodiacal longitude were 'both true',[17] he emphasized a brilliant mapping technique that he pioneered: astronomically accurate maps that showed lines for actual rising, setting, culminating and anti-culminating planets *in mundo*, rather than astrological ASC, DSC, MC and IC lines. He favored *in mundo* mapping so his orbs were distance based and given in miles.

My practice – which is just a matter of preference – is to look at maps with lines drawn for zodiacal longitude before looking at maps drawn *in mundo*. I probably do it this way because I emphasize the natal and relocated charts more than maps. The nice thing about this approach is that it allows you to use an orb measured in zodiacal longitude, or degrees. When using a degree-based orb, here's what I recommend: 8 degrees at most from any angle in the relocated chart.[18] Roughly, any planet within 3 degrees of an angle has 'strong' influence, any planet 3–6 degrees from an angle has 'moderate' influence, and any planet 6–8 degrees from an angle has a 'weak' though still important influence. The numbers can also be expressed as a fraction or percentage. For example, a planet 2 degrees from an angle has 75% of its maximum influence, or 6/8. A planet 3 degrees from an angle has 62.5% of its maximum influence, or 5/8.

Degree-based orbs aren't fully sufficient, however, when the *in mundo* position of a planet is significantly different from its position according to zodiacal longitude. For example, Pluto might be 4 degrees from the IC in the relocated chart, which is what I would say is 50% of a full-strength Pluto line. But *in mundo* that same Pluto might go right through the location in question, meaning that it's at full strength according to its *in mundo* position.

A similar problem can happen the other way around, though. When using distance as the basis for one's orb when looking at a map, both *in mundo* and zodiacal positions have to be considered. But a zodiacal degree-based orb doesn't work when looking at a geographical map drawn *in mundo*.

Distance-based orbs and zodiacally measured orbs can be hard to compare like apples to apples, because they're actually different. Using my own chart as an example, I've seen that when a sign of long ascension is rising, 8 degrees of zodiacal longitude (from the ASC) can work out to roughly 525 miles; when a sign of short ascension is rising, 8 degrees from the ASC can equal less than 300 miles. It's complicated.

I favor degree-based orbs while mapping with zodiacal positions, because that's in keeping with how we read natal charts and because that's what I've found to work so reliably. *In mundo* positions are also very important to consider, though, so in those cases I tend to 'eyeball' the range with a distance-based approach and in that event I use something like 500 miles as the outer range.[19]

Okay, now we can get back to what a medium-strength angular line would be, for those times when we want some of the energy of a major angular line but without too much intensity, as well as some of the mellowness of not living too close to major lines but without too much boredom. Measured in zodiacal longitude, to be safe, we're looking at something in the 4–6 degree range for a planet that we like fairly well; in other words, the planet should be between 4–6 degrees from an angle in the relocated chart. Using 6–8 degrees can definitely work too, but then the effect is weaker; however, this can be a safer, better choice when dealing with a natural malefic that we also like, such as a well-placed Saturn or Mars, or any planet in a very mixed condition (such as a planet with close, difficult aspects or some other very challenging condition).

When measuring the same thing using an *in mundo* map and distance, 200–350 miles is roughly the equivalent of a 4–6 degree range, and 350–500 miles is roughly the equivalent of a 6–8 degree range. Beyond that, in my experience the line isn't powerful enough to have a major effect. But I also think it's harder to be precise about guidelines for distance-based orbs, so you should use these distance-based orbs at your own risk.

A Chart Has Twelve Houses, Not Just Four Angles

Now the ironic thing for me is that in getting into a critique of some commonly held ideas about Astro*Carto*Graphy, I've so far ended up doing one of the things I wanted to warn people away from: putting too much emphasis on the angular lines. It's true that the angular lines are by far the most powerful influences, so it's very important to know how they work and how to work with them. But one of the big problems with Astro*Carto*Graphy as it is commonly practiced is that many people think so much about their angular lines and not *nearly* enough about the rest of the positions in the relocated chart.

It could also be said that many people focus on the angular lines to the exclusion of local space, parans or geodetics. All of these things are very important. But I've found that the relocated chart itself is an incredibly important tool and it's one that is ignored by too many.

I don't have the scope in this essay to go into great detail about how I work with the relocated natal chart. I'm working on a locational astrology book that I hope to complete sometime in 2012 or 2013, and I'll be focusing on relocated natal charts a great deal in that book. For now, I'll leave you with a simple, powerful traditional technique for analyzing a relocated natal chart, something as basic and fundamental as it gets.

Look at the condition and position of the ruler of the ASC in the relocated chart. If Libra is rising in the relocated chart and Venus is in the 12th House in her fall in Virgo dealing with some very hard aspects, you'll definitely want to make a note of it because Venus's placement will tell a reliably potent story about what it would be like for the individual to live in that location. In this location the person may feel intensely isolated, invisible to others or unpopular. He or she might feel extremely limited by financial conditions, or might have harsh experiences with intense or critical women. There may be a powerful feeling of entrapment, in general, or of being stuck in menial roles or difficult working conditions.

If Scorpio is rising and Mars is in Capricorn in the 3rd House and well aspected, then Mars's dignity will shine through in the 3rd House (for better or worse, but most likely for the better overall in this case) and that symbolism will describe a great deal about what the individual would experience living in that location. Maybe he or she will have a powerful drive to write, or to study some subject or to focus on creativity – which will lead to significant success or notoriety. Maybe the person will very effectively use communications technology, make good use of a scientific mind or communicate clear and specific ideas through his or her work. On the downside, maybe this person will argue too much with others or have intensely competitive relationships with siblings or friends. Maybe ambition and too much work, or too much mental energy or long commutes and too much traveling will become a problem, leading to a major imbalance.

For extra credit do the above in both tropical and sidereal astrology. It's not hard to do after you've practiced it. Just consider the placement of the ruler of the ASC in the sidereal zodiac as well as in the tropical zodiac and blend whatever you find, similar to how you would blend different bits of information in any given chart.

Maybe the person who has Libra Rising and Venus in Virgo in tropical astrology has, in the same location, Virgo Rising with Mercury in Virgo in the 1st House in sidereal astrology. That would change the picture quite a bit, wouldn't it? Although we would still expect the challenges shown by the Libra Ascendant with Venus in Virgo, the sidereal picture shows a very different story. We'd expect the person to be able to experience great success in a realm signified by Mercury or Virgo. Maybe the person still feels trapped and unloved (Venus in Virgo in the 12th), but nonetheless enjoys a great education or has a shrewd business sense that leads to a good income (Mercury in Virgo in the 1st) – along with great expenditures or losses (Venus in Virgo in the 12th). Maybe the person finds a good job that requires good organizational ability or technological knowledge (Mercury in Virgo in the 1st), but has major problems with female co-workers harming her reputation behind her back (Venus in Virgo in the 12th).

Our knowledge of astrology will always be imperfect. While technical proficiency is a wonderful goal, we're flawed human beings and there will always be a great deal more we don't know.

Still, we should always do our best for each client and we should study and research our craft as much as we can, because our work can change someone's life in dramatic fashion, for better or worse. We have to develop our humanity, because with some compassion and wisdom we can hope to make a positive difference in others' lives. Technical knowledge is precious but it is not as useful as a kind heart, a receptive ear and a humble spirit. Always do your best.

References and Notes

1. Martin Davis, *From Here to There*, The Wessex Astrologer, 2008, pp. 11–12.

2. *Ibid.*, p. 1. This includes, but is not limited to, correlating nations with zodiacal qualities. Also see footnote 7 on Wynn.

3. I have spent a considerable amount of energy researching this topic and I've spoken with Kenneth Irving, among others, about who first developed and wrote about the techniques of astrocartography. As far as I can tell at this time, Cyril Fagan seems to be the most deserving of credit for at least being the first to write about the basic approach of astrocartography for relocation purposes. And some of the other astrologers who are sometimes credited for developing astrocartography tend to be siderealists who were friends of Cyril Fagan, such as Firebrace, Duncan and Bradley. To me the evidence points toward astrocartography, as we generally think of it today, coming out of this group, with Fagan most likely candidate for the lion's share of gratitude. I'll continue to research this topic for my upcoming book on locational astrology.

4. Charles Jayne, *Considerations* magazine, Volume XIX, No. 1, p. 10. The article was written in 1985 but published in 2004. See http://issuu. com/considerations/docs/19-1

5. Cyril Fagan, *The Solunars Handbook*, 1976, p. 101. *The Solunars Handbook* is a collection of excerpts from Fagan's 1953–1970 'Solunars' column in *American Astrology*.

6. *In mundo* maps show astronomically correct rising, setting, culminating and anti-culminating positions for the planetary lines, rather than lines that correspond to zodiacal longitude, i.e. the ASC, DSC, MC and IC.

7. Wynn, in his own astrological magazine *Wynn's Astrology*, published a map in August, 1941 with mundane concerns related to World War II and Adolf Hitler; this map included some personal lines for Hitler, but those lines were geodetic positions rather than angular planets for Hitler (i.e. not A*C*G). Martin Davis writes that in 1957–58 Donald

Bradley published a hand-plotted map showing the rising, setting and culminating lines of all the planets (around the entire world) for the 1958 sidereal ingress of the Sun into Capricorn.

8. Jim Lewis, transcript from his 'Professional Training and Certification Seminar', 1993, p. 7 (produced by Continuum, edited and transcribed by Karen McCauley and Lori Osborne, June 1998).

9. *Ibid.*, p. 22.

10. *Ibid.*, p. 15.

11. *Ibid.*, p. 50.

12. I say, 'whichever *houses* it resides in', because it may reside in more than one house natally when we consider multiple house systems.

13. Pardon my gross estimation.

14. Lewis seminar, op. cit., p. 33.

15. One degree of latitude can be anywhere from 68.703 miles to 69.407 miles because of the Earth's slightly ellipsoid shape. So about 69 miles or 111 km.

16. Lewis seminar, op. cit., p. 26.

17. *Ibid.*, p. 25.

18. I've had people try to convince me that 9 degrees is a better orb, but I just haven't seen that angular planets have noticeable enough influence beyond 8 degrees.

19. And it may be the case that we should use different distance orbs with *in mundo* positions depending on how quickly the ASC/DSC axis is moving in any given region at any given time.

Frank C. Clifford
A Personal Biography

All charts in this essay:
Placidus houses
(except below:
Equal houses)

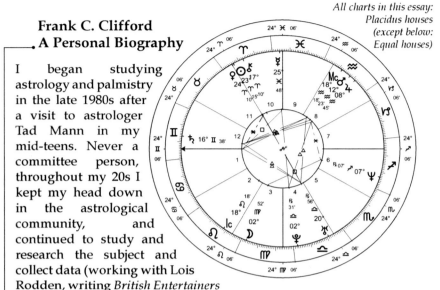

I began studying astrology and palmistry in the late 1980s after a visit to astrologer Tad Mann in my mid-teens. Never a committee person, throughout my 20s I kept my head down in the astrological community, and continued to study and research the subject and collect data (working with Lois Rodden, writing *British Entertainers* and creating a databank for Solar Fire). I then began to publish other astrologers' books (including Garry Phillipson's *Astrology in the Year Zero*) through my company Flare. I was also learning my craft by seeing clients, doing lots of media work (radio, TV and columns for weeklies and monthlies) and writing astrology books and palmistry titles for Random House (*Palmistry 4 Today*) and Hamlyn (*Palm Reading*), which had the good fortune to be published in eight languages. At 29 I plucked up the courage to start lecturing, and at 31 took over the running of the London School of Astrology, which had been founded by Sue Tompkins in 2000. Thanks to Sue's expertise and following, the LSA had already become the most popular astrology school in the UK. Being in charge of the school has occupied most of my 30s, and I have spent much of my time teaching, organizing conferences and classes, and inviting some truly great experts to teach my students. I like to joke that the LSA is one of a handful of 'full-time jobs' I manage to juggle in my life. I'm blessed with wonderful students at the LSA and they, along with some fascinating clients, teach me so much about my work and make my wonderful 'labour of love' so worthwhile. As my chart suggests, I'm driven to pursue new work avenues and determined to try everything and travel everywhere at least once! Writing books (including *Getting to the Heart of Your Chart: Playing Astrological Detective*) and columns for magazines (such as *The Mountain Astrologer*), having fun lecturing around the world, and working through my list of 'must finish' books are all current preoccupations that bring the most pleasure professionally.

www.flareuk.com • www.londonschoolofastrology.co.uk
info@flareuk.com

Chapter Nine

THE SUN, MOON & MIDHEAVEN IN VOCATION

FRANK C. CLIFFORD

The birth chart offers clear signposts that reveal vocational drives, career choices, work avenues and employment options. In this essay I'll be looking at three areas in the horoscope, ones that I most associate with vocation, everyday work routines and making an individual contribution to society. These are:

- The Sun – our calling;
- The Moon – our daily work needs;
- The Midheaven (Medium Coeli, the 'MC') – our social/ professional persona and contribution.

These three parts of our chart can point us towards paths of personal success and professional fulfilment. In order to make the most of each, we should consider:

- Following our Sun – by engaging in activity suggested by its placement and aspects, for we receive internal nourishment and external recognition by doing this;
- Feeding our Moon – by ensuring we are surrounded by nourishing people and supportive environments; and
- Directing the Sun through our Midheaven – by expressing our fundamental self in the outer world, building a legacy and contributing to a larger goal/greater good.

There are other areas of the horoscope that relate to work and career – from the Earth houses (2, 6, 10) to the Ascendant (our agenda and one-to-one interactions) and Mercury (our mental aptitudes) – but even though the chart should always be read as a whole, this essay focuses chiefly on the Sun, Moon and the Midheaven.

A vocation is something that gives our life meaning and significance; it occupies a place in us of creativity and fertility. It is something we feel compelled and 'called' to do (from *vocare*, to call, and *vocationem*, spiritual calling). The vocation is a fundamental area of our life to which we are dedicated. It may have little to do with our basic job or how we earn a living. Our vocation lies *within* us; it is at the core of our reason for being/living. It is understandable then that some astrologers, including me, link vocation to the astrological Sun rather than a house or horoscope angle.

Its link to the Sun in our horoscope suggests that our calling is something 'deep down inside ourselves' striving to appear, to make a significant personal statement and to stamp an individual mark (the Sun) in some way onto the world around us. In his eloquent and poetic publication, *An Astrological Guide to a Fulfilling Vocation*, astrologer Brian Clark writes:

> Vocation is an aspect of our fate, an integral part of our character which seeks expression... In contemporary terms we can imagine vocation as the calling to one's authentic role in the world. It is a calling from deep inside the self, an internal voice. The language of the soul speaks through images and feelings, not with literal words. Hence this inner voice, this calling, is often felt as a yearning to fulfil one's self creatively. The language of images needs to be engaged with, not deciphered. A vocation is not a literal pathway already existing in the world, but rather something that is shaped over the course of our lives as we come to know ourselves. Vocation is the calling to attend to soul in the world, not a literal mission.[1]

A calling appears to be beyond any single profession or line of work. The vocation isn't a clear job definition. It is what lies at the heart of the matter, the purpose behind the activity. Writing or composing is not a vocation per se; the vocation is the *life force and energy behind* the composition, the motivation that prompts a desire to write and communicate one's message. Astrology isn't a vocation either; it's a vehicle – a language, method, tool – to help us *fulfil our calling*. Each astrologer becomes a specific type of practitioner, and for very different, individual reasons (as seen in their natal horoscope). We have astrologers who are researchers, counsellors, the answerers of questions, wannabe gurus...

Consider these three questions: Have you discovered your own vocation? Are you actively engaged in this? And are you earning a living by following this calling exclusively?

The reality is that most of us don't work in the field that truly expresses who we are or want to be. We are on automatic pilot. Most of us are not aroused by the work we do. It's a means to an end, and perhaps that end is getting to a point of retirement in order to follow a cherished dream. It's no disgrace to earn your living without following your vocation, but it is a disgrace to put it off and wait 'until there's more time'!

Do we all have a vocation? In *The Soul's Code*,[2] James Hillman writes that each of us has a 'daimon', a guardian angel or spirit, that endeavours to help us fulfil our calling. Some of us have a very strong sense of vocation, often from early on in life. In the horoscope there is usually a repetitive pattern – a theme that recurs in so many ways that we cannot ignore it and have little choice but to express it. The more contradictory overtones and 'choices' in our charts, the more likely it is that we won't feel compelled to explore our vocation until later in life, if at all. One thing is for sure: people don't feel as condemned to accept their lot nowadays, and are more aware of a need to pursue work that expresses who they are (whether this is a hobby or paid employment).

As I wrote in *The Mountain Astrologer* (Oct./Nov. 2010):

> Getting in touch with our calling is a matter of defining it and being in a time/place/environment that allows it to be nurtured into manifestation and to bloom... Looking back on a life we may discover, as James Hillman wrote in *The Soul's Code* (Warner, 1997), that events have conspired to bring our particular calling (as carried by the daimon) to the fore to fulfil its function.

Elemental Considerations

There is no placement or planetary combination that says 'plumber', 'astrologer' or 'politician' or one that identifies us as the next 'pop idol'. (Although astrologers had a somewhat easier job a hundred or more years ago when there were fewer professional choices.) Trying to pinpoint an actual job for a client might be a thankless and unproductive task. It is better to work on identifying their needs, their talents and goals than to create a list of specific job roles. We can ask the client what excites them, what they are drawn to, and ask, for example, whether they consider themselves a:

- Communicator
- Educator/teacher
- Seller/agent/go-between
- Manager/organizer
- Constructor/builder/developer

- Maintainer
- Protector
- Campaigner
- Server/supporter

The horoscope reveals the motivations, qualities and passions that lie behind a person's work. For instance, here in the UK, barristers do a different job from solicitors. They have the 'right of audience' in court and, instructed by a solicitor, they are in the business of advocacy – pleading, arguing – before a judge. Although Mercury may 'govern' advocacy, the birth charts (and Mercurys) of these barristers will be as varied as their own individual motivations, professional styles and communication skills. These drives, styles and potential skills, rather than the actual jobs, are the parts that I believe can be seen in the horoscope. *Why* the person is doing their job is always more important than *what* they're actually doing for a living. (The 'why' can be seen in repetitive chart themes, key planetary placements and elemental balances/imbalances.)

For instance, consider the elements of the Sun, Moon and MC signs. Is our calling (the Sun) an earthy one? Does our daily working environment (the Moon) need an airy outlet? What is the fundamental motivation behind gaining recognition and contributing to the world around us (the MC) – is it fiery, earthy, airy or watery? Perhaps one element dominates the trio.

The elements reveal what motivates us – what stimulates, inspires and spurs us on towards goals and personal fulfilment; our incentive.

Fire ignites in fields offering challenge, competition, excitement and risk. Fiery people seek glory, greatness and recognition of their individuality rather than money or position; they wish to enthuse others, and are fuelled by passion and optimism. They are hustlers, (self-)promoters, evangelists, visionaries, inspirational teachers or leaders/motivators/life coaches/instructors.

Earth works well in fields offering safety, expediency/usefulness and tangible results. Earth signs wish to leave the world a better place than they found it. They seek routine and a steady income; they stay with the known and familiar and are security-conscious. Gaining pleasure from a job well done, earthy people are reliable providers, dependable 'rocks' and productive, purposeful 'realists'. They are craftsmen, builders (of anything, from homes to empires), lovers and supporters of their countryside; they are sensualists and work directly with their bodies (sports, physical work).

Air comes alive in fields offering exchange, dialogue and debate. These individuals seek interaction, variety and travel; they want to learn, read, question and communicate. Air people are interested in theory, concept, the abstract, formulas, patterns; they analyse, deduce and reason. They are fascinated by *people* and make natural communicators, salespeople, persuaders and advocates.

Water seeks work in fields offering an emotional connection. Water people focus on human values and aim to be of service to the human condition, and endeavour to help, care and develop emotional ties. They perceive that which has not been verbalized and connect to that which cannot be articulated. Water signs are empathetic and sympathetic; their antennae scan atmospheres and pick up nuance; they have spot-on judgments and gut instincts. They are the carers, counsellors, therapists and intuitives.

Before we look at the Sun and Midheaven as principal components of *realizing* and *manifesting* our vocation, let's look at the Moon and its role in our working life.

The Moon

- Our 'backpack' of needs
- The working environment
- The routine job and our attitude towards it
- Fundamental relationship needs

What do we need at work? What kind of work will *feed* us on a daily basis? What sort of environment will make us feel comfortable, safe and secure? The Moon has much to say about our daily rhythms, feelings and habits, and as most of us spend one third of our adult life at work, the Moon is a fundamental consideration. The office needs to be a place we want to go to in the morning!

Noel Tyl has written of the planets and 'need fulfilment', and the Moon sign being the 'reigning need' of the personality. In his chapter from *How to Use Vocational Astrology for Success in the Workplace*, he writes:

Fulfilment of our personal reigning need in life must somehow be abetted by the work atmosphere, pace, energy, growth stimulus, and image trappings of our job, cued by the Moon and its sign... We see how important it is, indeed, that the job situation assimilate, support and/ or reward the need fulfilment behaviours.[3]

The Moon indicates what we're *sensitive* to. It's fascinating how some people are drawn to (or compelled to engage in) daily routines that challenge this most vulnerable area of their lives/charts. Some of my actor or singer friends and clients have Moon–Uranus contacts, suggesting that they rebel against (Uranus) sedentary 9 to 5 office work (Moon) and are sensitive (Moon) to rejection (Uranus). Yet many have to audition or perform on a daily basis, where the threat of rejection or a pie in the face is forever present. Somehow they gravitate towards a scenario that pushes their most sensitive of buttons. Here we can also sense the calling (Sun) being stronger than simple daily needs (Moon).

If we wish to consider the most suitable environment at work, we must look to the Moon complex (its placement and aspects). What is our favoured working habitat? A Moon sign in Air needs light, space and an airy office – without being swamped by emotional, clingy co-workers. Fixed signs need a permanent desk, not some swap-and-change office environment! The Moon in Aries needs a busy environment and the autonomy to make decisions, and to spearhead their own ventures and set targets. The Moon in Cancer needs a nest, to feel a sense of belonging at work. The Moon in Libra favours a working environment of discussion, debate and joint decision-making, where there is respect for each other's opinions. Astrologer Faye Cossar suggests that we go further by considering lunar synastry with a company's horoscope to see whether we will feel 'at home' there.[4]

The Moon represents the level of deeper communication between co-workers, those non-verbal interactions that make up a relationship and go beyond the exchange of information, facts or gossip (Mercury) or the pleasantries (Venus). It is essential to help a client acknowledge their Moon, which will give them permission to want (and ask for) more at work. Identifying their office needs is often a client's first step towards improving their daily working lives.

A few years ago I read Judith Hill's book *Vocational Astrology*, which presents a wonderful collection of 100 horoscopes of individuals who have successful jobs *and* enjoy their work. I started to realize the importance of the Moon and its dispositor in describing the work, routine and rhythms that *nourish* us. For instance, if the natal Moon is in Scorpio, the daily job and regular activities need to allow some room for penetrating, probing analysis. People with the Moon in Scorpio want to engage in the investigative process; they are drawn to everyday work that is deep, and in which they can express passion. Often they are involved in work that regularly brings up life-or-death matters, crisis-driven situations or political undercurrents.

The Moon's dispositor (i.e. the planet that rules the Moon sign) provides additional, specific information about what lies behind our working needs. Continuing with our Moon in Scorpio example, Mars and Pluto become the dispositors (but I'd recommend leaving Pluto for more generational matters, and focusing on the placement of Mars). If Mars were in Virgo, this would suggest a craftsman-like approach to tasks and a need to be helpful/useful in whatever penetrating, probing work (Scorpio) is pursued.

So, what do Scorpio and Virgo have in common and how do they differ? Both signs are concerned with research, service, perception, control and health matters (the sickness and the cure) – Scorpio from a watery, emotional perspective, Virgo from an earthy, practical and expedient angle. Scorpio seeks respect and privacy but has a strong instinct to merge with another, while Virgo works well in a cloistered environment and is comfortable with its aloneness, cherishing periods of solitude.

One example I have of this combination belongs to a client born with Moon–Neptune in Scorpio who looked after his sick mother in the family home for twenty-nine years. She had had a stroke when he was thirteen years old, and rather than becoming a flight attendant and travel the world (a childhood dream), he trained as a nurse – partly in order to attend to her. Over the years he quite literally saved her life on a number of occasions,

moving mountains, against the odds (Scorpio) when she became sick (Virgo) and doctors held out no chance of survival. For my client, the reason behind (dispositor) the desire to engage in deep, transformative work (Moon in Scorpio) was a need to get things back in order and functioning efficiently ('healthily') again (Mars in Virgo). Put another way, an innate desire *to be in control* of one's daily environment (Moon in Scorpio) stemmed from a deeper fear of chaos or sickness (the dispositor Mars in Virgo).

The Sun

- What makes our heart sing
- Labours of love
- Following our inner self and sense of purpose
- What we were born to do
- Vocation

The astrological meaning of the Sun is often dismissed or simply reduced to adjectives and keyword traits of its sign position. Perhaps this is because one's *core* is more difficult to capture, articulate and elucidate. Yet those adjectives hammered into us early on in our astrological education are useful here. Each sign's characteristics are valuable when remembering the qualities we can bring to our professional lives.

What are we *really* here to do? The Sun says much about our true purpose in life, and what we're striving to become. The focus we place on the Sun in Western astrology suggests how much we value the idea of having an individual purpose, a destiny to discover or a life path that is special and unique in its message. Perhaps the reason Sun-sign astrology (in columns and books) is so popular and widespread is that it puts us at the centre of our universe, serving as a daily reminder of who we essentially are, our identity, life force and individual journey – what makes us special and different from the crowd. Yet astrology's enduring appeal lies in its ability to combine this specific sense of individual destiny with particular birth chart groupings (e.g. Air signs), signatures/overtones (e.g. Mercury-themed charts) and types (e.g. Geminis), so we know we are not alone in this pursuit of a unique path.

Astrologer Kim Falconer reminds us that:

> We don't automatically have all the solar traits indicated by our Sun sign. It is much more an assignment than a published thesis, and we have to work hard for most or all of our lives to complete it... Understanding our solar needs can go a long way toward developing natural abilities.[5]

One of our jobs as astrologers is to speak to the very core of who our clients are, to illuminate their Sun, to share what astrology says about who they were born to be; we must help them recognize and live out their Sun archetype. It is often said that we shine and feel alive when we engage in activity suggested by our Sun. This process of helping clients to rekindle their life mission should take into account the Sun's complex: its sign and house position, as well as aspects.[6]

The Sun is our type of *heart*. For instance, the Sun–Neptune person needs to connect to a spiritual centre, to follow their compassionate, intuitive and empathetic heart – one with heightened sensory ability, colour, flair, art and imagination.

When we define the natal Sun, we and our clients can begin to *realize* and *manifest* this most personal and compelling of journeys. Ideally we can do this for ourselves, rather than having someone act it out for us (e.g. marrying someone who epitomizes our Sun complex). And if we don't constructively engage with the messages of our Sun sign, we languish in the opposite sign. The warning is to follow your Sun or wallow in the worst of its polar opposite!

The Midheaven

- The best pathway to recognition
- Our definition of success
- A facet of our public persona; our reputation
- Making a contribution to the world around us
- Aims, direction, status, goals

The Midheaven shows the qualities we admire, elevate and wish to emulate. It can also be a 'social shorthand' for the ways in which we describe to others what we do, and in turn phrases that are used by others to introduce and describe us. As the most elevated point in the horoscope, the MC is the route up from our inner, private world (IC) and out into the world. We put ourselves 'out there' through our MC sign, whether that's in society, in a local group or on national TV. It is descriptive of our reputation. Rather than our character (Sun) or personal temperament (Moon), the MC reveals our image and, along with the Ascendant, it informs how we 'dress ourselves up' and construct a public persona.

Success in the horoscope is symbolized by the MC – it's the attainment of a goal and some form of recognition for our strivings. In *Money: How to Find It with Astrology*, Lois Rodden describes the MC as the best pathway to social recognition and worldly success – the conduct we need in order to succeed and achieve status and recognition. She writes, 'Success is shown in a chart by the extent to which we assume the role symbolized by the MC voluntarily and constructively.'[7] In essence, the MC says much about how and where we can express professionalism (lit. *to declare aloud or in public*, to profess one's vows).

The MC–IC axis reveals the early messages we received from parental figures about 'the big world out there' – ones that relate to personal, deep-rooted principles (Imum Coeli, the IC) and social/ work philosophies that affect our place in the world (MC). The axis says much about what was stressed as important by our parents. The MC is a call to leave the comfort zone and 'family name' of the IC and branch out on our own, to dare to create our own name and reputation. What is instilled early on in life at the IC (ideas, belief systems, messages from parents) is called up to be manifested in the world through the MC.[8]

The MC is very different from the zenith (90° from the Ascendant), although they can sometimes share the same degree. The zenith (the cusp of the 10th House by Equal house division) and the subsequent 10th House relate to mundane work and career matters. A transit/ progression/direction to the zenith (nonagesimal) degree brings up important work developments, while the same to the MC will coincide with something more meaningful about life direction and will have an impact on our reputation and perception of our social role. The MC is a more personal point that has links to deep-seated drives to achieve something significant in the outer world and resolve parental influences later in our social life.

Directing the Sun through the Lens of the Midheaven

Ideally, once we've identified and started attending to our daily needs (the Moon), we can concentrate on the bigger yet more intimate picture: fulfilling a personal, creative desire (the Sun as our vocation) and sharing this 'mission' with the people around us (the Midheaven).

The MC is the culmination and summit of the chart (literally and figuratively, as the most elevated point a planet can reach in its daily cycle). It is the means by which we can channel other features of our horoscope (revealing our talents, needs and desires) into society or a public/social/work arena.

Working the message of the Sun (the inner light) through the filter/lens of the MC (the external prism) is a way of fulfilling our destination/destiny/role in a social or public context. It is not necessarily about achieving acclaim or public renown – or even earning a living in the area of our vocation. It is about finding a way to project our solar philosophies, purpose and creative endeavours through the lens of the MC and make a meaningful, personal contribution (the Sun) to the world around us (the MC). It's about 'putting our vocation' *out there* and inspiring, helping, awakening, supporting and educating others.[9] The MC complex is the signpost to how we can do this successfully and have others recognize our contribution.

Consider the Sun like a 'beam of light' (the colour of this light is seen by the sign placement, the motivation by the element of its sign, the force/energy by aspects from the planets). Imagine it when projected through the prism of a particular MC – when it's refracted into society. The MC is the most ideal way of actualizing potential (the Sun) in order to 'become ourselves' in society – it shows how we can bear fruit socially and professionally. How we manifest in society what we feel summoned to do is shown by how well we are able to integrate the MC complex (its sign and aspects) with the Sun complex. Are these points immediately compatible? Is their conversation fluent, the message easily accessed and understood? Or perhaps these two complexes require more effort and awareness to make manifest one's essential 'heart' (the Sun) and receive some sort of recognition and validation.

The MC, like the other three angles, is linked to the path of the Sun. The Sun is on the MC around noon each day, so many people born in the late morning/early afternoon will have both Sun and MC in the same sign, suggesting that their purpose, calling and innate qualities (as shown by the Sun) can be 'seen' and recognized easily 'out there' (MC). In other words, their essence is on display, their reputation (MC) clearly linked to their calling (Sun).

For most people, the Sun and MC signs are different, and our job as astrologers is to blend these two signs (and complexes) and articulate their range of possibilities to clients. We must ask ourselves what these signs (and complexes) have in common and what they, in combination, can create that is fruitful. For instance, it might be 'easy' for someone with the Sun in Aries to shine this through an MC in the fellow fire sign of Leo, but how can someone with the Sun in Cancer shine through an MC in Aquarius? Still, any combination, no matter how disparate, is capable of working together and producing something remarkable and individual!

Combining the Three Points; Some Client Stories

Brian: Sun in Sagittarius, Moon in Aquarius, MC in Aries

Sagittarius, Aquarius and Aries are signs value freedom, independence and have a desire to speak up, speak out and *experience* life to the full. Each of the three has opinions on how the world can be improved! Sagittarius is a natural front-of-house meet-and-greeter. It is a sign linked to publishing, sport, sales and promotion. In Brian's chart the Sun is in the 5th House: he's a playful, free spirit and a man-boy in his late 30s who has never quite grown up. But the Sun makes a tight opposition[10] to Saturn in Gemini: he has always spoken of a need to prove himself to, and impress, his father, who is an established name in publishing (Sagittarius). This opposition saw Brian follow his father into magazine publishing as an office worker who spent his days on the phone selling advertising space in a small, traditional firm. On a daily level this job suited Brian's friendly nature and desire to chat with strangers and regular customers (Moon in airy Aquarius conjunct the Descendant) – the only concession was taking out his earring before he walked through the door each morning! – and he stayed in this role for a decade (note the fixed Moon). But working for someone else in an establishment-type, 'serious' job to please his father (Sun–Saturn), where there was no room for promotion or self-determination, never really appealed to his Aries Midheaven. Eventually he got in touch with this MC by becoming a personal trainer. Aries is a sign of the motivator. Aries needs targets and goals, to pit itself against some form of opposition. It is a sign at home with provoking others into taking control of their own lives. Aries offers a minimum-step program (it couldn't abide *twelve*!) and wouldn't have the patience to put up with someone who returned each week just looking for a sympathetic ear. It needs to see results fast. Aries wants to breathe new life into an existing idea, to race in front of the pack and get *ahead*. Like the Sun, the Midheaven sign can take some years to fully express its many facets. With Brian, he expressed his Aries MC as a rather cocky, sex-driven teenage 'lad' – impulsive and a bit reckless, leaving a trail of one-night stands behind him. Later, his contagious enthusiasm proved essential to his success as a trainer.

Kim: Sun in Taurus, Moon in Virgo, MC in Virgo

When the Moon and the MC share the same sign, the parts of life that provide succour, comfort and nurturance can be areas that one becomes known for in one's professional or social environment (MC). Often, what is naturally done well at home can be of benefit to the person and others in the outside world. In Kim's chart all three vocational components are in the element of Earth. She is, at heart, a collector, a hoarder, someone who wishes to build something of enduring, practical value (Sun in Taurus). At her home I encountered her Moon. I remember being struck by the large collection of bottles and jars stacked away in cupboards in her kitchen. And they were all labelled (Virgo) or in the *process* (mutable) of being labelled (Virgo's work is never done!). Over the years I have marvelled at the time she has dedicated to specific tasks (Earth is *slow*) and she told me recently of an Alice in Wonderland party she had at her home – one that took *twelve months* to plan. At work (five years as a Creative Director of music videos), Kim used these natural tendencies (Moon), and her attention to detail, efficiency and kindness (Virgo) were personal traits that media clientele admired in her. Together, these created her reputation for excellence (MC in Virgo). Later, Kim became a full-time artist and has since staged a number of award-winning exhibitions. One of her most memorable pieces of artwork is truly Virgoan: 800 antique test tubes (filled with resin and inks referencing colours and forms of *bacteria*) set within a large white frame in a circular, mandala pattern. Her website lists the key themes inherent in her artwork (revealing her Taurus–Virgo combination, plus the Pluto overtone of Scorpio Rising and Pluto on the MC): preservation vs. organic decay, rhythm and repetition, the precise vs. the organic, bacteria as life-enhancing/life-destroying. She writes, 'Labels are used for defining and identifying; bottles distil or preserve' (Virgo–Taurus).

Amy: Sun in Pisces, Moon in Aquarius, MC in Gemini

Two of Amy's vocational trio have mutability (Sun, MC) and Air (Moon, MC) in common, underscoring the Gemini MC placement and a fundamental desire for variety, movement and space (mutable Air). Amy is, in essence, a rescuer who needs to be of service to others, particularly in the emotional realm (Sun in Pisces in the 7th). During the time I've known her, she has counselled people, devoted time to charities and supported sick friends. Amy needs breathing space in her daily working life and has lived alone for many years (Moon in Aquarius). Originally an office PA for a banker in the City of London (MC in Gemini), Amy gave up this well-paid job when she felt called to pursue studies in metaphysics and tarot (Pisces). A period of learning numerous, related subjects turned into a multi-faceted career as a teacher–consultant–supervisor–facilitator of many mind–body–spirit disciplines (Gemini MC has a hyphenated reputation!). She now runs her practice in two towns and travels to and from them regularly (Gemini). Pisces has an instinct to save, empathize and merge. It seeks an emotional connection and spiritual exchange that Airy Aquarius and Gemini can't fathom. But Aquarius (along with Gemini) stands back, observes and clarifies from a rational, detached viewpoint. It avoids getting swamped or smothered by the needy. This Sun–Moon blend could suggest a struggle to find a freedom–closeness balance in personal relationships (for the longest time, her two cats have been Amy's only companions). But at work she has used this combination to develop a reputation by word-of-mouth (Gemini) of running workshops in her home (Moon) with groups who share her interests (Aquarius), articulating a variety (Gemini) of metaphysical ideas and spiritual practices (Pisces), including inner-child therapy (Moon in the 5th).

Heather: Sun in Gemini, Moon in Taurus, MC in Leo

Heather worked for many years to combine her dual interests (Gemini) of music and astrology, writing songs about her own horoscope. When I knew her, she spent much of her time talking about herself and bolstering an overblown but perhaps fragile ego (Gemini, Leo). Heather's key pursuits appeared to be fame and recognition (Sun–Jupiter conjunction, Leo MC) – and her pushy personality generated much publicity and fanfare for her ventures but provoked much opposition and scorn from others. A natural deal-maker (Gemini, plus Scorpio Rising) and delegator (Leo has a knack of 'encouraging' others to take on Leo's workload!), she ran a business promoting a select group of psychological astrology consultants that thrived for a short while. But Leo MC is not a team player, and the business fell apart amid personality clashes (Leo) and disputes over rightful shares of daily income (Moon in Taurus). The Moon in Taurus showed itself in Heather's need to accumulate money and, with Sun–Jupiter in the 8th, she had a philosophy that warned 'what's mine is mine, and what's yours will soon be mine!' With good investments and support from her husband's job (Moon in Taurus in the 7th), she built a nest egg that enabled her to move to another country and set up a health and beauty spa to pamper clients (Taurus, Leo).

Antonia: Sun in Pisces, Moon in Libra, MC in Cancer

With two vocational points in cardinal signs and two in Water, the vocational message is to seek challenge, make things happen and initiate (cardinal) matters of an emotional nature where human values and being of service to the human condition (Water) are prerequisites. With strong cardinality, Antonia needs to be in charge, ideally in joint-charge (Libra) with someone who does a different, valuable job in the office. At best, Water people have gut instincts that turn into spot-on judgments and work well for them. At worst, there can be a series of emotional crises, an attraction

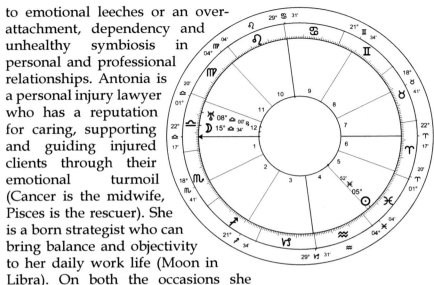

to emotional leeches or an over-attachment, dependency and unhealthy symbiosis in personal and professional relationships. Antonia is a personal injury lawyer who has a reputation for caring, supporting and guiding injured clients through their emotional turmoil (Cancer is the midwife, Pisces is the rescuer). She is a born strategist who can bring balance and objectivity to her daily work life (Moon in Libra). On both the occasions she worked for someone else, she encountered an imbalance of power and daily conflict (Libra) from difficult, irrational and sometimes tyrannical bosses. Antonia's Moon in Libra was called upon to mediate, calm, appease and restore harmony. When she worked for herself, she ended up supporting both (male) personal partners. Libra needs to be liked and have its ideas accepted – but when confident, it begins to rely less heavily on others and uses charm and persuasion/manipulation to have its *own* needs met. Here, the Moon in Libra (conjunct Uranus) is far less malleable or emotionally attached than people think or the Pisces–Cancer might suggest.

Follow Your Chart and Your Heart

We do our best work as astrologers when we encourage clients (and ourselves!) to follow the messages written in their horoscopes. I'm thankful to astrologer Faye Cossar for introducing me to the work of Barbara Marx Hubbard, who said, 'The vocation is the genius of the individual wanting to be expressed.' Hubbard uses the term 'vocational arousal' to describe that powerful spark that gets ignited when someone you meet *moves you forward* in a powerful way towards your own calling. This is what we have the potential to do as astrologers.

Some become nurses, teachers or fundraisers because 'good people do that'. Others are embarrassed to take up a pursuit because of what friends and family might say. This reminds me of the month in 2011 when my Ascendant (representing one's physical environment/surroundings) moved into regal Leo by Solar Arc (where it will stay for 30 years). I was asked to give consultations at the lush, splendid and salubrious Royal Crescent Hotel in Bath, England, and invited to stay over in one of their thousand-dollar-a-night suites (I could certainly get used to that for the next 30 years!). With my new environment (Solar Arc Ascendant) now in Leo, I encountered three (of the six) clients that first afternoon who had acting ambitions (Leo), all of whom felt that such things were flights of fancy – silly and childish. Part of each of the sessions dealt with the possible ways they could learn to act, and when I returned earlier this year, two of the three had joined amateur dramatic groups and were loving it to bits!

One of the attacks on modern astrology by some astrologers is that we encourage people to become *anything* they like – we do have our limits and certain practical considerations must be taken into account. But the key to our work as modern astrologers is to help clients discover what they truly love and encourage them to pursue it one way or another. It may not matter whether they win awards or are judged successful by others – what matters is that they love what they do, which brings its own feeling of accomplishment. At one conference I remember being horrified to hear an inexperienced astrologer recall discouraging a client from following a cherished dream because her chart didn't show *eminence* in that field. The astrologer had missed a chance to encourage the client to pursue it anyway!

Despair, it is said, comes from choosing to be someone other than ourselves. Being an Aries, I'm all for 'self-centred astrology': doing what makes us happy. We should encourage our clients to do the same. Remind them of who they were born to be – they already know this deep inside. They'll hear your words and recognize that special, burning desire they perhaps set aside many years ago... a fire that is still simmering. They just might need someone to open up avenues, possibilities and passions that they hadn't dared to consider – or rekindle.

Novelist Edith Wharton wrote, 'There are two ways of spreading light: to be the candle or the mirror that reflects it.' We astrologers can do both jobs in consultation. We're the mirror (the Moon) when we're able to speak to our clients, reflect their inner drives and talents, and then 'turn them on' to their calling. And we're the candle (the Sun) when we personally demonstrate what it is to work in a field like astrology – to engage in a true labour of love. In doing so we create an energy around us that brings opportunity and advancement for us all; it inspires others to stay with what truly makes them deeply happy – to 'follow their bliss', as Joseph Campbell often said.

In my book *Palmistry 4 Today*, I wrote of the three Ds: discipline, determination and drive, and the need for courage. **Courage + Talent + Energy = Success in Life**...

> Courage is essential... We need courage to channel our energies in order to explore our talents and express ourselves. We must never lose sight of the wonderful realities in our lives as well as our dreams – a loyalty to both keeps us alive. We must always dare to travel uncharted waters, to take risks, to grow, learn and live. Success starts with a way of thinking and being... None of us can change the past, but past circumstances and choices have helped to bring us to the place where we stand today. In knowing this, we can cast aside regret and expectation, and create our future by working now – in the present – to reach out and experience challenges, adventures and relationships. And it's never too late to start over.[11]

References and Notes

1. Brian Clark, *An Astrological Guide to a Fulfilling Vocation*, Astro*Synthesis, 2010, p. 3–4.

2. James Hillman, *The Soul's Code*, Warner, 1997.

3. Noel Tyl, *How to Use Vocational Astrology for Success in the Workplace*, Llewellyn, 1992, p. 42–3.

4. See Faye's book *Using Astrology to Create a Vocational Profile*, Flare, 2012.

5. Kim Falconer, *Astrology and Aptitude*, AFA, 2001, p. 90.

6. I would use only the conjunction, square, opposition and any very tight trines, within a 3° orb.

7. Lois M. Rodden, *Money: How to Find It with Astrology*, Data News Press, 1994, p. 191.

8. I shall be writing about the MC–IC in greater detail in my book *The Midheaven: Spotlight on Success*, due in 2013.

9. Transits, progressions or directions that ingress into our MC or Sun sign signal periods of activation – times when we are most easily able to reconnect with our aims, goals and calling.

10. Oppositions to the Sun can distract or draw us away from the pursuit of our goals, while oppositions to the MC can act as an anchor (or a millstone) to the development of a reputation or our social persona. At best, oppositions aid us in an understanding of the polar signs involved and bring out the best in the Sun sign and MC sign.

11. Frank C. Clifford, *Palmistry 4 Today*, Flare, 2010.

Recommended Reading

Frank C. Clifford, *Getting to the Heart of Your Chart*, Flare, 2012

Faye Cossar, *Using Astrology to Create a Vocational Profile*, Flare, 2012

Carol Eikleberry, *The Career Guide for Creative and Unconventional People*, Ten Speed Press, 2007

Kim Falconer, *Astrology and Aptitude*, AFA, 2001

Judith Hill, *Vocational Astrology*, AFA, 1997

James Hillman, *The Soul's Code*, Warner, 1997

Lois M. Rodden, *Money: How to Find it with Astrology*, Data News Press, 1994

Sue Tompkins, *The Contemporary Astrologer's Handbook*, Flare, 2007

Noel Tyl, *How to Use Vocational Astrology for Success in the Workplace*, Llewellyn, 1992

Joanne Wickenburg, *In Search of a Fulfilling Career*, AFA, 1992

Branka Stamenkovic
A Personal Biography

All charts in this essay: 7 visible planets Placidus houses + True Node, Part of Fortune

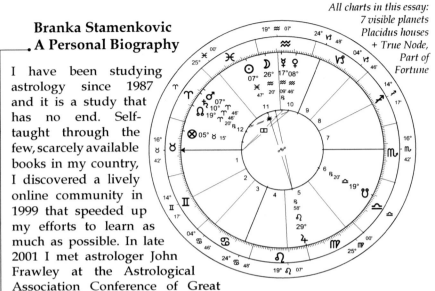

I have been studying astrology since 1987 and it is a study that has no end. Self-taught through the few, scarcely available books in my country, I discovered a lively online community in 1999 that speeded up my efforts to learn as much as possible. In late 2001 I met astrologer John Frawley at the Astrological Association Conference of Great Britain in Cirencester, UK, and soon after that graduated from his horary school. It is from that moment on that traditional astrology became my main focus of interest. In late 2002 I started my own horary correspondence course with students from five continents, and as of 2005 I have been lecturing around the world at various prominent international astrology conferences. My work has also been published in several international astrology magazines, including *The Astrological Journal* and *The Mountain Astrologer*. With a fellow Serbian astrologer (Aleksandar Imsiragic) I founded an annual astrology conference in Belgrade in 2001, just five months after Serbia reopened to the world, and I participated in the organization of the first two events. Currently I am completing studies for the MA in Cultural Astronomy and Astrology at the Trinity Saint David University in Lampeter, UK.

www.brankastamenkovic.com
info@brankastamenkovic.com

Chapter Ten

CHARTS ARE LIKE PASSPORTS
Some Offer More Freedom than Others

BRANKA STAMENKOVIC

Freedom of movement across this globe of ours depends greatly on the quality of the passport we hold, which in most cases is linked to our country of birth. If the passport we hold is not of the greatest quality, we can try 'willing' ourselves into getting a better one, but it is not going to work. We are simply stuck with it; this is our 'fate'.

If you happen to be a Serbian passport holder, chances are that you've experienced every conceivable limitation on the freedom of movement that you can think of. And the name of the limitation is: a visa requirement. For example, until recently a Serbian passport holder could not visit Denmark simply as a tourist. For quite some time the country of Denmark issued only family and business visas for Serbian passport holders. Want to be a tourist in Denmark? No can do. It simply did not exist as an option. If you are a UK passport holder, you don't even need a visa of any kind. You just jump on the plane and *voilà*, there you are, admiring the statue of Hans Christian Andersen's Little Mermaid the very same day.

The situation is pretty much the same with our natal charts. We are born into them and their quality greatly affects the amount of freedom of movement through our life. Some life experiences are simply not possible in certain charts. Want to marry Brad Pitt? No can do. It is an option in Jennifer Aniston's chart and Angelina Jolie's chart – it might or might not be an option in some other woman's chart – but it is probably not an option in yours.

That said, there is really no need to feel depressed over this fact of life. Fate vs. free will should not turn into a gloom vs. happiness game. There is no such thing as limitless fate or limitless free will. Just as fate and free will co-exist, gloom and happiness co-exist too. Life is large enough for both. But it pays to know your limitations (fate) and to know the scope of your life options within them (free will), so that you don't waste time and effort trying to attain the unattainable. In other words, if you live in a room with few doors it is better to focus on the doors that exist than to bang your head against the wall, looking for a nonexistent door. Give it a try and you will soon realize that even if you have just one door at your disposal, it will still provide you with enough opportunity to exercise your free will.

Birth charts are supposed to be the maps that help us navigate more easily through life. And if they were to show total and unlimited free will, they would have every planet in every sign and every house of the chart. As we very well know, that is not the case. We all get just one Saturn per chart, and if it is a Saturn in Aries, no amount of 'free-willing' will magically turn it into a Saturn in Libra. Saturn in Aries is our fate. A free will exercise would be choosing to work with this natal Saturn or some other, maybe better positioned planet in our chart. Maybe our chart also has Venus in Libra. In that case, our free will consists of choosing Saturn or Venus: whether to go through life (or various situations) as a grumpy or a jolly person. Both options are there.

Choosing the Best Option or Running on Autopilot?

If you want to make the most of your chart and use it the best possible way, you first need to identify its *best part* and then consciously focus on using it in life most of the time. The planet that is the chart's best possible option is known as the 'Lord of the Geniture'. However, Sometimes the Lord of the Geniture is easily accessible (because it's also the 'automatic pilot', see below) but it usually is not. When it is easily accessed, very little effort is needed on the person's part to use it – they use it naturally most of the time. When it is not, the person needs to focus on the Lord of the Geniture to express it more consciously and fight the urge to express the automatic pilot, which might represent a difficult part of themselves.

Given that the majority of charts have at least one good option for our free will to chew on, it is amazing how often we neglect to exercise that free will and make that good choice. So often – too often, I'd say – we simply switch to the 'automatic pilot' planet and let the fate take us where it will. The automatic pilot planet is often the most used option because it is easily accessible. Here, we allow ourselves to express the *most prominent* part of our chart rather than the *best part*, be that Saturn in Aries or Venus in Libra. The lucky ones will have Venus in Libra as their automatic pilot. But the others who have Saturn in Aries will need to put in an effort to bypass that most prominent placement, and instead push Venus in Libra (or another good option) to the forefront.

The Lord of the Geniture

To identify the Lord of the Geniture you first need to analyze the essential and accidental dignities and debilities of the seven traditional celestial bodies (Saturn, Jupiter, Mars, Sun, Venus, Mercury and the Moon). Personally, I do not use Uranus, Neptune and Pluto in my astrological work at all, but if you hold them dear to your heart, feel free to continue using them. However, when it comes to identifying the Lord of the Geniture, please keep them out of the picture.

Once you analyze the essential and accidental dignities and debilities of the seven traditional planets, you will have a clear picture of the quality of the different parts of your chart. The planet that ends up having most of both essential and accidental dignity will be your Lord of the Geniture.

Essential Dignities and Debilities

The essential dignity or debility of a planet describes its strength and either its constructive or destructive inclination in exercising that strength. There are three possible major dignities of a planet (rulership, exaltation, triplicity), two possible minor ones (term and face) and two possible debilities (detriment and fall).

Major Essential Dignities (Rulership, Exaltation and Triplicity)

Most astrologers and astrology students are familiar with the dignities of rulership and exaltation. Saturn rules Capricorn, so it is very strong (essentially dignified) when it is positioned in Capricorn. The other major rulership dignity for Saturn is Aquarius. Jupiter is dignified by rulership when in Sagittarius and Pisces, Mars in Aries and Scorpio, Venus in Taurus and Libra, Mercury in Gemini and Virgo, the Sun in Leo and the Moon in Cancer.

While most planets have their rulership dignity in two signs (except for the lights, Sun and Moon), when it comes to the dignity of exaltation each can have such dignity in one sign only. Saturn is exalted in Libra, Jupiter in Cancer, Mars in Capricorn, Venus in Pisces, Mercury in Virgo, the Sun in Aries and the Moon in Taurus.

Rulership and exaltation are the strongest dignities of planets, with rulership being a bit stronger than exaltation. Therefore all the planets in your chart which are positioned in their signs of rulership and/or exaltation will be your candidates for the Lord of the Geniture.

	Dignity by rulership	Dignity by exaltation
Saturn	Capricorn, Aquarius	Libra
Jupiter	Sagittarius, Pisces	Cancer
Mars	Aries, Scorpio	Capricorn
Venus	Taurus, Libra	Pisces
Mercury	Gemini, Virgo	Virgo
Sun	Leo	Aries
Moon	Cancer	Taurus

Table 1: Rulerships and Exaltations

If you don't happen to have any planet in its rulership or exaltation, all is not lost. The third major dignity that a planet can have is the dignity by triplicity. Unlike rulership and exaltation, triplicity is not that widely known among contemporary astrology students, as mainstream modern astrology does not pay much attention to it. Therefore triplicity needs to be explained in more detail.

To establish whether any planet is in its triplicity, you first need to discern whether you are working with a daytime or a nighttime chart. This is easy enough to do: if the Sun is positioned above the horizon (Ascendant/Descendant) line (i.e. if the Sun is in house 7, 8, 9, 10, 11 or 12), it is a daytime chart. If the Sun is positioned below the horizon line (i.e. if the Sun is in house 1, 2, 3, 4, 5 or 6), you are dealing with a nighttime chart. The tricky business will be to discern this in the sunrise and sunset births – those charts where the Sun is close to the Ascendant or Descendant degree. Even those charts that have the Sun positioned below the Ascendant/Descendant axis, if that Sun is less than 5 degrees below the Ascendant (in the 1st) or Descendant (in the 6th), the chart should be counted as a daytime chart.

Once you have established this, refer to the following table:

	Triplicity rulership by day	Triplicity rulership by night
Fire signs	Sun	Jupiter
Earth signs	Venus	Moon
Air signs	Saturn	Mercury
Water signs	Mars	Mars

Table 2: Triplicity Rulers

If you are working with a daytime chart check whether your Sun is in any of the three fire signs (Aries, Leo, Sagittarius). If so, then it is essentially dignified by triplicity. Next check if your Venus is in any of the Earth signs (Taurus, Virgo, Capricorn). The same applies to your Saturn (if it is in any of the air signs: Gemini, Libra, Aquarius) and for your Mars (if it is in any of the water signs: Cancer, Scorpio, Pisces).

If your chart is a nighttime chart check whether your Jupiter, Moon, Mercury and Mars are in the corresponding triplicity signs specified in the above table.

Any of your planets that have essential dignity by triplicity will also be a candidate for the Lord of the Geniture in your horoscope. Most charts you work with will have at least one planet in one of those three major essential dignities: rulership, exaltation or triplicity. You will also come across charts in which there are planets in one or more of these dignities. For example, Mercury in Virgo will at the same time be in two major dignities: rulership and exaltation. Venus in Taurus in a daytime chart will be in its rulership and triplicity dignities. These dignities are cumulative, so a planet in two of its major dignities will be stronger than a planet in just one. But having more than one planet in any of these dignities is good news. It gives you more good options in the chart – and therefore better options in life.

Minor Essential Dignities (Term and Face)
Sometimes a chart will have none of the planets in any of its major dignities. Then you will be forced to look at the minor ones. A planet in minor dignity is nowhere near as strong as a planet in major dignity, but it is much better than a planet with no dignity at all.

Unlike the major dignities, where we are looking at the position of a planet anywhere in a certain sign, when it comes to minor dignities we will need to pay attention to which degree of a sign a planet occupies. This is because the minor dignities of term and face rule just sections of signs.

Saturn, Jupiter, Mars, Venus and Mercury have their terms in certain segments of degrees of each sign. The number of degrees in those chunks and their position within the sign will vary. Therefore, to determine if any of those five planets in your chart have their term dignity, you will need to consult the following table:

♈	00.00–05.59 ♃	06.00–13.59 ♀	14.00–20.59 ☿	21.00–25.59 ♂	26.00–29.59 ♄
♉	00.00–07.59 ♀	08.00–14.59 ☿	15.00–21.59 ♃	22.00–25.59 ♄	26.00–29.59 ♂
♊	00.00–06.59 ☿	07.00–12.59 ♃	13.00–20.59 ♀	21.00–24.59 ♄	25.00–29.59 ♂
♋	00.00–05.59 ♂	06.00–12.59 ♃	13.00–19.59 ☿	20.00–26.59 ♀	27.00–29.59 ♄
♌	00.00–05.59 ♄	06.00–12.59 ☿	13.00–18.59 ♀	19.00–24.59 ♃	25.00–29.59 ♂
♍	00.00–06.59 ☿	07.00–12.59 ♀	13.00–17.59 ♃	18.00–23.59 ♄	24.00–29.59 ♂
♎	00.00–05.59 ♄	06.00–10.59 ♀	11.00–18.59 ♃	19.00–23.59 ☿	24.00–29.59 ♂
♏	00.00–05.59 ♂	06.00–13.59 ♃	14.00–20.59 ♀	21.00–26.59 ☿	27.00–29.59 ♄
♐	00.00–07.59 ♃	08.00–13.59 ♀	14.00–18.59 ☿	19.00–24.59 ♄	25.00–29.59 ♂
♑	00.00–05.59 ♀	06.00–11.59 ☿	12.00–18.59 ♃	19.00–24.59 ♂	25.00–29.59 ♄
♒	00.00–05.59 ♄	06.00–11.59 ☿	12.00–19.59 ♀	20.00–24.59 ♃	25.00–29.59 ♂
♓	00.00–07.59 ♀	08.00–13.59 ♃	14.00–19.59 ☿	20.00–25.59 ♂	26.00–29.59 ♄

Table 3: Dignity by Term

While the Sun and Moon do not have terms, they do have dignity by face, along with the rest of the five planets. Face dignity divides each sign into three equal parts of 10°. To check whether any of your planets are in dignity by face, consult the following table:

♈	00.00–09.59 ♂	10.00–19.59 ☉	20.00–29.59 ♀
♉	00.00–09.59 ☿	10.00–19.59 ☽	20.00–29.59 ♄
♊	00.00–09.59 ♃	10.00–19.59 ♂	20.00–29.59 ☉
♋	00.00–09.59 ♀	10.00–19.59 ☿	20.00–29.59 ☽
♌	00.00–09.59 ♄	10.00–19.59 ♃	20.00–29.59 ♂
♍	00.00–09.59 ☉	10.00–19.59 ♀	20.00–29.59 ☿
♎	00.00–09.59 ☽	10.00–19.59 ♄	20.00–29.59 ♃
♏	00.00–09.59 ♂	10.00–19.59 ☉	20.00–29.59 ♀
♐	00.00–09.59 ☿	10.00–19.59 ☽	20.00–29.59 ♄
♑	00.00–09.59 ♃	10.00–19.59 ♂	20.00–29.59 ☉
♒	00.00–09.59 ♀	10.00–19.59 ☿	20.00–29.59 ☽
♓	00.00–09.59 ♄	10.00–19.59 ♃	20.00–29.59 ♂

Table 4: Dignity by Face

If a chart does not have planets in any of the major dignities then any of the planets in either term or face will be your candidates for the Lord of the Geniture. These cases are rare. More often the situation you will be dealing with is that certain planets will have both a major and a minor dignity. For example, Mars positioned at 4° Scorpio will be in its major dignities of both rulership and triplicity, but also in its minor dignities of both term and face.

When several planets have both major and minor dignities, a guideline in determining the strongest planet is to give 5 points to rulership, 4 points to exaltation, 3 points to triplicity, 2 points for term and 1 point for face. So if you have a chart in which Mars is in Scorpio and Mercury is in Virgo, Mars will score 11 points and Mercury will score 9 points. Both are extremely and essentially strong and both are very good candidates for the Lord of the Geniture. However, just one of them can hold the title, so in this case it would be Mars.

Major Essential Debilities

Just as the major dignities of rulership and exaltation are widely known to contemporary students in mainstream modern astrology, so are the major debilities of detriment (sometimes also called exile) and fall. Planets will be in their debility of detriment if they are positioned in the signs opposite their signs of rulership, and they will be in their debility of fall if they are positioned in the signs opposite their signs of exaltation. These are given in the following table:

	Debility by detriment	Debility by fall
Saturn	Cancer, Leo	Aries
Jupiter	Gemini, Virgo	Capricorn
Mars	Taurus, Libra	Cancer
Venus	Aries, Scorpio	Virgo
Mercury	Sagittarius, Pisces	Pisces
Sun	Aquarius	Libra
Moon	Capricorn	Scorpio

Table 5: Debilities

A planet will acquire strength by being positioned in its debilities of detriment or fall, just as it will acquire strength by being positioned in its major or minor dignities. But the difference between those strengths is of the utmost importance, and it boils down to the way a planet will be inclined to demonstrate that strength. The simplest way to look at this is to think of dignities as constructive, positive strength, and of debilities as destructive, negative strength. A planet in its dignity will be inclined to show the better side of its nature, while a planet in its debility will tend to show its least desirable side. Each planet, be it labelled malefic or benefic, possesses both sides. A dignified malefic Saturn will feature strongly in a chart and in a life, and it will bestow the qualities of great self-discipline, responsibility and a serious approach to life. A debilitated Saturn will tend to show the opposite potential: the lack of discipline or sense of responsibility, as well as a gloomier and depressive approach to life. The great benefic Jupiter, when dignified, shows a desirable quality of generosity; when debilitated, exaggerated promises that are rarely delivered.

In our search for candidates for the Lord of the Geniture, we can immediately dismiss any debilitated planet. The Lord of the Geniture is intended to represent the best part of our chart, and a debilitated planet – regardless of the fact that it is strong – does not meet that standard.

Mixed Essential Dignities and Debilities

Sometimes you will run into seemingly contradictory situations: a planet is in both its dignity and debility at the same time. For example, Mars in Cancer will be in both its dignity of triplicity and its debility of fall. Mercury at 16° Pisces will be in its debilities of detriment and fall, and at the same time in its minor dignity of term.

These planets will fare slightly better than those that are debilitated only, but nevertheless we have to disqualify them as possible candidates for the Lord of the Geniture. Although they do posses the potential to behave well sometimes, most of the time the debility will be the first thing that they tend to express.

Peregrination

A planet that is neither in any of its major or minor dignities nor in any of its debilities is termed a peregrine planet. Such a planet is very weak in the true sense of that word, as it does not possess any strength for individual action, be it constructive or destructive. Some old texts refer to debilitated planets as 'weak', a weakness that stems from *the lack of strength to do good*. Peregrine planets are weak in that they are dependent on other planets to exercise any sort of action, good or bad. They are like 'homeless wanderers' (as old texts often call them), having no base in a chart from which they can draw strength, but instead are dependent on their encounters with other planets to sway them into demonstrating the more or less desirable sides of their nature.

Peregrine planets are not very good candidates for the Lord of the Geniture, and if you have any other planet in any of its dignities, you should disqualify all peregrine planets. However, every once in a while – very, very rarely – you will come across a chart in which there are no dignified planets, but all of them are either debilitated or peregrine.

Major Accidental Dignities and Debilities
While essential dignity gives a planet the strength to act, accidental dignity occurs where a planet is in a house position that allows it to act easily. Accidental debility, on the other hand, puts a planet in a house position where it has difficulties expressing itself. Therefore we should check all the candidates for the Lord of the Geniture against the accidental dignities and debilities. What we are looking for is, of course, a planet that will have both essential (sign position) and accidental (house position) dignity. That will be our Lord of the Geniture.

The main accidental dignity/debility that determines this will be the quality of the houses that our essentially dignified candidates fall into. If a planet is positioned in an angular house (houses 1, 10, 7 and 4, in that order of strength), it is strongly accidentally dignified. It can easily act out its essential strength. If, however, a planet is positioned in a cadent house (houses 12, 6, 3, 9, in that order), it is strongly accidentally debilitated. It cannot easily act out its essential strength. It is like a very powerful animal that has fallen into a trap. Outside the trap the strength of that animal is easily expressed. Inside the trap it is ineffectual. Therefore, no matter how essentially strong a planet is, if it is positioned in a cadent house we should consider the next best planet. Take another essentially dignified planet, even if its essential dignity is less, and check whether it is better positioned by accidental dignity.

If none of your essentially dignified planets are positioned in any of the angular houses in the chart, all is still not lost. Check if any of them falls in the succedent houses (11, 5 and 2, in that order of strength). Steer clear of the 8th House. Although it is a succedent house, traditionally it is part of the trio of 'bad houses' (houses 6, 8 and 12) and therefore not fit to be a place of accidental dignity.

The second major accidental dignity that we should check is the joys of the planets. Each planet has a house in which it particularly enjoys being. It is happy there. And if a planet is happy it will be inclined to show its true nature freely. If a planet in the house of its joy is essentially dignified it will show the more desirable side of its nature. If it is essentially debilitated then it will show the less desirable side more freely.

As a balance to accidental dignity of the houses of joy, we have an accidental debility of the houses of gloom. These are houses in which planets are not happy. And when they are not happy, even if they are essentially dignified they will have problems and difficulties expressing themselves.

To establish whether any of your essentially dignified candidates for the Lord of the Geniture are accidentally dignified or debilitated by being in their houses of joy or gloom, check the following table:

	Accidental dignity – house of joy	Accidental dignity – house of gloom
Saturn	12	6
Jupiter	11	5
Mars	6	12
Sun	9	3
Venus	5	11
Mercury	1	7
Moon	3	9

Table 6: Accidental Dignities

For most charts, reference to these two major accidental dignities and debilities (angular/cadent houses and joy/gloom houses) will be enough to arrive at a definite conclusion about which planet is the Lord of the Geniture. Sometimes, however, the situation is not going to be so clear-cut and you will need to be creative. For example, if there's only one planet in a major essential dignity, while all the others are either peregrine or essentially debilitated, but that one and only good candidate is in a cadent house, it must be named the Lord of the Geniture. It is not going to be a perfect Lord of the Geniture, but the very fact that it is not in a position to easily express itself will be part of the story and delineation of the chart. The person will have to work very hard – much harder than other people – to express the best qualities and potential of the planet.

Also, if you come across one of those special charts that consist of peregrine planets only, your choice of the Lord of the Geniture will fall on the planet with the most accidental dignity, as there are no essentially dignified ones to pick from.

There are also certain other accidental dignities and debilities (such as combustion), but for the purpose of identifying the Lord of the Geniture they will mostly be just secondary factors, so we will not dwell on those here.

Identifying the Lord of the Geniture – Some Examples

What follows are a few examples (data from birth certificate but withheld for reasons of confidentiality) of how to determine the Lord of the Geniture in a chart. Some of these are examples of the extreme cases you can come across, and this will hopefully equip you to deal with such situations when they emerge.

First, disqualify any essentially debilitated planets. In **Example Chart 1**, three planets are in their fall: Moon, Venus and Saturn.

Next, look at the state of the remaining planets. Jupiter is peregrine, so not a good candidate. Mars is in Scorpio, the sign of its rulership and triplicity, so it is very strong and therefore a very

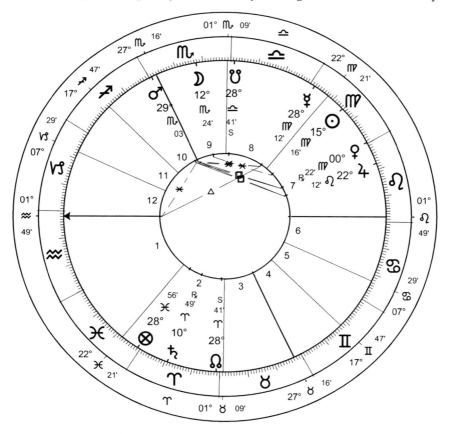

Example Chart 1

good candidate. The Sun is peregrine, so not a good candidate. Mercury is in Virgo where it has major dignities of both rulership and exaltation, as well as the minor dignity of face, so it is a very good candidate.

All in all, we are left with two candidates: Mars and Mercury. Which one is essentially stronger? This is a situation in which a point system might help.

We will assign Mars 5 points for its dignity of rulership and 3 points for triplicity – a total of 8 points. Mercury will get 5 points for rulership, 4 points for exaltation and 1 point for face – a total of 10 points. Mercury is essentially stronger than Mars, so it is a better candidate for the Lord of the Geniture.

However, next we need to look at the accidental dignities of those two strong candidates. Although essentially stronger, Mercury is accidentally weak by being positioned in the 8th House. Mars, on the other hand, is in the 10th House and conjunct the MC angle, making it more powerful. Therefore Mars wins the title of Lord of the Geniture.

In **Example Chart 2**, not one planet in this chart is essentially debilitated, so we can't immediately disqualify any of them. Instead we need to establish the amount of dignity all the planets have and discern which one is essentially strongest.

- Saturn is in its face (1 point) – a total of 1 point.
- Jupiter is in its rulership (5 points), triplicity (3 points) and term (2 points) – a total of 10 points.
- Mars is in its exaltation (4 points) and face (1 point) – a total of 5 points.
- Sun is in its exaltation (4 points) and face (1 point) – a total of 5 points.
- Venus is in its exaltation only – a total of 4 points.
- Mercury is in its face – a total of 1 point.
- The Moon is peregrine, so we can automatically disqualify it.

The planet with the strongest essential dignity by far is Jupiter with 10 points. Second place is shared by Mars and the Sun, each having scored 5 points. Third place goes to Venus with 4 points, fourth to both Saturn and Mercury with 1 point each.

What a wonderful setup, don't you think? Six out of the seven planets have at least some essential dignity and therefore qualify as candidates for the Lord of the Geniture. What this tells us is that

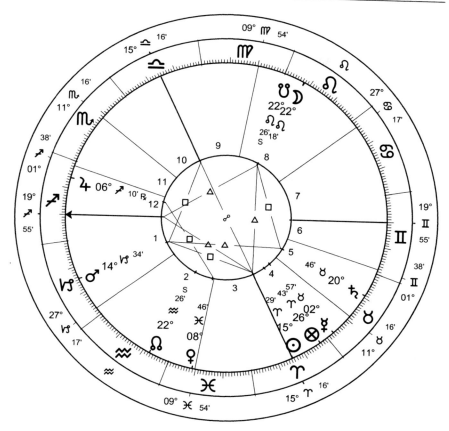

Example Chart 2

this person really has a lot of good options in her life. This is a holder of the UK passport, not the Serbian one! Even though we have not yet looked at accidental dignities or debilities, we can state this for sure. Even those essentially strong planets that we find in accidental debilities will still be a great asset for this person. They might not be so readily accessible and easy to express, but positive expression exists as an option.

However, just one planet can be the Lord of the Geniture and that will be the planet with best essential *and* accidental dignities. It is a pity that Jupiter, which is by far the strongest planet by essential dignity, is at the same time accidentally debilitated by being positioned in the cadent 12th House. This is not good at all. It will take a lot of time and effort for this person to draw the qualities of this Jupiter out of her. So we have to disqualify Jupiter.

Venus is also in a cadent house, so we must disqualify this planet too. Since we have three planets in angular houses, we should

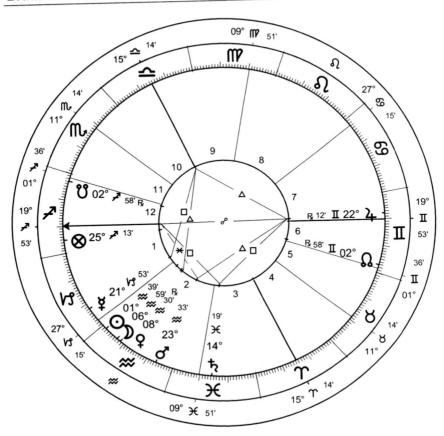

Example Chart 3

disqualify Saturn in the succedent 5th House. Of the remaining three angular planets, Mercury has the least essential strength (1 point), so we can disqualify it as well.

What we are left with is Mars in the 1st House and the Sun in the 4th. As Mars is deep into the 1st House, far away from the angle and in a sign that is different from the sign on the Ascendant, we will opt for the Sun, which is exactly conjunct the IC angle of the 4th House. The Lord of the Geniture for this person will be the Sun.

In **Example Chart 3**, we can immediately disqualify the debilitated planets: Sun and Jupiter in detriment. Examining the rest, we find that Saturn, Mars, Mercury and Moon are peregrine. The only planet with any essential dignity at all is Venus, which is in its face. So here we have no other choice but to take Venus as the Lord of the Geniture, despite the fact that it suffers from an accidental debility of combustion.

Example Chart 4 is one of those special charts without planets in any essential dignity. All we have to deal with are either debilitated or peregrine planets. The task of finding the Lord of the Geniture boils down to identifying the least 'bad' thing in the chart.

First, dismiss Mars and Jupiter, as they are essentially debilitated. The remaining five planets need to be examined for accidental dignity. Two are cadent and can be disqualified: the Moon and Saturn. If a planet is up to five degrees before a certain house cusp, it is conjunct that cusp and therefore counted as though it were in the next house. Consider Saturn to already be in the 3rd House. This is the reason to disqualify Mercury and Venus too, as they are on the cusp of the 8th House.

What we are left with is the peregrine Sun, positioned in the angular 7th House. Even though it is far away from the 7th House cusp, as well as in a sign different from that on the cusp, it is our best available option in this chart and will be the Lord of the Geniture.

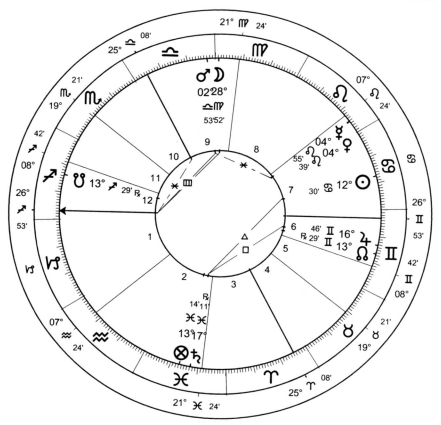

Example Chart 4

Automatic Pilots

As already mentioned, the Lord of the Geniture is our best option in the chart, and therefore the *type of energy* that we should consciously strive to express and employ most of the time in most of the situations we come across in life. But it is more than the potential *in us*. It is also the potential around us. When choosing friends and partners, furniture or houses, business or holiday trips, we should strive to choose those that fit the symbol and energy of this planet.

This is all much easier said than done. Most of the time the majority of people don't invest effort in consciously focusing on the best possible option, but instead let life throw things at them. The planets that describe our usual way of behaving when we are simply 'going with the flow' are what I call our *automatic pilots.*

These automatic pilots are quite easy to identify. Any angular planet will be one. If it is essentially dignified then our automatic pilot is quite safe. If it is debilitated, however, we are in for a turbulent flight through life. By the same logic any planet positioned in the house of its joy will be an automatic pilot too and, if it is debilitated, the need to consciously focus on using the Lord of the Geniture will be so much greater.

If we look again at **Example Chart 1**, where we have identified Mars as the Lord of the Geniture, what about the automatic pilots? None of the planets are positioned in the houses of their joy, but we do have four angular planets: Sun, Jupiter and Venus in the 7th, and Mars in the 10th. These four planets are the automatic pilots. The fact that Mars is an automatic pilot as well as the Lord of the Geniture is very good

news indeed. This woman expresses the best possible option with great ease, almost automatically. When she taps into this Mars, she exhibits great fighting spirit and energy when approaching life. She gets things done, without procrastination or hesitation. She's efficient and on the move.

If, however, she chooses to let any of the other three automatic pilots take over, we might see her exhibit a different attitude. Let's imagine that life threw a promotion her way. Her immediate, automatic reaction might come from one of the four automatic pilots. Peregrine Sun's reaction: 'But I don't want to be a boss, I don't have the necessary authority.' Peregrine Jupiter's reaction: 'But I don't want the pressure of having to inspire people, I don't have the necessary vision.' Debilitated Venus's reaction: 'I can't possibly be as nice to people as the position requires, and I don't want to have to be nice to everybody all the time!' Dignified Mars's reaction: 'Great! I'll get things done!' Obviously the best possible reaction she can have is the one stemming from Mars, her Lord of the Geniture.

In **Example Chart 2**, we again have no planets in the houses of their joy, but we do have two angular planets which will be this person's automatic pilots: the Sun and Mercury in the 4th House. Again we have a chart setup in which the Lord of the Geniture, the Sun, is at the same time an automatic pilot. Even the second automatic pilot has a little bit of dignity, as Mercury is in its face. Whichever automatic pilot she chooses to exercise in any

life situation, she'll fare well. The exalted Sun will drive her to take a leadership role with great integrity and build a good reputation, while Mercury will make sure she thinks before she acts. Most of her instinctive and automatic reactions to whatever life throws her way will guarantee success and bring rewards. She does not need to invest *great effort* to tap into the best option in her chart, as the most accessible options are positive and the best options.

In **Example Chart 3**, once again we have no planets in the houses of their joy, but we do have one angular planet which will be this person's automatic pilot: Jupiter, placed in the 7th House. The Lord of the Geniture for this person is Venus in the 2nd House. And here is where we have a big problem. The automatic pilot (debilitated Jupiter) is so much more accessible than the Lord of the Geniture

(Venus). If this person 'goes with the flow' and allows himself to *automatically react* to whatever life throws his way, he'll end up exhibiting the worst characteristics of the debilitated Jupiter most of the time. He will be making many promises he never keeps, he will be unrealistic and see opportunities where there are none, he will overspend and overreact... And this comes to him as the most natural behaviour. If he wishes to change his ways he needs to really focus on consciously drawing out the potential of the only dignified planet in his chart: Venus. Listening to his wife's ideas of how he should approach life might be one of the possible delineations of this configuration.

In **Example Chart 4** we have just one automatic pilot, as there is only one angular planet: the Sun in the 7th House. This is also this person's Lord of the Geniture, meaning that her automatic reaction to what life throws her way is at the same time her best possible reaction. The problem here is that this Sun is peregrine and therefore weak, so we might suspect that an instinctive reaction to life challenges or opportunities boils down to her turning to some authority figure in her life for guidance. Given that much of the rest of the chart is also peregrine, this really is the best possible option for this woman. Left to her own devices, she just might not do anything at all and just passively accept whatever comes her way, never fighting the challenges nor using the opportunities.

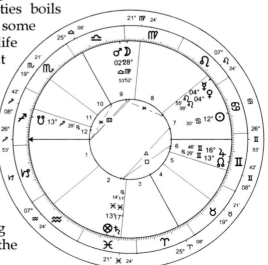

Same Fate, Different Outcome

In our times, when fertility drugs and artificial insemination result in many more births of twins and triplets than ever before – and these babies delivered by C-section births are merely minutes apart, we are surrounded with examples of how two or more people born with the same chart end up using it in quite different ways.

During the past sixteen years I have had the chance to follow the development of two boys – fraternal twins – born just one minute apart. They are as different as day and night, as the Sun and Moon, and have been so obviously different ever since I first saw them, just seven days after birth. Below is their chart (**Example Chart 5**).

Their Lord of the Geniture is Venus; their automatic pilots are Sun and Jupiter (positioned in the angular 10th House) and Saturn and Mars (positioned in the houses of their joy). Three of their four automatic pilots are essentially debilitated, which is not good news.

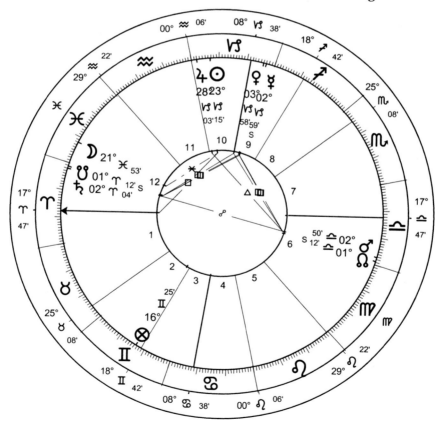

Example Chart 5

To counter that, their Lord of the Geniture is very easily accessible, being so angular. So in a way, it is as accessible as any other automatic pilot. But they still have a choice between those easily accessible planets. What will they choose? Debilitated automatic pilots, or the Lord of the Geniture?

From the time that they were babies, it was obvious that (most often) the older twin used Saturn in the 12th and the younger used Mars in 6th. The older one was a dream baby who slept all the time, provided he was dry and fed. The younger one was very sociable, spending lots of time seeking attention. When they learned how to walk, the younger one would enjoy jumping up and down in his crib, and quite often ended up jumping out of it, landing on his head. The older one enjoyed watching this from the confines of his crib, laughing at his brother's activity but never attempting it himself.

As they grew older they also divided their most enjoyable activities along this Saturn/Mars split. The younger one was outside all the time, chasing the ball, enjoying active games. The older one preferred passive or solitary entertainment: watching TV or playing computer games.

When they started elementary school and the time came for their first school play, they were given roles in *Snow White and the Seven Dwarfs*. The younger one (Mars) was assigned the role of the prince – by popular demand of all the girls in class. The older one (Saturn) shocked us all when he told us that he volunteered for the role of Dopey. Why oh why, dear child? He answered, 'He can't speak, so he has no lines, so I don't have to spend any time learning anything. I can just show up and goof around, and that's it.' Lazy, debilitated Saturn indeed! Well, at least his younger brother discovered the power of the charming Venus, his Lord of the Geniture.

For the first fifteen years of their lives it has been quite obvious how the older twin chose to use debilitated Saturn in the 12th House most of the time, as well as how his younger brother opted for the debilitated Mars in the 6th House. And even though both used their Lord of the Geniture from time to time – mostly in emergency cases to charm themselves out of the trouble that their debilitated Saturn and Mars behaviour got them into – it is also obvious that the younger twin has employed it more than the older one.

As life progresses and childhood challenges turn into more serious life problems, my hope is that they will both choose to use this Venus most of the time, and that their choices of partners, jobs and friends will be from this dignified Venus variety, and not from the other three debilitated automatic pilots.

The choice is up to them. Fate has been kind to them, providing them with a pretty good passport. Will they be smart enough to make the best choices? This depends on their willingness to exercise their free will within the 'fate' of their horoscopes.

Benjamin Dykes
A Personal Biography

All charts in this essay:
Traditional 7 planets
Whole Sign houses
+ True Node and Part of Fortune

I first discovered astrology as part of my general esoteric/occult studies. But I found that the modern astrology I tried to learn did not resonate with me or the other traditional occult practices I followed. After many years of fits and starts, I finally discovered Robert Zoller's medieval astrology course while I was teaching ancient ethics, and knew it was for me. Since 2005 I have been translating Latin astrology texts from the ancient and medieval periods, and making them available to contemporary astrologers for the first time. I am excited to be part of the traditional revival in astrology, because I believe it, along with many different forms of traditional ethics and outlooks, has serious contributions to make to astrological practice and thought, especially: powerful techniques, a sympathy for the human condition, cultivating patience, and focusing on realistic choice. I received my PhD in Philosophy from the University of Illinois, and this has helped me to understand what traditional philosophy can bring to astrology and other esoteric studies. The result is an ongoing series of MP3 lectures on traditional philosophy, astrology, and magic, titled *The Logos & Light Series*. In 2007 I published a complete translation of Guido Bonatti's classic *Book of Astronomy*, a major text in traditional astrology. Since then, I have worked to publish numerous texts to create a well-rounded body of traditional works: *Works of Sahl & Masha'allah*, five works on nativities and annual predictions in *Persian Nativities I-III*, two introductory books for beginners, and more recently a three-volume set of horary astrology: *The Search of the Heart*, al-Kindi's *The Forty Chapters*, and *The Book of the Nine Judges*. In 2012 I will begin to publish translations of electional and mundane astrology. I also do readings for clients worldwide.

www.bendykes.com
benjamin_dykes@msn.com

Chapter Eleven

TIME LORDS IN TRADITIONAL ASTROLOGY

DR. BENJAMIN DYKES

One of the distinguishing features of traditional astrology is its use of what are called 'time lords' (Gr. sing. *chronokratōr*) in predictive techniques. As with modern astrology, traditional practice recognizes a specific starting point for events or series of events, but it conceives of them differently and applies them in a different way.

In much modern practice predictive techniques are closer in conception to what in physics has been called a 'point event', a particular definable event occurring at a specific time. If, say, a particular progression or transit becomes exact or even within orbs, we should expect easily identifiable, discrete events at that particular time; but if a given planet is not making a transit or progression to anything, we should not expect anything from it at all. Moreover, the starting and ending points of the events, and their power, are often based on the motion of the planets: a Saturn transit may define events over a longer span of time, simply because Saturn is a slow planet, while a Mercury transit might be fleeting and not particularly noticeable.

This is not to say that traditional astrology rejects discrete events. Rather, traditional practice usually begins by dividing one's life (and even different areas of life) into periods, such that every moment of life is somehow governed by one planet or another: the planet ruling the period is called a time lord, and is considered to be active over the whole period. This has several consequences. First, an 'event' is viewed as developing over time, and is not necessarily confined to a particular day or sequential and discrete set of goings-on. Second, since an entire period of life will have the same time lord, periods of life have thematic meanings and qualities which help tell the story of one's life in larger chunks, as opposed to the intermittent occurrences of progressions or transits. Third, since different techniques are meant to be used in concert with one another, a period in one technique might have its intensifications (indicating discrete events) when that same time lord appears as a different kind of time lord or even as a transiting planet. These features help a traditional astrologer explain why certain predictive techniques, used on their own, sometimes do not yield events. For example, many people have the experience of waiting for a positive Venus transit to take place... and then nothing happens. From a traditional perspective transits are often supposed to be used in the context of time lords, so that if (say) Venus had not been a time lord during that period, we would not necessarily expect her transit to indicate anything in particular. Let me give two examples, using techniques I will flesh out below.

Profections (lit. 'advancements', Lat. *profectiones*) are a simple but powerful technique in which some point in the chart (usually the Ascendant) is advanced by one sign per year. Once the profection reaches some sign, the planet ruling it becomes the 'lord of the year'. This planet gives primary information about the themes and activities of the year, both by its natal position *and by its ongoing transits* throughout the year. Moreover, the sign of the profection, along with others, identifies key places where these transits become especially active. For example, if the profection reaches Scorpio then Mars becomes the lord of the year, and his transits and stations – particularly in Scorpio and certain other signs – give primary timing periods for the year. It is these transits of the lord of the year which most often give the kinds of discrete events people seek. In other words, the technique not only identifies what planets are most important, but also what kinds of planetary activities matter most, and where to look for them.

Likewise distributions (sometimes called 'directing through the bounds/terms') identify a pair of planets which work together as time lords for broader spans of life. But if the distributor (the primary planet involved) also happens to be the profected lord of the year during that period, it identifies a particular year in which the distributor's natal meaning becomes especially pronounced. In the meantime the division of life into these episodes helps to tell the story of the individual, including his or her state of mind, meaningful activities and so on.

You should be able to see that this approach to prediction provides several tools to the astrologer. For one thing, it offers overall meaning-giving themes for life even when it seems like no particular event is happening at the moment. Also, by arranging techniques into a hierarchy with triggering methods at the 'bottom' (such as transits), it helps identify what things are most important to look at in any given part of life, rather than getting lost in details which might otherwise be hard to distinguish in their significance. In the following two sections of this article I will describe profections and distributions in greater detail, to see how they work in practice.

Profections

Profections were a mainstay of traditional practice, described all the way from Dorotheus and Ptolemy in the earliest centuries CE, to William Lilly in the 17th century. As I mentioned before, some position in the chart with a particular meaning (such as the Ascendant, for life as a whole) is advanced by one sign per year, starting with the Ascendant at age 0. In fact, there were a couple of approaches and ways of reckoning the advancement, but I will stick to the simpler method of counting by whole signs.

Suppose that the native (lit. 'the one born') has a Scorpio Ascendant. This means that for the first year of life, from age 0 to 1, Scorpio provides the theme of the year, along with the lord of the year, Mars. When the native turns 1 year old the Ascendant advances to Sagittarius, with its lord of the year, Jupiter. No matter what you are profecting, the profection will always return to its starting sign every 12 years. So this native will have Scorpio/Mars as his profection again at ages 12, 24, 36 and so on. In astrology we often talk about people's lives being characterized by cycles: in profections this is given an immediate and literal application, by circling around the chart sign by sign. Following is a diagram illustrating the years which fall in the angular signs, for easier reference.

Simple profections are interpreted in the following way. First, the house identified with the sign of the year will provide some topical information, such as if the profection reaches the 5th House. Then, planets natally in the sign will color the year, according to their general qualities and dignity (if any), along with the nature of the houses they rule: for instance, if the natal planet in the sign of the year rules the 12th then 12th-House matters will be brought into the year. Finally, the nature, position, condition and aspects of the lord of the year in the natal chart will give yet more information about how and where the business of the year is carried out: if the lord of the year is in the 3rd perhaps siblings or other 3rd-House matters will be instrumental in what the thrust of the native's life is for that year.

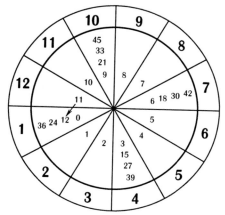

Profection Ages from the Ascendant

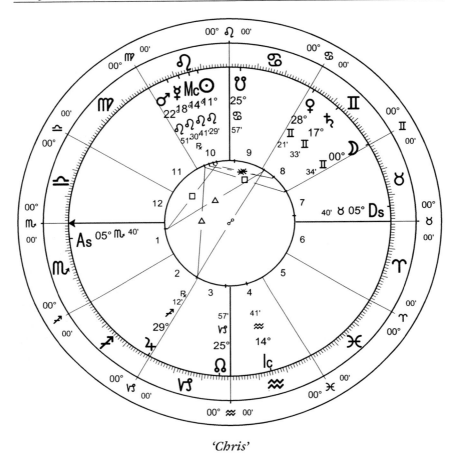

'Chris'

Let's look at the example of a native ('Chris') with Scorpio rising. After several years pursuing a higher, liberal arts degree at a major American university, he fell into a number of personal conflicts and failed job prospects, before finally settling on self-employment in writing and publishing. (We'll learn more about him later.) Let's look at some of the major themes of the year at age 37, when he had been working for himself for several years. You can see by the Figure 1 that his profected Ascendant would have come back to Scorpio at age 36, and so age 37 corresponds to Sagittarius and the 2nd House. Because Jupiter rules Sagittarius, Jupiter is the lord of the year.

The first thing we can say, then, is that within the context of his whole life, financial matters (2nd House) should be key this year. Following the interpretive plan I provided above, we would next look to see if there are any planets in the house: indeed, Jupiter himself, the lord of the year, is there. This emphasizes again the role of finances, since traditionally Jupiter (not Venus) is a wealth planet, and he himself rules the 2nd House. We might even say that because he is in his own sign and so is dignified, it shows something of personal control and management, perhaps issues of self-sufficiency. But Jupiter is also retrograde, which often shows reversals, delays, having to cover old ground and so on. So although things might look good for the management of finances and self-sufficiency, there might be delays or a need to wait a while for those activities to bear fruit.

What kinds of aspects are there to this sign? Actually, all of the planets aspect the sign of Sagittarius, from two of the most powerful aspects: the opposition and the trine. One way we can whittle these down to the most important would be to look at the closest aspects to Jupiter himself (since he is the lord of the year). Two planets make close applying aspects to him: Mars in the 10th by trine, and Venus in the 8th by opposition. Mars is in the 10th (profession, reputation), and rules the 1st (personal identity and life) and 6th (illness, hard work, stress); Venus is in the 8th (debt, anxiety, mortality), and rules the 7th (relationships) and the 12th (illness, enemies, isolation). That is a lot of material to consider, and for now we are only trying to get a general profile of the issues involved in the year. So we could expect that the native's year, which has a lot to do with finances, will also be related to his sense of mission and professional development (Mars), as well as relationships (Venus), probably with a good deal of stress and hard work.

At age 37, after having worked on some successful projects for a couple of years, the native designed an ambitious writing project to increase his professional profile and make more money, but by design the project would take about five years to complete. He was working hard and in isolation for many months on one of the more difficult writing projects he had already begun, but by the middle of the year he had produced a successful book, raised more money than he had expected to through public engagements, and by the end of age 37 his new business plans had been put into place, suggesting an ambitious and difficult but ultimately stabilizing business model.

Now, in the introduction to this article I noted that traditional astrology often combines techniques, especially using the time lord (Jupiter, the lord of the year) in transits. How does this work? If we follow the practices and logic of the Persian and Arabic writers there are two things to consider. First, we want to observe Jupiter's transits throughout the year: any ingresses, transits to important natal planets (including to his own natal position), stations and retrogradation, and the points at which he enters the Sun's rays or appears from them, at about 15° on either side of the Sun. Second, we also want to observe four primary places in which these transits (but possibly the transits of any other planet) will take place. These places are the sign of the year itself (Sagittarius) and the other three signs which form a cross with it – namely, the squares and opposition of Sagittarius: all of the common or mutable signs, Virgo, Pisces and Gemini. This helps us identify not only a particular planet, but also places which have a direct impact on the sign of the year. Of course, since Jupiter is a slow-moving planet, we cannot always hope that he will make an ingress or station or something else in one of these signs – that is far more likely with a faster-moving lord of the year.

At age 37 (in 2009) both of the malefic planets were in key signs I identified: Saturn in Virgo, and Mars in Gemini. Since one of the main themes of the year is finances, having these planets in such places had a depressive and difficult impact on finances while they were in them: he was running out of money and almost got dragged into what would have been a big financial mistake. But after a few months both Saturn and Mars moved out of those signs, and virtually to the day after they were both gone, his financial situation improved. This coincided, within a couple of weeks, with Jupiter's stationing direct – an indication of change and movement in the primary meanings of the year. Then in early 2010 transiting Jupiter entered Pisces, which is one of the key signs I mentioned before. Within about a week of this ingress, several important events occurred: first, he was well received and his public standing improved at an important conference; second, he made more money than he had hoped for out of a recent publication, and he ended a relationship he had been in at the time (the ending of the relationship also coincided within a few days of the square of the lord of his Lot of Marriage to the Lot itself, but that's another story). Jupiter continued in this sign for a few months, during which time he made further developments in his business plan and published additional material in service of it. After Jupiter left Pisces, but during Jupiter's last station during age 37 (in July 2010) he was hard at work and making breakthroughs on yet another ambitious writing project. Soon after that, the profection changed at age 38 to Capricorn, with a new house (the 3rd) and a new lord of the year (Saturn).

There were of course other trends and developments which could be seen by other methods, but I hope you can see that profections, with their hierarchy of techniques and focus on special planets and signs, help to provide a clarifying template for the astrologer trying to make sense of a native's year: its themes, meaning and highlighted periods. Now let's look at another technique and see how it applies to this native at the same time.

Distributions

This method, also very ancient, is sometimes known as 'directing through the bounds/terms', indicating that it is related to primary directions. Let's first look at what the bounds (often called 'terms' in English-language astrology) are. These are divisions of each zodiacal sign into five unequal bits (ranging from 2° to 12°), each one ruled by one of the non-luminaries – that is, the five classical planets excluding the Sun and Moon. There are several schemes of bounds, and in fact Ptolemy (in his *Tetrabiblos* I.20-21) describes a few of them: one attributed to the Egyptians, one to the Chaldeans and one which he says he found in an ancient manuscript and proceeds to favor himself. I work with the most popular and established one, the Egyptian. Here is the generally agreed version of the Egyptian bounds:

♈	00.00–05.59 ♃	06.00–11.59 ♀	12.00–19.59 ☿	20.00–24.59 ♂	25.00–29.59 ♄
♉	00.00–07.59 ♀	08.00–13.59 ☿	14.00–21.59 ♃	22.00–26.59 ♄	27.00–29.59 ♂
♊	00.00–05.59 ☿	06.00–11.59 ♃	12.00–16.59 ♀	17.00–23.59 ♂	24.00–29.59 ♄
♋	00.00–06.59 ♂	07.00–12.59 ♀	13.00–18.59 ☿	19.00–25.59 ♃	26.00–29.59 ♄
♌	00.00–05.59 ♃	06.00–10.59 ♀	11.00–17.59 ♄	18.00–23.59 ☿	24.00–29.59 ♂
♍	00.00–06.59 ☿	07.00–16.59 ♀	17.00–20.59 ♃	21.00–27.59 ♂	28.00–29.59 ♄
♎	00.00–05.59 ♄	06.00–13.59 ☿	14.00–20.59 ♃	21.00–27.59 ♀	28.00–29.59 ♂
♏	00.00–06.59 ♂	07.00–10.59 ♀	11.00–18.59 ☿	19.00–23.59 ♃	24.00–29.59 ♄
♐	00.00–11.59 ♃	12.00–16.59 ♀	17.00–20.59 ☿	21.00–25.59 ♄	26.00–29.59 ♂
♑	00.00–06.59 ☿	07.00–13.59 ♃	14.00–21.59 ♀	22.00–25.59 ♄	26.00–29.59 ♂
♒	00.00–06.59 ☿	07.00–12.59 ♀	13.00–19.59 ♃	20.00–24.59 ♂	25.00–29.59 ♄
♓	00.00–11.59 ♀	12.00–15.59 ♃	16.00–18.59 ☿	19.00–27.59 ♂	28.00–29.59 ♄

Table of Egyptian Bounds

What this means is that every place in the natal chart will not only fall into a sign ruled by a planet, but also into a bound ruled by some planet. For instance, if your Ascendant falls at 15° Cancer the lord of your Ascendant is the Moon, but the degree of the Ascendant itself has Mercury as its bound lord. Bounds were used in a number of ways, but here we will concentrate on distributions. What are distributions?

The idea behind distributions (Lat. *partitio*) is something like this. Suppose your entire life is like a birthday cake baked at your birth. God, or the Cosmic Intelligence, or whatever you want to call it, has all of the planets lined up in a row waiting to take a piece of cake which represents a certain number of years of life – when they take the cake, they will become your time lord for a certain number of years. Because your life is being distributed piecemeal among the planets, any planet getting a piece is called the 'distributor'. First in line is the planet ruling the bound of your natal Ascendant, then the planet ruling the next bound and so on. If you live long enough all of the planets will have their share and then get back in line for seconds.

As an example, let's take the nativity, 'Chris', we looked at above. The Ascendant is at 5°36' Scorpio, which falls in the bound of Mars. So he will be the first distributor, getting the first piece of the cake of the native's life, and will be the time lord for however long the rest of his bound lasts (more on that later). The next bound is ruled by Venus, so she will become the distributor for the next portion of life; then Mercury, Jupiter, Saturn,

and then (when the Ascendant moves into Sagittarius) Jupiter again and so on. So the story of the native's life will be told by these distributors in turn.[1] But for how long will each planet be the distributor? For this we have to shift our focus to something called 'ascensional times'.

When we looked at profections we used only the zodiacal degrees, jumping from one sign to the next: each sign takes up exactly one year of life. But in distributions (which are related to primary directions) we have to take the actual diurnal rotation of the heavens into account. Now we all know that because there are

360° in the zodiac, and 24 hours in a day, each sign will be on the Ascendant for an average of two hours, and each degree will be on the Ascendant itself for about 4'. But this is only an average. First of all, because the ecliptic or zodiac is a bit askew from the celestial equator (the 'obliquity of the ecliptic'), and because the latitude of the birthplace changes the apparent angle of the signs, some signs will rise faster in the east and others will rise more slowly. Traditional astrologers had special words for these signs: the 'crooked' (faster) and the 'straight' (slower). In the Northern Hemisphere the signs from Capricorn through Gemini are crooked and will go across the Ascendant faster; those from Cancer to Sagittarius are straight and will go more slowly. But in the Southern Hemisphere (such as in Australia) these are reversed: Capricorn through Gemini are straight, and Cancer through Sagittarius are crooked. You can imagine in your mind why this is so: if a sign rises in a more upright position (straight) it will take longer to rise, but if a sign rises at more of a slant (crooked) it will not take as long.

The ancient astrologers decided to assign each sign a certain amount of years of life, depending on how long it took to rise across the horizon in the east: its 'ascensional time'. And the exact time was determined by counting how many degrees of the celestial equator passed across the meridian (where the Midheaven is), as the sign arose in the east, from start to finish. Don't worry about the math – the point is that if you have a straight sign (rising longer) then normally more than 30° will pass across the meridian during the time it takes for that sign to rise; but if a crooked sign, fewer. For example, at my location at 45° N in Minneapolis, Scorpio (a straight sign) has 30° in the zodiac itself, but about 39.7° will pass across the meridian by the time Scorpio is fully across the horizon in the east: so it has 39.7 ascensional times. On the other hand, by the time Aries (a crooked sign) fully passes across the horizon, only about 16.2° will have passed across the meridian, giving Aries 16.2 ascensional times. These ascensional times are directly equated to years, so that for Minneapolis, Scorpio equates to 39.7 years of life, and Aries to 16.2 years of life.

The upshot of this is that as we direct the Ascendant through the bounds, each bound will be worth a different number of years of life, depending on what sign is rising in your chart: a 5° bound for a chart with Scorpio rising will last longer than a 5° bound in a chart with Aries rising. This is one reason why an exact birth time matters: if you are off by even a few minutes, especially if a crooked sign is rising, it will throw the predictions off by at least a year. But it also means that distributions can be of great aid in rectification. Currently the only astrology program I know of that calculates ascensional times for each sign is Delphic Oracle, which places the ascensional times in the center of the chart diagram. You may also download a free PDF with ascensional times of my own calculation from my site.[2] With a little division or multiplication you can easily find out exactly how many months or years of life each degree in your chart is worth.

Now that you understand the basics, let's turn to interpretation principles and then to an example. When you know what planet is the distributor for a given period, look at the following things: (1) the planet's general nature and significations (such as love and pleasure for Venus), (2) its natal house position, and (3) what houses it rules in the natal chart. By listing these you can begin to draw up a profile of what the theme of the period is, with one little addition: (4) the planet making the closest aspect to the distributor will tend to show mood, state of mind and what the native is thinking about.

In our example chart the native has 5°36′ Scorpio rising. Since we know that the ascensional time of Scorpio at the birth location is 39.7, each degree of Scorpio is worth about 1.32 years of life.[3] With a little division and multiplication we can tell that he will enter into the bound of Saturn at about age 24.3, lasting from early 1997 to late 2004. So Saturn

is his distributor during those years. The closest aspect of Saturn in the natal chart is Mercury, which will say something about his mindset and mood at that time. What can we expect? Well, Saturn by his nature suggests burdens and hard work, isolation, ancient things, pessimism, asceticism and so on. He is in the 8th House, suggesting concerns about mortality and debt and business partnerships. By rulership he governs the 3rd and 4th Houses. So we could say that Chris is working hard, perhaps lonely, interested in writing and education (Mercury, 3rd House), and perhaps with personal links to family and death, having some financial concerns related to poverty and business arrangements.

A few months after the Ascendant entered this distribution the native took a tremendous pay cut by entering graduate school at the university I alluded to before. He studied ancient literature, was obviously doing a lot of writing, as a graduate student he was teaching and he was finding that his new life of the mind (accompanied by poverty) was turning him more inward, serious, pessimistic and lonely. During this time his last grandparent and family patriarch died (4th House, Saturn in the 8th). And so this Saturn–Mercury combination well described what life was like during these years. After leaving the university and getting a teaching job elsewhere he also formed a business partnership with a friend which was full of burdens and oppression, and during his most active time in the partnership he made no money.

As you can see from the table of bounds, the bound of Saturn is the last bound in Scorpio. After that, the distribution continues into Sagittarius, whose first bound belongs to Jupiter. It's a long bound (12°), and since Sagittarius at this latitude has about 36.4 ascensional times, each degree is worth about 1.21 years, and the full bound about 14.5 years.[4] So from late 2004 on, he has been in the distribution of Jupiter. Above, we noted a few things about Jupiter's significations, along with the fact that his closest aspect is with Venus. So we can expect that this period will be generally characterized by relief, pleasure-seeking and financial matters. After withdrawing from the doomed business partnership, the native changed jobs to one that made a decent wage, got a new apartment with better furniture, felt a lot more free about life and set about creating the new writing career which I described above.

This new Jupiter distribution now allows me to re-introduce something I described before: the doubling-up of the same time lord across techniques. In distributions the meaning of the period is supposed to be enhanced and intensified (and so resulting in concrete events) when one or both of the following things happen: when the distributor also happens to be the lord of the year by profection, and when the distributor actually transits through or aspects the bound itself. In this case we want to see when Jupiter happens to be the lord of the year, and even when he transits through or aspects these first 12° of Sagittarius.

In the late spring and summer of 2005 Jupiter was transiting through (and then stationed direct in) the early degrees of Libra, which are in a sextile to his bound in Sagittarius. During this time the native was offered a surprising job which then became the basis of his future writing (at the time, he was still considering teaching, and in fact had taught some in the previous year). But seeing that this new writing job could be more lucrative, he threw himself into it.

In late 2006 and early 2007 Jupiter again transited the bound, this time by body. During these months he was invited to move in with a friend, who had just bought a luxurious new house. He did move in, and when Jupiter turned retrograde and re-entered the bound (again, with a station) between June and August, he made a great deal of money after publishing his first book.

In early 2009 Jupiter transited the bound by a sextile from Aquarius, and although his living situation had changed drastically, he started work on a complicated new writing project and conceived of a new body of lectures and teaching, to supplement his writing business. He was much more optimistic about life and felt freer.

So far, then, we've seen the theme of the distribution (finances and their management, freedom, etc.) manifest particularly when the distributor transits the bound. Now let's look at a period in which Jupiter was both transiting the bound *and* acting as the lord of the year. In the section on profections above, we have already seen when Jupiter became the lord of the year: at age 37, when the natal Ascendant profected to Sagittarius itself. Likewise we have seen that when Jupiter transited through one of the whole-sign angles of Sagittarius at age 37, there were concrete events mirroring the meaning of the year (increased wealth and laying down future business plans). Now we see that this profection and transit were also intensification periods for the distribution, precisely because Jupiter was playing all three roles: as distributor, lord of the year and transiting planet). There is only one more detail to add: when Jupiter was actually transiting the first 12° of Sagittarius by that square from Pisces, the native had a meeting with a friend who introduced him to a new, less expensive and more lucrative way of carrying out his business. Over the period of a couple of weeks he transitioned his business model over to the new format, which made the whole series of writing projects now more financially feasible. Again, these projects are more long term and will probably take until the end of the Jupiter distribution to really come to full fruition; but it was during this Sagittarius/Jupiter profection, and his transit to these 12°, that the projects actually became practicable through a concrete event (meeting with the friend).

Traditional astrology is full of time lord techniques, some of which have not even been tried for many centuries and are only now being translated into modern languages. I hope that you can see the value of these two well-known techniques, which can be integrated into any astrologer's regular practice.

References and Notes

1. In the full method of distributions, there are also certain 'partner' planets which give additional information. The distributor's partner is the planet which the directed Ascendant has most recently encountered, by body or ray. So for example, suppose that the Ascendant is in the bound of Jupiter and while in that bound it encounters a square from Venus: Venus is described as the 'partner' of Jupiter until the Ascendant comes to the body or ray of some other planet (which may be close by or far away), at which time that next planet becomes the partner. The partner tends to show people, events and activities the native meets and is engaged in. In this article I have left out the partners in order to concentrate on the basic technique.

2. http://www.bendykes.com/reviews/ascensions-table.pdf

3. Keep in mind that this is a little rough. Since the signs are curved and have signs of greater or lesser ascensions on each side, not every degree will really be equally as big as neighboring ones. So although I am instructing you to divide each sign's ascensions into 30 equal parts for the sake of convenience, the degrees at one end of a sign might in reality be slightly longer or shorter than those at the other end. Programs such as Delphic Oracle are able to calculate and apply these slight differences more precisely than a simple table of ascensions can.

4. Again, this is by dividing the ascensions of the whole sign equally into 30 parts. Since the degrees earlier in Sagittarius are of slightly longer ascension than those at the end, the period will actually last about 15.25 years, as shown in Delphic Oracle.

Part IV

Psychological Astrology &
Archetypal Awakenings

John Green
A Personal Biography

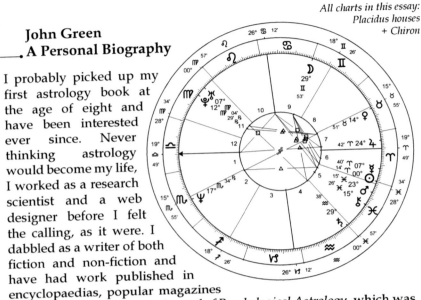

All charts in this essay:
Placidus houses
+ Chiron

I probably picked up my first astrology book at the age of eight and have been interested ever since. Never thinking astrology would become my life, I worked as a research scientist and a web designer before I felt the calling, as it were. I dabbled as a writer of both fiction and non-fiction and have had work published in encyclopaedias, popular magazines and articles in *Apollon, the Journal of Psychological Astrology*, which was published from 1998–2001. Finally taking the astrological plunge, I studied at the Centre for Psychological Astrology, qualifying with their Certificate and Diploma. Currently, I work as an astrology consultant and as a tutor for the Centre for Psychological Astrology, both in the UK and online. I am also editor of *The Astrological Journal*, the international bi-monthly publication of the Astrological Association. *The Journal* allows me to read all the latest work being done in the astrological field as well as indulge my love of graphic design by creating all the cover art and layouts. My main astrological joy is teaching and I am very happy to have developed a new Intermediate Course for the CPA in 2011. With my Sun in Aries and Moon in Gemini I've always been one for chopping and changing in my careers, but finally I seem to have found something that I can stick at. My website is at www.psychologicalastrology.com.

www.psychologicalastrology.com
john@psychologicalastrology.com

Chapter Twelve

THE ASTROLOGY OF THE SELF

JOHN GREEN

Psychological astrology has been a big part of the astrological world since the latter part of the 20th century, not just as a separate study but inveigling itself into many more traditional areas. Is psychology a good bedfellow for astrology? Is all astrology actually psychological astrology? Has this movement improved astrology or made it worse, and what is the future for psychological astrology? This essay will attempt to answer all of these questions and more.

Introduction

The times, as the song goes, they are a-changin'. As we stare, a little bleary-eyed, into the second decade of the twenty-first century, with all the outer planets having recently changed signs, it seems that the world is not going to remain the same. Astrology is not going to remain the same. The art, or science if you prefer, of astrology has been with us for so long it is natural that it should evolve, change and mutate over time, and I would argue that it is inevitable that astrology would fit the times we are living in. We get the astrology we deserve – but what will that astrology be?

Over the course of the last century psychological astrology emerged as one of the major players of the various types of astrology open to us. What I want to examine here is whether psychology is a good match for astrology and whether it has made our astrology better or worse. In the course of looking at this I want to see what the future may hold for it as a discipline. Has psychological astrology had its day?

I should start by saying that I am a psychological astrologer, so obviously the subject has held enough interest for me to study, teach and work with it. However, that doesn't mean that I don't sometimes have doubts about the course it is taking or question how the subject is taught or practised.

What is Psychological Astrology?

I was originally going to start by asking what psychological astrology is but soon realized that I have to take it back a stage and ask first what psychology itself is. While the dictionary definition today tends to refer to it as 'the scientific study of the human mind and its functions, especially those affecting behaviour in a given context',[1] the original meaning is somewhat different. 'Psychology' literally means the study of the soul, and comes from the Greek *psyche* meaning 'spirit', 'breath' or 'soul' and *logia* meaning 'study of' or 'research'. The earliest known reference to the word 'psychology' in English was by Steven Blankaart in 1694 in *The Physical Dictionary* which refers to 'Anatomy, which treats of the Body, and Psychology, which treats of the Soul'.[2]

If we use that original premise it might be pertinent to ask: What do we actually think of as soul? To me it suggests something spiritual, perhaps something intangible – an idea more linked to philosophy than science. This seems to have been one of the changing processes in psychology and perhaps the original word no longer really fits what science calls psychology today. From these philosophical beginnings we have moved forward to a psychology practised in the twenty-first century with branches in development, cognition, evolution, neurological, clinical, forensic and social psychology alongside the analytical approach.

I would say that what many people think of as mind or soul is different from many of the more modern psychological definitions. We tend to associate ourselves with our mind and see it as the essential 'me-ness' of ourselves. We don't see it as having neurological processes, or evolutionary ones. Although we can understand the logic to these, we glimpse ourselves as being something unique and special that exists outside of that. The popular, though mistaken, idea that the human body weighs 21 grams less after death appeals to our idea of a 'soul' as something uniquely us which is not part of the physiological makeup of the body.

Over the years there has been a split in some circles of psychology – one that has seen the branches that focus on the idea of the unique self, such as analytical psychology, being dismissed as pseudo-science. Much like astrology, I might add, where it is no longer seen as the founding father of astronomy but rather the grubby illegitimate cousin no one wants to discuss. The scientific world we live in only wants to deal with statistics: that which can be replicated over and over again in tests. Psychiatry would rather deal with cheaper fixes such as Cognitive Behaviour Therapy and drugs than the long-winded processes of psychoanalysis and the like, even though all these have been proven in the 1977 paper *Meta-Analysis of Psychotherapy Outcome Studies*[3] to be no more or less effective in clinical practice. In fact this paper summarises that the typical therapy client is better off than 75% of untreated individuals, a result that seems to have been ignored in more modern scientific journals. The scientific process really seems to have no time for the concept of 'soul' anymore.

So what about psychological astrology, then? Looking for a definite starting point may be fruitless; astrology, like psychology and the rest of our knowledge, is built upon the past. Freud did not wake up one day and say 'I have a dream' and thus change the world. In the same way, no one person started psychological astrology, though there have been many claims as to when it began and who started it. In Angela Voss's book *Marsilio Ficino*[4] she talks about how Ficino, an Italian astrologer and priest born in 1433, saw astrology as helping us understand our spiritual nature with the planets represented within the soul or *psyche*. It was much later that the term 'psychological astrology' would be coined. Patrick Curry in *Astrology, Science and Culture: Pulling Down the Moon*[5] sees the strand of astrology termed 'psychological' as rising at the beginning of the twentieth century from the astrology system of Alan Leo. Leo's work rejected the idea of astrology being about predetermination and our fate, and instead stated that it was more concerned with character analysis, with the planets not deciding our destiny but showing how our personality would react to situations – in effect, giving us some free will over our fate. This is a key idea in psychological astrology.

Throughout the early twentieth century, psychology was growing in popularity due to the works of Sigmund Freud and, later, Carl Jung and many others. As interest in this grew, alongside changes in mass manufacture, it helped give rise to modern capitalism and, with that, the rise in the idea of individualism. Products of differing types could now be manufactured cheaply and so people could pick and choose what they bought and display their own style, preferences and individuality.[6] It was no longer 'any colour you want as long as it's black', but 'anything you want to show what an individual you are'. As these ideas grew in society it was inevitable that astrology would run alongside these new and exciting schemes. The thought that the planets were in charge of your every decision would no longer be as popular as the idea that astrology could show how unique you were and thus in charge of your individual destiny.

These views were furthered by the publication of Dane Rudhyar's book *The Astrology of Personality* in 1936. In this book, subtitled 'a re-formation of astrological concepts and ideals, in terms of contemporary psychology and philosophy', Rudhyar argued that it was no longer relevant to practise astrology based on how Ptolemy set it out thousands of years ago, that a new age needed a new approach to astrology. Rudhyar put his own model forward as one for the new era. Heavily influenced by the work of Carl Jung he wrote: 'We are, above all, stressing values and using a terminology which are found in C. G. Jung's works because we are deeply convinced of their inherent validity, and also because they dovetail so remarkably with the general set-up of astrological symbolism.' In the same paragraph he states '…Jung's "analytical psychology" is a psychology whose roots may be grounded in Freudian psychoanalysis, yet whose stem and flowering live in strata of being almost as far from Freudian thought as the vision of a Lao-Tze or a Plato is from that of a laboratory vivisectionist.'[7]

Psychological astrology's love affair with Carl Jung had well and truly begun and survives to this day. The works of psychologists such as Roberto Assagioli, Carl Rogers and James Hillman have also been popular among psychological astrologers, but the root seems to remain intrinsically Jungian.

In 1969 Rudhyar founded the International Committee for Humanistic Astrology, putting forward that astrology should primarily serve as a guide to the integration and transformation of personality. During the 1970s psychological astrology grew in prominence through astrologers such as Zipporah Dobyns, Richard Idemon, Stephen Arroyo, Liz Greene and Howard Sasportas. We now had a new astrology, one of the soul, of myth and one which fed our desire for finding our about inner selves.

The humanistic movement in both psychology and psychological astrology seemed to be a good match with the prevailing counterculture movement of the 1960s and '70s. This movement was defined by political opposition to a perceived conservatism and went alongside new approaches to sex, drugs, art and music. The concept of *finding oneself* through Eastern religions, gurus and mind-altering drugs became of interest, and interest in conventional Western religion began to wane. God was losing his status and, as a consequence of psychology, we became the keepers of our own soul. Age-old questions like 'Who am I?', 'What am I here for?', and 'How can I find my true purpose?' were no longer the domain of the priest, but that of the counsellor and the psychological astrologer.

One important tool in psychological astrology is the use of archetypes. An archetype is a universally recognized symbol found in almost every form of storytelling across different times and cultures. The use of archetypes to explain human behaviour was pioneered by Carl Jung, although the origins of the archetypal hypothesis date back as far as Plato. Jung himself compared archetypes to Platonic ideas, which were pure mental forms imprinted in the soul before it was born into the world. Psychological astrologers see the planets as archetypes and the horoscope is analysed through these to gain psychological insight into an individual's psyche.

The '80s and '90s saw the rise of schools and courses specialising in this type of psychological astrology, and many of the older schools and institutions widened their scope to include this new breed of astrology. The quest to find out more about the self continued unabated in society, and psychological astrology helped to feed that desire. Astrology appeared to be following the path set out by psychologist Abraham Maslow in his theory of the hierarchy of needs.

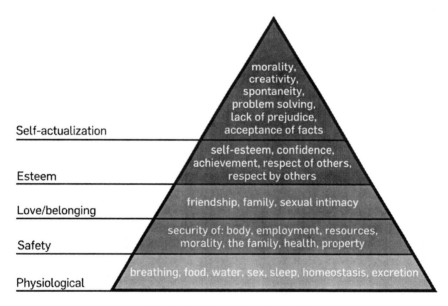

Maslow's Hierarchy of Needs[8]

Maslow's Hierarchy of Needs is often illustrated as a pyramid, as it is here. At the bottom are the most fundamental needs of us all such as food, water and sleep. As these needs are met we start to focus on and desire those further up the pyramid until we are concentrating on the top level of self-actualization. This level of need pertains to what an individual's full potential is and to realizing that potential. Maslow described this as 'the desire to become more and more what one is, to become everything that one is capable of becoming'.[9]

In effect, while we are struggling just to survive, to find food and shelter, we are not going to focus on the idea of 'becoming who we are meant to be'. An astrology that focuses on the self is of no use to the populace until those other needs are satisfied. Only then can we become more interested in looking inward, in finding our true self. In times past, astrology reflected this: court astrologers were employed to look at matters of government for their monarch and the peasants' lives were in the hands of their leaders – the idea of free will must have seemed ludicrous to most. As the world developed and more needs were satiated, astrology changed while still maintaining a fatalism at heart. It was not until more recent times – as we began to feel more in charge of our lives with increasing freedom, financial security and so on – that astrology could develop to address our internal questions.

Is Psychology a Good Bedfellow for Astrology?

It may be easy to understand how psychology and astrology became interlinked but perhaps a more important question is to ask whether psychology has harmed astrology. Some would argue that its influence on astrology has distorted the true essence of what astrology once was. Astrologer James Brockbank says '…the meaning of the houses has been completely changed in modern times, and… modern planetary meanings are barely recognisable from their Hellenistic antecedents. The modern meaning of Leo is closer to the Hellenistic meaning of the Sun than the modern meaning of the Sun. Saturn and Mars are no longer seen as malefic, while Jupiter and Venus are not purely benefic; the squares and oppositions are now seen as "opportunities for growth".'[10]

Brockbank is not alone in this, and there does seem to be a feeling among many traditional and horary astrologers that psychology has diluted the original astrological meanings. But should astrology not adapt to fit in with a changing society? Or in the same way that medicine or science progresses as society learns and evolves, is it not possible that psychological astrology just reflects the period in which we live? In ancient times, seeing the planets as gods who rained down gifts or punishments seemed acceptable and fitted the prevailing model of the universe. When life seemed more black and white, a traditional, more event-focused astrology matched the feeling of a population that believed they were victims of the whims of rulers, gods and the elements, and that they had little or no control over what happened to their lives. Now humanity tends to perceive life in various shades of grey. Surely it requires a more person-centred approach to astrology? Life is rarely purely malefic or benefic, and these shades of uncertainty are depicted in the more modern interpretations of the planets.

One could argue that all astrology is now psychological. If we are interacting with another human being when we are reading a chart, does psychology not come into play? Even if I am doing a horary reading for someone, surely I cannot rule out that their psyche and my psyche are involved. What I say may well have an influence on their thoughts on the matter, if not their actions. If so, surely it is more responsible to consider the effects on the client rather than to give them 'just the facts' and let them get on with it. If I go further and start to give them details of their character in a natal chart reading, psychological or not, I am still affecting their psyche and they mine. In addition, I need to consider my own prejudices, ideas and conflicts to ensure I am giving clients something truly useful to work with, and I must consider their reactions to what I say.

But what about mundane astrology, that most ancient of astrologies which looks to the cosmos to understand world affairs and events? Surely we can't say that is psychological. Well, if we are prepared to consider the existence of the archetypes in the collective, as we do in psychological astrology, then we must consider the idea of a national psyche in a country's chart, the psychology of those in charge of it and the population involved. Indeed archetypal astrology, a branch of psychological astrology, studies the connection between the changing positions of the planets in the solar system and archetypal patterns in human experience.

Returning to individual consultations, I think that the introduction of psychology benefited astrology by allowing client sessions to become more counselling-orientated. When you are helping someone discover the various depths of who they are, it is necessary to have some idea of what this does to a person. Many psychological astrologers take the time and effort to train in counselling or psychotherapy in order to give clients a fuller, more in-depth understanding of what their chart says about them. This seems a far more responsible approach to what many may dismiss as 'fortune telling'. I am often aghast at those who purport to give knowledge of the psyche, or information about what is to come, to others but have no training. Many astrologers would like astrology to be accepted by the populace as something more than a parlour game or an end-of-the-pier attraction. It seems to me that to gain respect in this area, we must take the client–astrologer dialogue far more seriously. A thorough knowledge of counselling adds to this. A good bedside manner is important for any doctor, and if we are taking on the role of the advisor or priest of old, we need to understand all the responsibilities and ethics this entails.

Astrologer and psychologist Mike Harding in his book *Hymns to the Ancient Gods* puts it as follows: 'What psychotherapy *does* have to offer the counselling astrologer is its very considerable expertise in understanding *process*. That is "what goes on in people" and "what goes on *between* people" – client and therapist included. Here, psychotherapy's record of clinical observations is impressive indeed. There is a vast catalogue of all the nuances of projection, transference, denial, displacement, conversion and what have you. There is an enormous literature on the ramifications of that essentially simple act of therapy – two people talking to each other – that offers profound insights into the mechanism of our behaviour and the intricate pathways our inner needs follow on their journeys to the surface of our lives. It is a guidebook of human behaviour and a literature of discoveries that counselling astrologers ignore at their clients' peril.'[11]

A downside to this is that some astrologers may think that the very nature of psychological astrology gives them the right to act like a therapist to a client. I have been left dumbstruck at astrologers who feel it is their right to pressurize a client for a psychological breakthrough, rather than referring them to someone better qualified to undertake such in-depth psychological work. With occult knowledge such as astrology, there are always those who revel in the power that it gives them and seek to use it for influence or control over others. Once again much of this could be eliminated with sound psychological training, but it is not the 'fault' of psychological astrology per se.

Some astrologers may see that psychological astrology's move away from its traditional roots has made astrology more 'airy fairy', giving it a New Age or spiritual slant, which they think does not have a place alongside 'true' astrology. In truth, though, astrology has simply been applied to the arena of the modern world. Since the 1960s the Western mind has been in search of truths about the self, seeking out what life is about and what we are here for. In recent years everyone from *X Factor* contestants to Miss World finalists talk about their *journey*, often to the point of the ridiculous, but it is an inescapable fact that the idea of being on a quest or journey through our life is undoubtedly part of the modern age.

In actuality I think psychological astrology, rather than making astrology more New Age-y or spiritual, has taken it more into the realms of the intellect. On the plus side it allows us to consider the arguments of fate and free will. In the book *The Astrology of Fate*[12] Liz

Greene admits that psychological astrologers have often sought to disown the more traditional astrological view around these issues. She agrees that astrology had to be more deterministic hundreds of years ago because people lacked an awareness of psychological insight, but many changes have taken place in how we look at the world around us. Greene suggests that this new way of looking at the chart is not about escaping our fate but rather it is concerned with understanding the chart and relating to it from a different perspective. She acknowledges that the birth chart shows us a moment of time outside of our conscious will and is thus 'fated'. But, on the other hand, it also contains all of the individual's potentials in life – the opportunity to express these is a sign of our free will. Thus psychological astrology allows us to consider the chart as a seed moment from which we may grow, rather than an inescapable pattern of fate that we were born with. On the negative side many can use it as an intellectual exercise and not seek to integrate the notion of mind, body and spirit to form one individuated whole. In essence this would be a mistake for any astrologer, as the very nature of the links between planets, the physical world and our own psyches allows us to contemplate and unite the whole paradox of how we fit into the mundane world when our soul may feel so separate from it.

Finally, perhaps an overlooked benefit to psychological astrology is that it has expanded clients' choices. Some people may be looking for a simple answer to a question that is bothering them, such as: Should I buy a house? Should I start a business? While others need a more person-centred approach to understand what they can make of their lives and to see the various complexes within them that they may be struggling with. Looking at the chart and giving insight into why certain events keep repeating in people's lives can be of enormous help to a client. Surely it is therefore beneficial to astrology as a whole that all areas of life that the client considers important have a field of astrology dedicated and ready to help them.

The Future of Psychological Astrology

So where does psychological astrology go from here? Some astrologers have been sounding its death knell. Bernard Eccles in his dissertation *Astrology in England in the Twenty-First Century* notes:

> Astrology turned inwards on itself in the last two decades of the twentieth century, rediscovering its roots

and traditions in what we have referred to earlier as the traditional revival. This meant that astrology's preferred reference points, which had until then been placed somewhere at the end of the nineteenth century with the Theosophical astrology of [Alan] Leo, and not far away in time from the beginnings of psychology and psychiatry with Freud and Jung, jumped back by another three hundred years to the seventeenth century, or earlier still. As well as providing a defined path leading back to the dawn of written history and the first forms of astrology, the traditional revival moved astrology's viewpoint and it found itself no longer in such close alignment with psychology.[13]

This is certainly true to some extent; particularly in the last ten years there has been a noticeable re-emergence of interest in the astrology of William Lilly, and others. However, I'm not sure that this would signal the end of psychological astrology. I think many disciplines, from time to time, require a period of rediscovering their roots, and this can be invaluable if it is used as a new starting point on which to build. It may well have been the case that many astrologers in the latter part of the twentieth century ignored the traditional past in astrology but now matters are being reset, bringing about a broader interest in astrology's history.

Eccles gives a second possible cause for concern that psychological astrology may be on the wane: the decline of psychology itself. He says, 'Thirty years ago psychology and its attendant disciplines were enjoying a wave of popularity very similar to astrology's, bound up with the desire to discover the inner self which was so much a part of the social revolutions of the 1960s, but since then changes in society have placed an increasing emphasis on material and financial gain, and psychology is seen as outmoded or irrelevant. In a series of articles in *The Times* in May 2003, Peter Watson claimed that: "Psychology... has failed big-time. Furthermore, it has failed not just in the sense that more people are ill or unhappy, it has failed technologically, philosophically, and is in an advanced state of decomposition."[14][15]

Once again this is an interesting point, although I would disagree with Watson's view that psychology is dead. There has certainly been a change in public perception of both psychology and psychotherapy. The renowned psychologist James Hillman wrote a book called *We've Had a Hundred Years of Psychotherapy and the World's Getting Worse*[16] in which he argues that psychotherapy requires a major re-visioning in order to be fully relevant to the modern world. I think that the perception of psychology has been tainted in the public's mind. They have seen certain individuals undergo years of psychotherapy and not appear to be the better off for it; they have seen the use of psychology in the black arts of advertising and political spin doctoring and are rightly wary of its use to help the average person. In addition, the insistence of scientists that everything must be absolutely proven through double-blind clinical trials leaves both psychology and astrology wanting, as neither discipline fits well into that technique. Maybe what we need is for psychology to re-establish itself as the study of the soul again and to worry less about its place in the modern scientific forum.

Another problem with the psychological approach is that depth psychology involves putting in a lot of hard work to uncover the various complexes at the heart of the psyche, and then even greater work to fully integrate these and make the self complete. I think that in this speeded-up and time-short world, many find they are not prepared or able to put that amount of time or effort into their 'becoming whole', as Jung would have put it. Perhaps we are back to Maslow's pyramid where the priorities of food, shelter, warmth and work require a quick fix from the astrologer more than a complex assessment. In addition, it is unusual for astrologers to see the client frequently, and depth work requires this in order to be successful.

Then there is the huge shadow of Jung that still hangs resolutely over psychological astrology. Mike Harding makes an astute point on this matter:

> If we examine the attempts that we have made so far to reconcile astrology with the observations and theories of psychologists, then it would appear that the term 'psychological astrology' is applied almost exclusively to varieties of Jungian archetypal theories, and their development by others.

> There could be no quarrel with this approach were it possible to demonstrate convincingly that these theories were *correct*. Indeed, were this the case then the path we have already begun to take would be the only sensible track. But it is *not* the case. Whatever we may learn from Jung – and there is much that we may want to consider – his theories have not been universally substantiated and

there is a real risk that, in embracing his position, we may take on board much more than we realize.

By adopting the currency of Jung's language we buy our way into a system of thought which has implications which are not always immediately recognized by astrologers, and which contain attitudes that are not necessarily in astrology's best interests.[17]

Jung himself had perhaps more in common with the mystic than the scientist, and many of his ideas, as Harding notes, are no longer considered important in psychological circles, despite many being common knowledge for the general public – such as the idea of the shadow or the collective unconscious. Does this mean that we should be seeking to move away from the Jungian theories that psychological astrology makes much of? While I would agree that many of Jung's ideas are a very good way of examining the chart, we should beware of allowing psychological astrology to stagnate by not considering more recent advances in psychology such as those in the areas of developmental, positive, social, personality and evolutionary psychology. These may lead us to having a fuller and more meaningful model of psychological astrology.

Fashions come and go in astrology, as they do in other disciplines. The flavour of the moment may well be towards the more ancient forms of astrology, but as soon as thought turns more inward, then psychological astrology will, once again, be called upon and utilized. I don't see psychological astrology disappearing, nor even just becoming a footnote in astrological history as some of its detractors would perhaps like it to be. Like it or not, psychology in whatever form will always be with us; we cannot stuff the cat back into that particular bag and hope it will disappear. In addition, for as long as man philosophises about his purpose and wants to know about the inner workings of the self, then studies that explore the psyche in depth will always be popular. They may change and grow but it seems impossible to imagine a time when man will not ask himself 'who am I?'.

References and Notes

1. Oxford Dictionaries online, http://oxforddictionaries.com/definition/psychology (accessed 2/11/11).

2. Wikipedia, http://en.wikipedia.org/wiki/Psychology#Etymology (accessed 2/11/11).

3. M. L. Smith and G. V. Glass, 'Meta-analysis of psychotherapy outcome studies', in *American Psychologist,* 32, 1977, pp. 752–60.

4. Angela Voss, *Marsilio Ficino,* North Atlantic Books (US), 2006.

5. Patrick Curry, *Astrology, Science and Culture: Pulling Down the Moon,* Berg Publishers, 2004, Chapters 4–9.

6. For further information regarding the role of psychology in capitalism and individualism see Adam Curtis' BBC TV series *The Century of the Self.* Details at http://www.bbc.co.uk/bbcfour/documentaries/features/century_of_the_self.shtml (accessed 7/11/11).

7. Dane Rudhyar, *The Astrology of Personality,* Aurora Press, 1991, p. 81.

8. By Factoryjoe (Own work) [CC-BY-SA-3.0 (www.creativecommons.org/licenses/by-sa/3.0) or GFDL (www.gnu.org/copyleft/fdl.html)], via Wikimedia Commons.

9. Abraham Maslow, *Motivation and Personality,* Harper and Row (New York), 1954, p. 92.

10. James Brockbank, *A Model for Astrology,* MA Dissertation for the University of Kent, 2003, p. 15. Available online at http://www.the9thhouse.org/dissertations.htm (accessed 10/11/11).

11. Michael Harding, *Hymns to the Ancient Gods,* Arkana, 1992, p. 18.

12. Liz Greene, *The Astrology of Fate,* Thorsons, 1984.

13. Bernard Eccles, *Astrology in England in the Twenty-First Century,* MA Dissertation for Bath Spa University College, 2004, p. 22. Available online at http://www.the9thhouse.org/dissertations.htm (accessed 10/11/11).

14. *The Times,* 14 May 2003.

15. Eccles, op. cit., p. 23.

16. James Hillman and Michael Ventura, *We've Had a Hundred Years of Psychotherapy and the World's Getting Worse,* Harper Collins, 1992.

17. Harding, *Hymns to the Ancient Gods,* p. 21.

Rebecca Crane
A Personal Biography

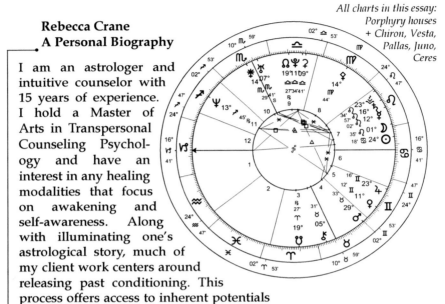

All charts in this essay:
*Porphyry houses
+ Chiron, Vesta,
Pallas, Juno,
Ceres*

I am an astrologer and intuitive counselor with 15 years of experience. I hold a Master of Arts in Transpersonal Counseling Psychology and have an interest in any healing modalities that focus on awakening and self-awareness. Along with illuminating one's astrological story, much of my client work centers around releasing past conditioning. This process offers access to inherent potentials and the divine perfection that lies inside of us all. My serious involvement with astrology took off around my first nodal return (age 19). The extent to which astrology can describe the nuanced personality of the individual was astounding to me. I was convinced that combining astrology with a person-centered psychology could effect change in clients exponentially faster than traditional psychotherapy. It has been incredibly fascinating to discover how these modalities fit together in practice. I love connecting with fellow astrologers online and at conferences. I felt strongly about making astrology conferences and education more readily available to astrologers just starting out, so I became involved in the formation of the Association for Young Astrologers (AYA) in 2003. It was exciting to participate in a movement that has helped make the field of professional astrology more accessible to the upcoming generations. Through the AYA I was invited to speak at astrology conferences in 2006 and 2007. These were wonderful experiences but I have not pursued speaking to large groups since then, as I prefer one-to-one astro-psychological work with clients. Perhaps the number of planets in my natal 7th House has something to do with that! Through my commitment to being of service to the field of astrology, I now serve on the Steering Committee for the Association for Astrological Networking (AFAN) as the Chair of Correspondence and Facebook. Through this organization, teaching, contributing to this book and continued involvement at astrology conferences, I am honored to participate in the growth of astrology as a respected, professional field in the new millennium.

www.rebeccacrane.com
rebeccacraneastrology@gmail.com

Chapter Thirteen

ESSENTIAL SKILLS FOR THE COUNSELING ASTROLOGER

REBECCA CRANE

There are some key components of psychological counseling that I would like to share with astrologers who are seeing clients. Each of us has a unique approach to the kind of astrology we do, but simply delivering astrological information is not enough if we want to see results of healing and change for the clients in our practice. We must cultivate skills such as reflective listening, awareness of biases and projections, respect for boundaries and confidentiality and non-judgmental handling of difficult issues that may arise. These are just a few components of a session in which the client feels heard and validated, and walks away feeling more empowered than when they came in.

Since this topic could be a book on its own, here I will offer a brief reference guide to familiarize you with some psychotherapeutic basics and share some of what I have learned through working with clients over the past ten years. I will also raise some questions for you to consider in the context of your own practice and experience. From my perspective the field must adapt to humanity's currently accelerating evolution, and it is my hope that this essay will help plant some seeds for the development of responsible and ethical astrological counseling in the next generation of astrologers.

Confidentiality

Maintaining confidentiality is perhaps the most important professional skill one can cultivate as a counseling astrologer. It goes without saying that sensitive information shared in the session must stay between the client and practitioner. Often there can be circumstances in which the practitioner becomes overwhelmed or excited about the exchange happening in the room and wants to share it. It can be healthy to relieve oneself of the psychic energy built up in the session but I would only do so under certain conditions: the first being that if you are going to talk to a trusted friend or colleague about a particularly insightful, effective or difficult session, under no circumstances should you reveal personal details about the client. This kind of sharing should focus only on how it was relevant to you and your process. An example would be if a client triggered you into learning more about your relationship dynamic with your spouse; only what that experience was like for you and nothing about the client's birth data, life situation or personal details should be shared. The second condition would be if you have a supervisor or therapist (which is recommended for anyone in a counseling role) and the information about the session would be beneficial to share in order for you to learn and grow as a professional. No one should be practicing in isolation and I strongly hope to see all counseling astrologers involved in ongoing professional consultation in the future.

What about seeing one half of a couple and discussing the other half in the session? Do you discuss the relationship, or even go so far as to obtain the birth data for the other half without his or her permission? I stay away from discussing a third party's horoscope unless that person has explicitly given his or her permission. I prefer to focus on the chart and relationship patterns of the person sitting in my office. If the client is desperate I will sometimes make an exception but I must admit it makes me uncomfortable. If I happen to know both people I always get permission from the other person first. I would not share any personal details I happen to know about him or her with the client in the room, keeping our session strictly about the psychological dynamics between them and the condition of each person's relationship houses and planets in their horoscope.

I used to be very much against conducting sessions with others present in the room, and traditional psychology maintains that it disrupts the psychic energy and makes it difficult to get clear information on the client. However, recently I have seen some people who come in with their significant others and they both would like the other to sit in on the session. It has gone rather well, as long as I focus strictly on the client and treat the other as an observer. Sometimes it is comforting or supportive for the client, or it has led to the other person becoming a client too because they have seen an example of my work. However, I will usually avoid talking about relationships or I keep this area extremely vague. I also state I am going to do this before the session starts, so it is clear to both people. Regardless, there is always *triangulation* going on (a phenomenon I will discuss in a later section of this essay) which alters the energy in the room and affects the outcome of the work. In the case of children or teens I will ask the parent to sit outside and wait. In the past, I've made the mistake of letting the parent sit in and I felt that I had to seriously edit myself in the session. All three of us were left feeling dissatisfied as a result. If the parent insists, I will allow it but I explain to them that the children are safe and will not hear anything 'bad' about themselves or that will give them nightmares. If you are going to say this make sure you can deliver on this promise by remembering what is age appropriate and having very clear boundaries.

Boundaries, Containment and Power Dynamics

Firm boundaries are the primary factor in the client's overall feeling of safety. The session is more likely to proceed without strong defensive mechanisms in play if you are holding a secure frame, or container, for the work. This sense of safety begins with the astrologer setting a definite time for the session, starting promptly and not running over. Disregarding this structure can cause both you and the client to feel vulnerable, and it throws the power dynamic off balance. If not initially clear, it is a good idea to state at the beginning of the session what time has been allotted. For example, 'In the hour we have together today...' which is also a nice lead-in to what you plan to address. I invite the client to ask questions whenever they arise so I'm not assuming too much of the power, which also helps me tailor the reading to their needs. If sensitive material arises at the end it is a good idea to first let the client know he or she is being heard by making a reflective statement and then politely suggesting another session. You must stay in control of the session. Being firm with that power establishes you as someone whom the client can depend upon, and it empowers them because they are receiving mirroring from someone reliable and present. They become more willing to allow healing and growth to happen. It is similar to the need for parents to establish strong boundaries and structure for their child. Doing so facilitates the establishment of a solid sense of self and enables the child to develop an individuated personality.

The space in which you are seeing your client should be clean and uncluttered, well-lit and set at a temperature that feels good for both of you. It is important that the setting be appropriate. I would avoid bedrooms and steer clear of noisy or public places, which interfere with concentration and a sense of safety. The more a person can relax, the better the work goes. However, if the client is too relaxed boundaries tend to become loose. There should not be too many personal items around – this can alter the client's perception of you, which creates the potential for them to adjust what they say and not stay true to how they really feel. Clients will, at times, project onto us anyway and react to ideas they have about what kind of people we are, but we should aim to keep the setting as neutral as we can. I will address this further in the section on transference.

This brings me to the topic of self-disclosure, which is another factor that, depending on its use, can make the client feel safe or unsafe. How much of your own life do you let your clients see, if any? When is it helpful and therapeutic to let them see certain aspects of you? Try never to tell a story about your own life unless you are absolutely certain it is relevant and would be helpful for the client to hear, and always keep it very brief. This can support understanding and a holding environment ('oh, it's nice to know I'm not alone!'), which promotes a sense of comfort and support. If you are not sure then it is best to err on the side of not sharing your story. You can tell that if the client's body language, facial expression and general energy drop as you are talking, it is best to stop and move on, and turn the focus back onto them.

If you are going to maintain 'dual relationships', i.e. interactions with a client outside of the sessions, in anything other than your professional role, be ready for tests of integrity. You will be asked to walk your talk. I have found that it is more trouble than it's worth to have ongoing sessions with a client *and* a relationship outside of these. The result is often a blurring of boundaries and confusion over how and when you are there for the person. Dual relationships with clients can have us hypervigilant about how we are acting in all of our relationships. It can be exhausting to maintain a number of roles at once or to make sure the primary role you present with is one that the client feels safe being around. I did a trade with a practitioner in another field once and in my mind the boundaries were still well defined as we became friends and colleagues. However, later he stated to me that he did not feel safe sharing any further personal information with me because what I had disclosed to him about myself had triggered certain reactions in him. In short, always be aware of what you are sharing with clients and in what capacity you choose to interact with them outside of the session.

Reflective Listening

How do we make our chart interpretation useful for the healing processes of our clients? What do we say to help them feel witnessed and validated? How can we align with the client to bring out their inherent wisdom and growth instead of telling them what to do? Learning to become a good listener who is engaged in contextual dialogue is imperative to the energetic exchange that needs to happen between you and your client. It is important to focus on *process*, not just content and information. The interaction you are having with the client is just as important as, if not even more important than, the information you are telling them. A mentor of mine holds the position that, beyond the direct and practical handling of particular crises, when we are sitting with a client we are actually just distracting the mind while we let the love come through; entertaining and occupying the ego while we are giving them unconditional positive regard, as Carl Rogers would define it. I have been testing this for ten years and listening with my heart seems to always give me true access to what the client is really saying. Not everybody is coming to us for healing; they may just want to hear the astrological viewpoint. However, this approach can be a significant component to building rapport. In *The Astrologer, the Counsellor and the Priest* by Juliet Sharman-Burke and Liz Greene, it is stated that the client and practitioner must always develop some kind of relationship for healing to occur. Even if you are only seeing the client one time an attitude of openness and caring can communicate your availability and build a climate of trust. This allows clients to relax their defenses enough to potentially shift their ingrained psychic patterns, which are usually the cause of their problems and inability to see past their current circumstances.

Reflective listening is a tactic of repeating what the clients have just said to you in different words than they used. This signals to the brain that you have really heard them, which again builds confidence and trust, and can stimulate self-realizations and insights that they would not have been aware of otherwise. It can also be useful to reflect a client's body language to them, as people often do not realize that a physical reaction they had or how they are sitting can describe a lot about what's going on for them. 'I notice you crossed your arms in front of your chest when we began talking about your father,' for example. Use your discretion when naming these things in the session and be aware of what you *don't* name too, as this can be indicative of your own discomfort or blocks.

Transference and Countertransference

Often clients will re-enact with the practitioner the dynamics they've had with significant people in their lives. This is known as *transference*, a phenomenon where preconditioned exchanges with people who had great influence over us in the past become played out with others. In the counseling realm this is a positive exchange because it gives the client an opportunity to have a 'corrective experience' when the astrologer does not react in the way the client is used to people responding. This happens as a result of you as the astrologer holding a (mostly) objective and neutral position in the interaction. It requires that you stay diligently aware of your own biases and judgments and do your best to keep them out of the session completely. This is the second requirement that Sharman-Burke and Greene in *The Astrologer, the Counsellor and the Priest* deem necessary for healing to occur in the session: continually doing your own work in order to stay aware of your personal emotional state and be able to resist reacting to your client based on personal feelings.

Have you ever had a client trigger you into behaving like he or she feels? People often unconsciously treat others how they have been treated. This is useful in therapy through the phenomenon of *countertransference*: when the practitioner begins to feel like the client feels, as relational patterns are repeated through the relationship dynamic presented in the session. There is a way in which the client unconsciously disowns their feelings in the interaction and if the practitioner is open and neutral, the natural inclination is to accept that energy and take on the role of the client. This can be extremely useful because the client gets to experience the other side of how they've been treated. They can assume the position of perpetrator of circumstances heretofore outside of their control, which can be empowering, revealing and incredibly informative. A strategic approach to addressing this is to try to verbalize what is happening, and normalize it. This could include a statement like, 'I'm feeling _____ in response to what you're saying. Have you ever felt like that? It sounds similar to what you've described to me when _____ was happening.' If it feels appropriate you may even suggest a way in which you would prefer to be treated in such circumstances, which can encourage clients to feel more confident in breaking the conditioned pattern and asking those in their lives for similar treatment themselves.

In terms of dealing with countertransference, when you begin to speak about a planetary placement or configuration, notice what goes on in your body. Track your feelings in your gut and observe what you are inclined to say in particular. Don't over-analyze it to the extent that it ends up altering what you say because you are being careful – just notice. Listen through your witness/observer self and make some mental notes as the session proceeds. There is a lot of information available simply in how you speak to the client. What words do you generally use for the Moon that you omitted with this client? Are there any aspects to your Moon from the client's chart? Does he or she remind you of someone you know? How do you typically respond to that other person and are you reacting to this client in similar ways? It is important to remember that, within reason, the way in which you are naturally reacting to this client is most likely appropriate, as they came to you for the experience you are in a position to give them. It is beneficial as long as you keep being aware of yourself and stay primarily in the spirit of giving. This creates an exchange in which both parties come away feeling 'filled up'.

We will not always have the time or space during consultation needed to ponder the answers to these questions – it's usually in hindsight that the astrologer comes to a deeper understanding of what was going on while sitting with the person (this is one reason I love seeing clients for more than one session because these interactions can be addressed in later sessions). However, it is all for good learning, and increased awareness of our biases and triggers is always progress. Again, by the law of resonance, the client comes to *you* because of the reflection you have to give. The clearer you can be around your own inclinations and issues, the better mirror you can be for them.

Challenges Specific to Counseling Astrologers

The primary issue counseling astrologers face is *triangulation* with the chart. The birth chart confounds the traditional psychotherapeutic relationship. In other words, the chart is an additional element that is introduced into the dynamic and it distracts from the relational exchange between the client and practitioner. This can turn out to be helpful, as it decreases the level of tension in the room at key times, which can open the client up to new insights and perspectives that they might not have been able to access before, due to feeling put 'on the spot'. The maintenance of defense mechanisms perceived as necessary for psychic survival can prevent these insights from being readily available. A not-so-useful instance of triangulation is when clients blame everything happening to them on the chart and refuse to take responsibility for their life situations. There have also been times when we are just about to uncover or gain access to significant insights and the client decides to shift the attention to the chart and away from themselves because the psychic material is too confronting and challenging to take on board. It is important to allow this to happen and not attempt to redirect them, especially if you are only seeing them once. Just observe and make note that it happened. If the same material is brought up later and it happens again with the same client, it may be prudent to mention in a non-judgmental way that you noticed it.

We as astrologers have an advantage over traditional talk therapy in that the birth chart is our shortcut to the real issues at hand. We do not need to sit with the client for weeks in order to gather relevant strands of information. How can the astrological chart indicate therapeutic goals to be addressed in counselling, and which parts of the horoscope do we look to for this information? I always take some time to assess how the clients are presenting themselves that day (body language, mood, mannerisms, grooming) and what they initially say – and look at this in the context of the natal temperament and their current transits. The first thing I look at when a client presents in crisis is what is going on with the chart's angles. Transits and progressions to the four angles will often manifest as upheaval in one of the four main areas of life ruled by these angles (home, career, relationships and self/body). In addition, hard aspects or conjunctions to the Sun and Moon, especially from the slower-moving outer planets, can elicit sudden panic when something that has been brewing under the surface becomes unavoidable and compromises the client's daily life. As Donna Cunningham wrote in *The Counseling Astrologer's Guidebook*, outer-planet transits usually bring crisis, and crisis usually means loss.

It is my opinion that outer planets are responsible for information that is not in plain sight, so we can often be blindsided by their effects. There cannot be 'a-ha!' moments all the time. These planets rule the levels of the subconscious and also the higher consciousness – these are the routes through which they work; the only way the energy can get to us. It does not usually happen by direct consciousness. People with personal planets conjunct outer planets in the natal chart are often channels or hold the awareness of the superconscious realms in their waking consciousness or their bodies. These people are often the biggest counseling challenges because functioning in the mundane world can be difficult and it often asks for greater effort from them. What kind of practical suggestions can we give clients who are bringing this level of knowledge or experience into the conscious mind and body? What can we offer to those who are communicating with other worlds and having spiritual experiences for which they do not have a context?

In cases of outer-planet transits the client usually wants to know right away, 'When will it be over?' I will look ahead and tell them when the difficult influence will subside somewhat, but then I always bring the discussion back to the moment. I emphasize to them that the current moment is the only place where we have any control over how the transit or progression will go for the rest of the time. I will ask them what they have been doing and what hasn't been working for them. I often suggest some coping strategies in the flavor of the archetype linked to the transiting or progressed planet. With Neptune it usually takes the form of surrender and the loosening of rigid patterns. With Uranus it's often anxiety management and a creative outlet. With Pluto I suggest further exploration of repressed feelings and ways of coping with traumatic circumstances.

It is important to consider how much to say to these folks who often already feel incredibly overwhelmed. What level of frankness and truth can this person handle right now? Saying too much is a do-no-harm concern, but also what is vague or incomplete can leave the client feeling confused. I'm constantly searching for that delicate balance of tactful yet effective delivery. I also try to avoid using too much astrology when describing what's going on – this can confuse and bewilder clients to the point where they just disengage and don't hear the helpful information in between. I have found that stating the exact astrological conditions I'm attempting to interpret is really for my own sense of self-competency. Clients just want to know what is happening in words they can understand, and be given room to reflect on it in that moment. Psychotherapy holds that a lot can happen in the space of silence. We don't necessarily need to fill the entire time with talking; doing so may be somewhat detrimental because clients need to be able to take in and process what you are telling them in order to adequately digest it. This is part of the reason that I always make a recording of the session so the client can go back at their leisure and fully grasp what was said.

Again, we always want to stay aware of biases found in what we say to our clientele. What we choose to focus on in the consultation may unconsciously emerge because it resonates deeply with us. This phenomenon may in fact be of great assistance to the client, allowing him or her to feel heard and empathized with, promoting further insight and healing. However, we want to cultivate sensitivity and the awareness that our experiences may be very different from theirs. Regardless, the strategy is to maintain a firm but gentle nudge toward the 'a-ha!' moment. There is a difference between leading and pushing: leading is an offering; pushing is usually ego-driven. You will know if you've gone into ego mode if you start to feel attached to the client's 'getting it' or following your ideal agenda for them.

Be aware of the gifts available to *you* in the session as well. It is okay to receive guidance, healing and support while you are counseling others. The key, while conducting the session, is to be primarily focused on them and resist pursuing any need to be validated or fed yourself. There is a natural exchange that occurs through your selfless giving that benefits you as the practitioner. You may not see this right away but your soul and psyche are enhanced regardless. Often I think we attract clients who have lessons to teach us through the way they 'present' in the session. Sometimes it comes through their suffering, sometimes their joy. Sometimes just their statements about where they are in their lives can be catalytic for us. If you lead with your heart, stay conscious of your egoic needs and refrain from feeding them at the expense of the client, it is often a perfect and beautiful exchange – soul-contracted to propel both of you further into healing and higher consciousness. I will say that I tend to naturally attract a lot of clients with a Leo emphasis, perhaps due to my 7th/8th-House Leo planets – a part of me must unconsciously be seeking that kind of mirroring. What do you think? Do you attract clients with issues or planetary configurations similar to your own? As I've mentioned already, it is my understanding that by the law of resonance the client consults *you* because of the reflection you have to give, astrological or otherwise.

I've had clients say to me, 'This other astrologer said I would be having a rough time. Why aren't you telling me that?' When I look at the chart there is sometimes indication of potential difficulty, but I will wonder to myself why the astrologer made reference to it, and what made them frame the aspect in that particular way. Is it somehow a reflection of where the astrologer is themselves? Did the client have more of a (fill in the blank with perceived rough transit)-type of presentation that day, which the astrologer felt was necessary to interpret as 'rough'? What resources could the astrologer have highlighted for that person that could have left him or her more confident and supported, rather than scared and feeling resigned to have a difficult time? I'm not saying we should sugar-coat what's going on for the client. On the contrary, I think divulging as much of the truth as we can is part of our service to the client. Otherwise we are just being paid to tell them what they want to hear, or tell them what they already know, for entertainment purposes. I feel that we have an obligation to deliver an uplifting yet truthful perspective, and provide clients with a holistic point of view in order to give them the opportunity to decide what resonates with them. This is often a double-edged sword. I couldn't help but cringe when a client said to me once, 'Another astrologer told me that with the chart I have, I shouldn't still be alive.' She seemed to be stating this proudly, as if she were justified in having a tremendously difficult life. In hindsight I could see that this statement gave her permission to forgive herself for not having lived it better. The challenge here was to shift the focus from doom and gloom without taking away the sense of empowerment she derived from feeling validated in her struggle.

It is also a good idea to be aware of your own transits as well as what's generally going on in the heavens at the time of consultation – not just the transits to the client's chart. In preparing for a session I spend a few minutes looking at what's going on for me as well as the general vibe of the time. I don't always look at the synastry between us ahead of time but this can be another useful source of information. Or it can sometimes be detrimental. If I see that we have a Mars–Pluto square, for instance, I might choose my words more carefully, which can be a good or bad thing. If Pluto is highly emphasized in the client's chart they might feel unacknowledged if I mince words and try to stay 'safe' in the session – they could sense that I'm not telling them the whole truth. My gift to them as the practitioner is to be as real, clear and unadulterated in my delivery as possible, yet still tactful and compassionate. I would not go into a session being intentionally confrontational simply to give them a Mars–Pluto experience. These are individual circumstances which require one's best judgment in the moment. It's likely that the synastry will emerge somehow anyway, but your job is to stay as neutral as you can. This allows you to be a clear mirror for the client, which is the primary goal, so they can experience the benefit of unbiased reflection to understand themselves and make better choices.

Circumstances such as a Mars–Pluto square dynamic in your personal relationship, or a family member having a natal Mars–Pluto square, or a Mars–Pluto square in the sky, can all be triggers for the practitioner in the session. The goal is to diffuse unnecessary conflict and use the aspect to the client's greatest advantage. This may be tricky if you are only seeing the client once. In psychotherapy a bond of trust established by an ongoing relationship is the ideal arena in which to address such tensions. Again, the relationship between the client and practitioner provides a safe space, which is fertile ground for exploration of the kinds of conflicts the client may have had with others. In the session we can give the client the option of testing out different ways of being by exposing them to saner or more non-judgmental reactions than they've experienced elsewhere. This offers a wider range of choices around how to be in the world – without the consequences they may be used to expecting. Herein lies the 'corrective experience'!

Conclusion

I feel honoured, through this essay, to be sharing what I am learning in my work. I'm finding that astrology is an invaluable route through which we can rediscover our inherent gifts and potentials. At the time of this writing I'm noticing that the process of healing in my clientele is happening less through their learning and retaining new information and mostly through letting go of old conditioned behavior patterns and ingrained belief systems. As information management becomes more advanced it is easy to look up almost anything on the spot and there is less of a need to remember it. Packing more information into our heads distracts us from accessing the wealth of knowledge within, which I believe is the next step on our evolutionary path: the rebalancing of the left and right sides of our brains. What we have perceived through duality up until this point is being called toward unity. Perhaps a healthy integration of each axis of the zodiac is how astrology will be on board with this developing consciousness model.

I think we have an opportunity now to advance further than ever by releasing the blocks that prevent us from fully living out our divine potentials. We are purging lifetimes of inherited material and, as we do, our DNA begins to function in different and better ways, which allows our true abilities and gifts to shine through. This increased activation of the right side of the brain and its merging with the left side will allow us to naturally reflect upon circumstances in a more intuitive and holistic way. Astrology further assists with this process by validating what clients are experiencing and promoting compassion and self-forgiveness through a greater understanding of the archetypal stories.

It is my hope that the intuitive side of astrology becomes more prominent in the years to come, and that the old fate vs. free will debate is resolved with the understanding that we create our fate with our free will. Yes, the chart is a road map of the overarching themes in a person's life, but as a teacher of mine says, 'If you keep doing what you're doing, you'll end up where you're going.' The choices we make today help determine our paths tomorrow. This is how we astrologers can be of greatest assistance to our clients: we can show them the map, help them become aware of unconscious impulses and habits, and guide them toward their most appropriate routes ahead. We can reflect what they are saying from a neutral standpoint, and we can hold a safe contained space for them to explore their options. Along with a well-prepared chart delineation, I believe this will prove to be one of the most effective and expedient avenues to healing and human evolution in the years to come.

Sources

Donna Cunningham, *The Consulting Astrologer's Guidebook*, York Beach, ME: Samuel Weiser, 1994.

Robert E. Doyle, *Essential Skills and Strategies in the Helping Process*, Pacific Grove, CA: Brooks Cole, 1992.

Juliet Sharman-Burke and Liz Greene, *The Astrologer, the Counsellor and the Priest: Two Seminars on Astrological Counselling*, London: CPA Press, 1997.

Keiron Le Grice
A Personal Biography

All charts in this essay:
Koch houses
+ Chiron, Eris,
True Node

My interest in astrology began in 1989 when I taught myself the fundamentals of chart calculation, forecasting and interpretation, drawing on books by Margaret Hone, Grant Lewi, A. T. Mann and others. I soon discovered the work of Dane Rudhyar and Stephen Arroyo, which became the major influence on my approach to astrology. Without question, the most significant intellectual and spiritual influence on my worldview, however, has been Carl Gustav Jung. As an undergraduate I became engrossed in Jung's *Collected Works*, writing a thesis on his concept of individuation. During my late twenties, inspired by revisiting Joseph Campbell's *The Power of Myth* interviews, I began work on a book exploring how astrology could be used to illuminate the various phases of the hero's journey as a guide to psychospiritual transformation. To give this topic the foundation it required, I realized I needed to set forth a theoretical explanation of astrology within the context of an encompassing worldview – a project that was to hold my attention for the next eleven years, and which culminated in the publication of *The Archetypal Cosmos: Rediscovering the Gods in Myth, Science and Astrology* in 2010. Meanwhile, studying under Richard Tarnas I gained a Master's degree and Ph.D. in Philosophy and Religion from the California Institute of Integral Studies in San Francisco, where I have since worked as adjunct professor. I am also guest lecturer in the Jungian and Archetypal Studies Specialization at Pacifica Graduate Institute in Santa Barbara, and founding co-editor of *Archai: The Journal of Archetypal Cosmology*, for which I have contributed a number of articles, including astrological analyses of Jung, Bruce Springsteen and Rafael Nadal. My second book, *Discovering Eris: The Symbolism and Significance of a New Planetary Archetype*, published in 2012, explores the possible astrological meaning of the recently discovered dwarf planet.

www.keironlegrice.com • www.archaijournal.org
keironlegrice@gmail.com

Chapter Fourteen

THE ARCHETYPAL DYNAMICS OF INDIVIDUATION
Astrology, Myth and Psychospiritual Transformation

KEIRON LE GRICE

Individuation, as described by C. G. Jung, is a process of deep psychological transformation leading the individual towards the realization of the Self – the organizing center and the totality of the psyche. According to Jung, individuation represents an advanced stage of psychological development by which the individual 'I', the conscious ego, becomes aware of, and engages in a dialectical encounter with, the unconscious, encompassing both the repressed contents of biographical experience and complexes (the personal unconscious) and the universal stratum of the psyche (the collective unconscious). The individuation process is impelled and informed by archetypes – numinous formative principles and conditioning factors existing *a priori* in the depths of the collective unconscious that give a thematic predisposition and continuity to human experience. Jung saw archetypes – which include the shadow, the hero, the anima and animus, the wise old man, the mother, the father, rebirth, the spirit, the child and the trickster – as the fundamental motifs behind mythology and religion, the underlying determinants of human experience that are evident in numinous dreams and fantasy images, and that manifest in every typical life situation.[1] At root, although the archetypes function autonomously, they are all aspects of the Self, which initiates and draws forth individuation, imposing a labor of transformation on the individual ego. Individuation ultimately leads to the realization of a greater authority in one's life, a higher will beyond that of conscious willpower – a will that is akin, Jung thought, to the Will of God, to be uniquely realized within every individual life.[2]

As Jung and Joseph Campbell have demonstrated, the sequence of transformations occurring during individuation is symbolically portrayed by myths of the hero's journey.[3] These myths, Campbell suggests, tend to loosely adhere to a certain pattern or template – the *monomyth*, as he termed it – comprising three fundamental stages: separation or departure, initiation or transformation, and return or incorporation. The monomyth depicts, first, the hero's separation from the ordinary daylight world of consensus reality in response to a 'call to adventure', which is followed, second, by a threshold crossing, typically marking an initiatory 'descent into the underworld' and sequence of transformative experiences on a 'road of trials'. Lastly, the adventure culminates with the attainment of a boon or treasure, and subsequent return journey in which the hero brings back and disseminates the boon to the culture. The treasure, the 'pearl of great price', understood psychologically, might be interpreted as a symbolic representation of the precious gift of individual selfhood and, with it, the realization of a unique life destiny and calling.

In this article, by exploring connections between archetypal themes evident in human experience and particular planetary alignments in both natal charts and transits, I present the case that astrology can be used to help illuminate the archetypal dynamics of the individuation process and the hero's journey.[4]

The Planetary Archetypes

The universal principles associated with the planets in astrology seem to relate to Jung's conception of archetypes *per se*, universal forms underlying the archetypal images he identified, such as the shadow, hero and anima.[5] For example, the planetary archetype associated with Pluto – which is related to themes such as instinctual dynamism, the depths of experience, death–rebirth, transformation, evolution, compulsion and empowerment – is connected to the Jungian archetypes of the shadow (containing the repressed instincts and primitive drives) and rebirth, as well as the compulsive, possessive quality associated with all archetypes (particularly evident in what Jung calls the archetype of the mana personality) and the fated quality often associated with the Self. The astrological Moon is associated with the anima (the feminine principle within the psyche), and the archetypes of the mother and the child. Saturn is associated with the wise old man or senex, the father archetype, and with the inferiority complex and negative emotions contained in the shadow. Uranus has particular connections with the trickster archetype, especially in its association with creative disruption. The Sun, pertaining to themes such as the quest for identity, the heroic task of carrying the light of conscious self-awareness, and associated with the centralizing principle of the psyche, is naturally connected to Jung's concept of the hero archetype and to the realization of the Self. And Venus and Mars, to give two final examples, are associated with the idealized images of female and male contained in the anima and animus, respectively. In short, each of the principles associated with the planets in astrology seems to be related to one or more

Jungian archetypes and particular qualities exhibited by these archetypes.

The planetary archetypes are also connected to gods and goddesses of mythology, and to a number of prominent motifs of the hero's journey. Thus Pluto is associated with Hades, the Devil, Dionysus, Shiva, Mara, Kali, the Uroborus, the alchemical god-man Mercurius and many other mythic deities. It is also associated with kundalini power, the mythic underworld, hell and purgatory, and the motifs of 'descent into the underworld' and transformation. Neptune is associated with the principles of divine love and universal compassion, personified by figures such as Christ and the Buddha. It is also related to the yearning for paradise, and the quest for mystical experience of oneness or transcendence, central to the esoteric branches of all religious traditions. Saturn relates to the patriarchal authority of Yahweh in the Old Testament, to Chronos and Father Time, to the stern hand of fate, and to the spiritual wisdom and authority by the guru or wise old man figure.

Again, as these few examples suggest, each planetary archetype is connected to many different mythic figures from the world's religious and cultural traditions. Each mythic figure represents one or more different aspects or characteristics of the planetary archetypes, which possess universal meanings that cannot adequately be portrayed by any one single deity or concept. The planetary archetypes, as Richard Tarnas has emphasized, are multivalent and multidimensional principles.[6] That is to say, they are indeterminate creative powers that manifest in a wide variety of ways across all dimensions of reality. Although they always reflect an unchanging central core of meaning, these archetypes do not have a singular fixed mode of expression that might be exhaustively described using a few simple keywords. Nor can one determine from astrology alone how the archetypes will actually manifest in human experience. Astrology pertains to universal element of human experience – to general themes and motifs – not to particulars.

Indeed, conceived more broadly, the planetary archetypes in astrology are associated with the set of universal qualities and themes that do not vary across cultures or change over time – themes such as love, beauty, courage, death, faith, pleasure, destruction, creation, awakening, wisdom, transformation, mystery, illumination, sacrifice, freedom, a sense of the sacred and more. These are the great universal constants in human experience. To see these qualities as the expression of archetypes is to recognize that they exist independently of the individual human mind. We do not create these universal qualities; rather, they act on us, structuring and pervading the world and our experience of it. Archetypal principles are independent factors existing in the background level of reality. They form the context within which our experience of the world arises moment to moment.

Understood from this perspective, astrology offers a comprehensive cosmological–mythic–archetypal framework that can provide sustaining meaning and orientation for human experience.[7] Such orientation is particularly valuable during individuation when one's very identity undergoes a profound transformation, which naturally throws one into states of chaos, disorientation and perhaps even trauma. In this context one can use astrology to gain some objective perspective on and insight into the themes, dynamics and timing of such experiences. Natal astrology allows one to better understand the major mythic themes and archetypal dynamics expressing themselves through one's life experience as a whole; transit astrology and the study of progressions enable one to gain insight into which particular themes are prominent at particular times of one's life.

Mythic Themes of Transformation

The planetary archetypes associated with the outer planets (Uranus, Neptune and Pluto) are associated with experiences of enduring, consequential and deep-rooted transformation, and of all the planetary archetypes are therefore the most immediately connected to individuation.[8] The archetypal principles associated with these so-called transpersonal planets are, at once, powers of immense evolutionary, creative potential and of immense, life-annihilating destruction. They are instinctual and archaic in essence, and yet also transformative, spiritual and progressive. They can act to sensitise, inspire and deepen our conscious experience, but also to obliterate, dissolve and disrupt.

Uranus: Individualism, Awakening and Creative Genius

The Uranus archetypal principle is often experienced as the impulse to break free from patterns of conventional existence, to separate oneself from the common crowd. The motive power of this archetype is connected to the desire to go one's own way in life, to seek out one's own unique experience, to bring forth one's creative genius. It is connected with the impulse to become a unique individual, *sui generis*, a goal which is central to the individuation process, as Jung explained:

Individuation means becoming an 'in-dividual,' and, in so far as 'individuality' embraces our innermost, last, and incomparable uniqueness, it also implies becoming one's own self. We could therefore translate individuation as 'coming to selfhood' or 'self-realization'.[9]

Especially in those cases in which the urge to authentic individual experience is not consciously willed, we can observe the archetypal Uranus in its characteristic role as trickster, liberator and awakener, manifesting as the sudden awakening 'call to adventure', or the unexpected disruption in one's life that jettisons one onto a new life path. 'A blunder – apparently the merest chance – reveals an unsuspected world,' as Joseph Campbell observes in *The Hero with a Thousand Faces*, which 'may amount to the opening of a destiny'.[10] Such is the activating and releasing quality of the archetypal Uranus to prompt or impel one onto a path of individual development.

The Uranus principle is expressed through the capacity of the shadow archetype, informed by the deeper *telos* of the Self, to undermine one's conscious intentions, to trip up the ego, as it were, and to break apart the artificial certainties and protective strategies we often depend upon. To individuate, one cannot cling to the established forms and values of the past; one has to commit oneself to one's own emerging truth, as one seeks to emancipate oneself from the often staid and hackneyed patterns of conventional life. A developed expression of the Uranus principle brings a fresh, unique, ever-unfolding, indeterminate quality to experience.

Unsurprisingly, Uranus is prominent in the birth charts of many figures well known for their individualism or figures whose creative brilliance and individual genius sets them apart.[11] For example, the life and work of Friedrich Nietzsche, born in 1844 during a Jupiter–Uranus conjunction, are characterized by a rebellion (Uranus) against moral principles (Jupiter), a championing of the 'free spirit' and an impassioned commitment to individual excellence and nobility – themes all connected with the combination of these archetypes. As is evident in Nietzsche's writing, the Jupiter–Uranus archetypal combination is associated with the emergence of new philosophies and worldviews, with the aspiration for a greater ascent of the spirit and with the activation of ever higher potentials; it correlates with the unexpected opening of expansive new vistas, the exhilaration of creative possibilities and the euphoric experience of freedom. Central motifs of this archetypal complex, as Richard Tarnas has noted, are well conveyed in the following passage from Nietzsche's *Daybreak*, both

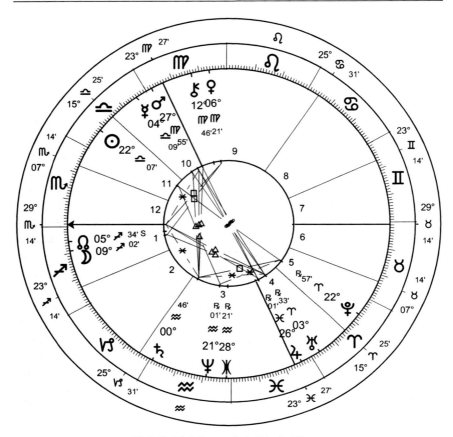

Friedrich Nietzsche's Birth Chart

through its vision of a future condition of greater strength and possibility, and in its symbolism of soaring birds and open expanses of space stretching into the unknown future:

> We aeronauts of the spirit! All those brave birds which fly out into the distance, the farthest distance – it is certain! Somewhere or other they will be unable to go on and will perch on a mast or bare cliff-face – and they will be even thankful for this miserable accommodation! But who could venture to infer from that, that there was not an immense open space before them, that they had flown as far as one *could* fly! All our great teachers and predecessors have at last come to a stop… But what does that matter to you and me! Other birds will fly farther! This insight and faith of ours vies with them in flying up and away; it rises above our heads and above our impotence into

the heights and from there surveys the distance and sees before it the flocks of birds which, far stronger than we, will strive whither we have striven, and where everything is sea, sea, sea![12]

Elsewhere, in another apt image of the Jupiter–Uranus pairing, Nietzsche describes the *Übermensch* Zarathustra – his vision of a future form of godlike human – as the nimble-footed 'cosmic dancer' who defies the 'spirit of gravity', climbing ever higher, reaching further into the distance and preaching a gospel of a greater, fuller future for the human being.

Similar themes are also evident in the life and person of Joseph Campbell (with a natal Sun–Mercury–Jupiter conjunction in a T-square with a Uranus–Neptune opposition) who held in high regard the pursuit of one's own individual path through life, an approach well exemplified, he thought, by the Knights of the Round Table who 'thought it would be a disgrace to follow the way or path of another' on the quest for the Holy Grail.[13] Campbell also professed his admiration for the pioneering space exploration program of the 1960s, bringing us a dazzling new holistic perspective on our planet, and for the technological brilliance that made possible the epic scale of the Manhattan skyline – both reflecting the Jupiter–Uranus complex's association with ascent, expanded perspectives and enormity of scale (Jupiter) combined with new innovation, brilliance and technology (Uranus). Generally, like Nietzsche, Campbell was an enthusiast for higher human possibilities, advocating a life-affirming individualistic philosophy.

Both Nietzsche and Campbell also had Uranus in major aspect to Mars (Nietzsche had a Mars–Uranus opposition, Campbell a Mars–Uranus trine), which in Campbell's case seems to have been expressed, in the early part of his life, in the field of athletic achievement (pertaining to Mars). As a young man Campbell went to Columbia University in New York where he excelled in what would today be called the 800 meters. He recounts with pride one particular race in which he was running the final leg of a relay and, after receiving the baton, was able to make up a thirty-yard deficit to catch the runner in front and power past him. In Abraham Maslow's terminology Campbell had a peak experience; he was 'in the zone', as we might now say. This experience seems to have made a deep impression on Campbell. Even late into his life, he retained an admiration for the nobility of athletic training and achievement, and the camaraderie and aspiration to excellence shared by men and women in this field. The ethos of the athlete appealed to Campbell's developed sense of Apollonian excellence and elegance in mind, body and spirit. Such themes – peak experiences, athletic excellence, the championing of individual freedom, the positive exuberance with which he advocated following a life path of one's own – are all directly related to archetypal dynamics associated with Campbell's Jupiter–Uranus square and Mars–Uranus trine alignments, which shaped his own particular path of individuation and his worldview. For Nietzsche, the same combination of archetypal principles found expression in the high spirits and good humour evident throughout his philosophy (alongside the polemic), and in his vigorous mountain hikes in the Alps or along the precipitous mountain path of Eze in the Côte d'Azur, where he composed his epic *Thus Spoke Zathathustra*. The same complex was evident, too, in his philosophy of abundant health of body and spirit, even as he was ailing under the pressure of the psychospiritual transformation process in which he was embroiled.

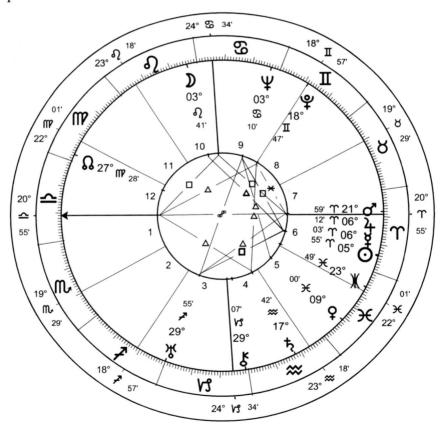

Joseph Campbell's Birth Chart

By themselves Mars–Uranus alignments are often expressed as a rugged and forceful individualism, as an ardent commitment to authenticity, as assertive rebelliousness and a restless craving for exciting new experiences – traits well exemplified by the Beatnik poets (Kerouac, Ginsberg, Cassady), each born with Mars and Uranus in hard aspect, and also by Jim Morrison (Mars–Uranus conjunction), lead singer of The Doors, who repeatedly screamed 'wake up!' during a number of live performances in the late sixties in an effort to forcibly jolt his audience out of its existential slumber. In archetypal terms Uranus is connected to the trickster, the rebel, the liberator and the awakener – dynamic patterns of being emboldened and energized in these figures by the Mars archetype, resulting in a fierce form of individualism and a rejection of the conformist patterns of conventional existence in favour of a life of constant change, experimentation and new stimulation.

The problematic forms of expression of archetypal complexes involving Uranus, especially as they relate to individuation, include an over-emphasis on individualistic freedom at the expense of the spiritual life and the discipline necessary for psychological transformation, willfulness, restlessness and an impatient recklessness, an inability to accept limitation of any kind, and a precocious brilliance out of balance with other aspects of the psyche. For instance, considering again the Mars–Jupiter–Uranus combination, alongside the more positive qualities of this complex we can see the exaggerated individualism and dissociated intellectual genius in the case of Nietzsche who proclaimed himself '6,000 feet above humanity' and who was unable to accept the more ordinary, commonplace aspects of human nature – an attitude that condemned him to a life of wandering and desperate solitude.[14] Nietzsche was totally separated from the dominant values of his culture, forced onto his own path by his philosophy and his worldview.

Similar themes are evident in personal transits, with the Uranus archetypal principle often serving a liberating or awakening function that draws forth one's unique creative talents and launches one onto a path of individuation. The archetypal Uranus electrifies, pointedly stimulates, and intensifies themes associated with other planetary archetypal principles. Under the influence of an activated Uranus, dormant complexes and drives in the psyche break into conscious awareness and cannot be ignored. Uranus thus facilitates the process of becoming conscious that is fundamental to individuation.

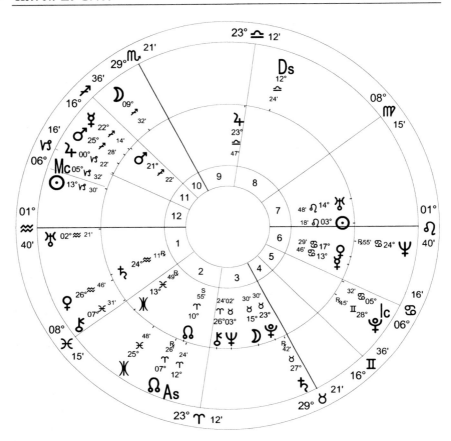

C.G. Jung's Birth Chart with Transits for 4 January 1913, Basel

For example, the period of Carl Jung's 'confrontation with the unconscious', beginning in 1912, coincided with a Uranus transit to his natal Sun–square–Neptune alignment.[15] This transit was particularly evident in a number of ways consistent with the meaning of the archetypes involved, exemplifying the significance of the archetypal Uranus for individuation.

First, it was at this time (in 1912) that the original version of Jung's *Wandlungen und Symbole der Libido* was published, setting out his own mythological interpretation of incest theory – a bold deviation from the established Freudian position with which he had previously been aligned. He subsequently broke away from Freud, resigning his position as President of the Psychoanalytic Association, and thus committed for better or worse to the uncertainty of his own unique life path – a typical occurrence during Uranus hard-aspect transits to the Sun. The chart above shows

Jung's transits for 4 January 1913, close to the date Jung received a letter from Freud beseeching him to 'take your full freedom' and 'spare me your supposed "tokens of friendships"' – a letter that virtually finalized the rupture between the two men.[16]

Second, the Uranus transit to Jung's natal Sun–square–Neptune also coincided with a series of destabilizing and revelatory experiences during his encounter with the depths of the unconscious. Reflecting Neptune's association with myth, dream, fantasy, altered states of consciousness and so forth, the Uranus transit to Neptune brought forth a stream of vivid fantasies, throwing Jung into states of profound disorientation and confusion, undermining his capacity to function in the world. He experienced jolting disruptions to his ordinary conscious experience, and encounters with numinous personified spirit figures, such as Philemon, that were to serve as guides to his own psychospiritual development.

Third, it was out of the weltering confusion of this experience that Jung developed his understanding of the individuation process. Reflecting a major theme associated with the Uranus–Neptune archetypal combination, he pioneered a new individual approach to spiritual experience that has since been extremely influential on contemporary forms of spirituality. The individualistic, inventive and creative qualities of Uranus were here brought to bear on the Neptunian archetypal and spiritual dimensions of experience.

In sum, then, during the Uranus transit to his natal Sun–Neptune alignment Jung effectively found and forged his own life path, entered the critical period of his own individuation process, and developed his unique individual approach to the unconscious from which all his subsequent creative work emerged.

Neptune: Transcendence, Dissolution and Synthesis

Turning now to the Neptune archetype, in respect of individuation this principle is associated, as we touched on above, with the realm of the collective unconscious. The Neptunian sensibility – expressed through dreams, fantasies, the imagination, visionary capacities, the religious instinct, the eye for symbol – is the means by which one engages with the collective unconscious during individuation. Neptune is specifically associated with the symbolic reading of one's life experience, the quest to cultivate a mythic perspective on life, and the desire to recover a more enchanted, magical way of being in the world. Through the Neptune archetype one attunes to spiritual ideals and inspiring visions, or one seeks transcendence through mystical experience, or one mythologizes and perceives the underlying connections and unity between all things. The

312 *Keiron Le Grice*

aspiration to discover the Kingdom of Heaven and the quest for
paradise are Neptunian phenomena.

In Jungian terms Neptune is connected to the Self and the
incarnate 'god-image', to the archetype of the spirit, and to
an encounter with the numinous dimension of reality. The
Neptunian principle is associated with the activity of the
transcendent power of the Self that, behind the scenes, orchestrates
the spiritual adventure and leads consciousness on the journey
towards individuation. In the soul that is inwardly ready, the
Neptunian principle manifests in the spiritual realization or
enlightenment experience which turns one's gaze away from the
external things to the inner world of the spirit. This principle can
also manifest as a regressive longing to return to a womb-like
state of blissful preconscious unity to escape the painful alienation
of ego-consciousness. Indeed, the regression of libido, as Jung
called it, when energy is withdrawn from the extraverted activities
of life and directed inwards, is essential for individuation,
stimulating the fantasy-making activity of the unconscious.

During individuation, when psychospiritual transformation
begins in earnest, the Neptune principle is often first observed
in the dissolution of the existing form of the ego-structure – the
'dissolution of the persona', to use Jung's term.[17] Through this
process the former cohesive unity of the personality disintegrates
into separate parts, and there is a return to the undifferentiated
psychological state the alchemists called the *massa confusa*. The
boundaries separating the ego and the unconscious are partly
dissolved, and the clear demarcation of the conscious ego-
personality from the unconscious is blurred. The problematic sides
of this experience include narcissistic self-absorption, delusory
states of consciousness, a schizophrenic detachment from reality
and an unconscious identification with the archetypes – all of
which reflect the characteristic Neptunian themes of dissolution,
confusion, lack of clarity, delusions and projections.

By giving in to the regressive longing to return to the paradise
of the womb, to a state of pre-conscious unity, one is exposed
to all those illusory ideals, wishes and images that lie in the
background of the psyche, subtly distorting one's experience. In
facing the unconscious, one has to attempt to become conscious
of the archetypal images that move consciousness without our
realizing. One has to differentiate the ego – the personal 'I' – from
the multitude of archetypes and instincts.

In mythic terms this experience is suggested by the 'belly of the
whale' motif, when the conscious personality is engulfed by the

unconscious, pulled down into the depths, which does indeed feel like being pulled underwater – an experience suggested, too, by the motif of the *night sea journey*, to use Leo Frobenius's term.[18] In the watery depths one is charged with the onerous task of cleansing the 'doors of perception', removing the distorting blemishes from the mirror of self-reflective consciousness such that one can see the world as it really is. The aim of individuation, according to Jung, is to arrive at a realistic view of oneself and the world, which can only be attained after one has liberated oneself from the unconscious compulsion and reality-distorting influence of the archetypes.

The danger, throughout individuation, is that one might give away one's unique conscious selfhood by unwittingly identifying either with an idealized image of oneself – a persona – or with an archetypal image in the unconscious, such that one's consciousness is possessed by the archetype and true individuality is lost: one becomes nothing but a hero, for instance, ever struggling tragically against adversity, seeking adventure and conquest; or one identifies completely with the wise old man (or mana personality) and solemnly believes oneself to be a being of superior wisdom devoid of less exalted traits; or one falls prey to the manic godlike inflation that comes from identification with the Self. The possessive quality here, it should be pointed out, is more directly related to the Pluto archetype, but Neptune represents the archetypal images themselves, and the illusion, the escapism, the self-loss, the hypnotic allure of the archetypal unconscious.

For all its great dangers, however, the dissolution of the persona and the ensuing absorption in the world of archetypal images is a prerequisite for the reintegration and reorganization of the psyche around the Self – the deeper center and totality of the psyche. 'Dissolution,' as Jung notes, 'is a pre-requisite for redemption.'[19] The redemptive quality of the Neptune principle is manifest, during subsequent stages of individuation, in the movement towards the synthesis of the disparate parts of the psyche around the Self. The redemption of the ego occurs by the re-establishment of psychological unity; one's 'eye is made single', to put this in the familiar words of the Bible, and the raging conflict between the disparate parts of the psyche is healed. To the redeemed individual the Neptunian principle might be recognized in the beatitude of Heaven, in the experience of 'paradise regained', and in the recovery of a magical enchanted sense of participation with the natural world. Myth has many fitting images of this attainment: ambrosia as the elixir of the gods, the fountain of youth, the mystic marriage of the individual and God. In alchemy the archetypal Neptune is well described by the *aqua permanens* – the 'wonderful waters of transformation' – that are contained within the Philosopher's Stone, the endpoint of the alchemical opus.[20]

As one would expect, many of the above themes are evident in a number of people born with major Sun–Neptune aspects. This archetypal complex is found, for instance, in many prominent figures for whom the spiritual dimension is a directly experienced reality: Jung himself (Sun square Neptune), Pierre Teilhard de Chardin (Sun conjunct Neptune), Saint Thérèse of Lisieux (Sun square Neptune), and Saint Teresa of Avila (Sun sextile Neptune). To this list we might add Roberto Assagioli, pioneer of transpersonal psychology and explorer of spiritual experiences (Sun square Neptune), and Sri Aurobindo, pioneer of integral yoga (Sun trine Neptune).

In persons of a mystical inclination, Sun–Neptune complexes can manifest as a Christ-like sacrifice of the individual self to the greater life of the spirit, a form of spiritual heroism in which one's consciousness, or even one's identity, becomes a channel for the divine. The emphasis in such cases is less on self-will and more on serving as an emissary for the spirit. Equally, as in Jung's case, there can be a struggle to preserve one's individual self against the potentially overwhelming influx of the archetypal unconscious, and the impulse to harmoniously align oneself with the spirit, with the Tao or the Logos – the principle of cosmic order.

Aspects of Neptune to other planets in the natal chart give an indication as to how such themes will be experienced in the individual's life. The Venus–Neptune complex, for example, is connected with a spiritualized expression of the anima, or the blurring of spirituality and romantic love, taking the form of anything from romantic flights of fancy and unconscious romantic projection to a mystic's love of the divine and a transcendence of personal romantic inclinations. The latter is clearly evident in Teilhard, whose love for the divine in the material world and the figure of Jesus Christ assumed a personal, almost romantic quality. The placement of Teilhard's Sun and Venus in Taurus is reflected in the characteristic earthly cast of his mysticism, which focused on the spirit in the heart of matter, and re-conceived Christianity in terms of the evolution of the material universe.[21]

With Mercury–Neptune aspects, by contrast, Neptunian themes evident during individuation – such as synthesis, mythologizing, a symbolic or metaphorical reading of life experience, access to subtle dimensions of reality – are typically expressed through the intellect. Thus we can observe the signature of Mercury–Neptune complexes in the grand philosophical synthesis of Hegel, the

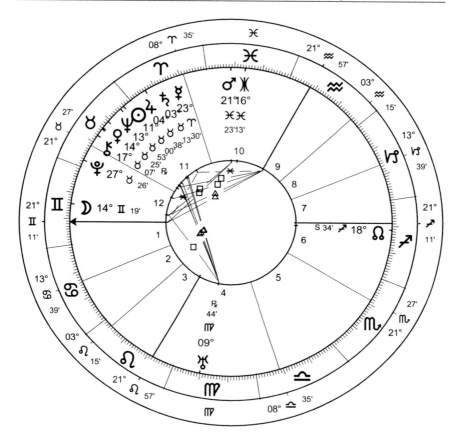

Pierre Teilhard de Chardin's Birth Chart

psychic knowledge and mystic philosophy of Rudolf Steiner, the mythic studies of Joseph Campbell and Robert Graves, and the metaphors and mythic imagery in the song lyrics of Bob Dylan and Bruce Springsteen – each born during major Mercury–Neptune alignments.

Similar motifs are evident during major Neptune transits and progressions to Neptune, which typically coincide with openings to the fantasy products of the unconscious, periods of hermetic withdrawal from the world, spiritual experiences, and periods of heightened mythic or artistic sensitivity, often with a prophetic or visionary quality.

Pluto: Instinctual Compulsion, the Underworld Descent and Death–Rebirth

Whereas the Neptune principle pertains to the spiritual dimension of reality and the imaginal realm of the collective unconscious, the archetypal Pluto pertains to the instincts, seething passions and irrational drives in the depths of the unconscious – impulses that need to be brought to the surface of consciousness and purged. Pluto symbolizes the dark spiritual power of nature that seeks its own evolutionary transformation in the light of human self-reflective awareness. The Pluto principle is thus associated with perhaps *the* major theme of the individuation process: psychospiritual death–rebirth. This theme is especially connected with the interaction of the Pluto and Saturn archetypes, indicated by natal alignments or by transits between the corresponding planets.

In psychology the Saturn archetype finds expression in the crystallized forms and rigid structures of the ego-complex. Saturn is connected, too, with the emotion of fear and the instinct for self-preservation that underlie the ego and its mechanisms of defense. Saturn symbolizes the old ruling principle of the psyche; it is associated with the principle of repression, control, censorship, and is thus well described by the Freudian notion of the superego. In mythic terms Saturn is personified both as an old king, symbolizing a negative, life-resistant form of the wise old man or senex, and as the 'guardian of the threshold' – the barrier that must be overcome if one is to live out one's own life adventure, realize one's potential and access the transcendent. In essence, before it is transformed during the work of individuation, Saturn represents the principle of negation and resistance in the psyche that manifests as a 'no' response to life: the inability to accept and affirm life in all its suffering and struggle, as well as its joys and pleasures.

The agent of transformation of the crystallized ego is the archetypal Pluto. Pluto symbolizes the elemental force of nature, ever destroying and creating, moving inexorably on, ensuring that life is always dying to the old and being born to the new, like the mythic Uroborus, the tail-eating serpent or dragon, consuming itself in the perpetual cycle of instinctual life. In Jungian terms Pluto is associated with elemental and instinctual power repressed into the shadow. It is connected, as well, with the Dionysian power of Nietzsche's *Übermensch* – and the daimonic force that empowers the individual to far greater deeds than would be possible by conscious willpower alone.

The transformative impulse associated with Pluto works by a process Stanislav Grof has called *pyrocatharsis*: the burning out and destruction of a psychological complex or pattern of behaviour by driving it to its extreme, intensifying it.[22] In the case of Saturn–Pluto combinations – whether in natal alignments or transits – experiences of fear, negation, contraction, resistance, limitation and repression can all be transformed through extremity of expression. This archetypal combination is thus associated with the experience of eternal damnation, the fiery torments of hell and the agonies of purgatory. Saturn–Pluto archetypal complexes can be experienced as a 'pressure cooker' of transformation, like an alchemical alembic, in which the ordinary human ego undergoes a death–rebirth. Indeed, the entire alchemical transformation process essentially reflects Saturn–Pluto dynamics, incorporating themes such as the transformation by fire (*calcinatio*), the *nigredo* phase of the death (*mortificatio*) and dismemberment of the old ruling king or dominant principle (*Sol*, the old Adam), and the purging of impurities, which symbolizes, Jung believed, the impulse to become free of instinctual compulsion.

As Mircea Eliade has shown, alchemy has its roots in both metallurgy, the mining of ores deep underground and smelting of the ores in fire to create metal, and in shamanism, in which the shaman undergoes a descent and death experience, often involving extremes of suffering and encounters with animal powers.[23] These themes – the underground realm, depth, fire, intense heat, the animal world – are all unmistakably Plutonic. The Pluto archetype is also evident in myth in the motif of the 'descent into the underworld', and it is symbolized by encounters with denizens of the depths and the confrontation with fearsome beasts, or as volcanic eruptions of elemental power and consumption by fire, and so forth.

With the Pluto archetype acting on Saturn, as it were, the repressed power of the instincts effects a transformation of the ego structure: the old crystallized forms of the Saturnian structure of the ego are destroyed; the normal limits of the human personality are broken down so that a new wholeness might be realized. Conversely, with Saturn acting on Pluto, the instincts themselves are to be contained and controlled – the prerequisite for their transformation. One must bring Saturnian discipline and control to bear on the passions, and one must invoke established moral values as one confronts the primitive uncivilized instincts in the unconscious. For it is only by such an endeavour that blind instinctual compulsion, which characterizes much of human existence, can be brought to an end. Individuation, mediated by the Saturn and Pluto archetypes, brings the 'death of the animal man'. In Christianity the primary symbol of this death, and of the overcoming of the unregenerate instinctual state of being, is the Crucifixion.

Unsurprisingly, we can see many of these themes associated with the Saturn–Pluto combination in the lives and works of figures who have explored experiences of psychospiritual transformation in depth, including spiritual philosophers Alan Watts and Sri Aurobindo, as well as Nietzsche and Jung – each born with Saturn and Pluto in major aspect. Aurobindo, for example, with natal Mercury, Saturn and Pluto in a grand trine, set out, in his voluminous written works, comprehensive in-depth psychological analyses of the experience of evolutionary transformation by which matter could be spiritualized through the medium of human consciousness. He remains one of the most systematic and insightful articulators of the labour of spiritual transformation. In Nietzsche's case, his exhortation to a life of more intense suffering – a descent 'deeper

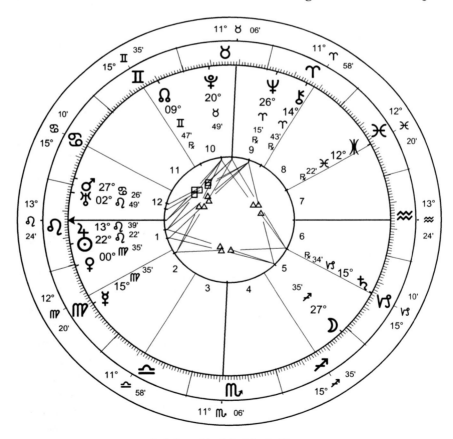

Sri Aurobindo's Birth Chart

into pain than I have ever descended' – as a prerequisite for further evolution, gives voice to one essential dimension of his Saturn–Pluto archetypal complex, as do his firsthand testimonies of the 'heartbreaking last hours' of psychospiritual death–rebirth.[24] Such themes are also evident in Jung, whose description of individuation as an arduous Herculean labour and whose testimony of his prolonged struggle with the dark forces of the unconscious are but two of many instances that reflect the Saturn–Pluto dynamics in his own life. Jung's experience of this complex is well conveyed in the following account of his 'confrontation with the unconscious':

> I was living in a constant state of tension; often I felt as if gigantic blocks of stone were tumbling down upon me. One thunderstorm followed another. My enduring these storms was a question of brute strength. Others have been shattered by them – Nietzsche, and Hölderlin, and many others. But there was a demonic strength in me... When I endured these assaults of the unconscious I had an unswerving conviction that I was obeying a higher will, and that feeling continued to uphold me until I had mastered the task.[25]

One can recognize the Pluto archetype here in the 'demonic' and 'brute' strength empowering and intensifying the Saturnian capacity for resistance and endurance. At the same time, the Plutonic power of the instincts was destroying the old structure of the ego and its persona, symbolized by the crashing blocks of stone and the elemental power of the thunderstorm.

As I have argued elsewhere, when considering the significance of the Pluto archetypal principle for individuation, one can, I believe, discern an underlying developmental trajectory often apparent in the lives of people who deeply engage the dimension of experience associated with Pluto.[26] This trajectory, to briefly summarize, is defined by several distinct stages:

1. An unconscious instinctual empowerment of the ego, when the drives associated with Pluto compel the emerging individual ego to assert itself in the world, to conquer and plunder, and to exert its power and try to satisfy its instinctually driven cravings.

2. A frustration of instinct by the Saturnian context of human life (the pressures of material existence, the hard facts of one's reality, the inherent limitations of life, the slow pace of

change, responsibilities and duties to others, and so forth) with a simultaneous intensification of the unfulfilled drives and desires associated with Pluto.

3. An increasing schism between the ego, attuned to an outer objective reality, and the instincts, hell bent on gratification – a schism that, if too extreme, can lead to the experience of alienation or estrangement from the instinctual basis of life and, with it, a loss of vitality, zest and life power.

4. A 'descent into the underworld' of the unconscious in order for the ego to recover lost power and potentials.

5. An ensuing death–rebirth struggle through which the ego and the instincts are both transformed.

6. And finally an ascent, resurrection and the realization of the greater wholeness of the personality in which the instinctual compulsion associated with the Pluto archetype is overcome.

As these brief examples illustrate, the archetypal principles associated with Uranus, Neptune and Pluto are the primary agents of individuation, representing themes and motifs that are central concerns of the world's mythic and spiritual traditions. By using archetypal astrology one can better understand one's unique relationship to these principles and thus discern how these themes are expressing themselves in one's own life experiences. In an age in which myths are widely dismissed as primitive truths superseded by science, which leaves the individual shorn of spiritual guidance and mythic orientation, archetypal astrology enables us to understand our own relationship to the gods, as it were. It provides an archetypal framework to give deeper context to our lives, and to help us navigate even the most challenging of experiences.

Endnotes

1. Many of these archetypes are discussed in Jung's seminal *The Archetypes and the Collective Unconscious*. The individuation process is discussed in his *Two Essays on Analytical Psychology* and is the central focus all his major works on alchemy, especially *Mysterium Coniunctionis*.

2. On the Self's association with the Will of God, Jung writes: 'The Self ... by virtue of its numinosity, compels man towards wholeness, that is, towards the integration of the unconscious or the subordination of the ego to a holistic "will", which is rightly conceived to be "God's will".' (C. G. Jung, *Letters II*, p. 14.) Following the convention in this quote, I am capitalizing the Jungian concept of the *Self* to distinguish it from the usual connotation of the term individual *self*, which is more or less synonymous with Jung's term the *ego*.

3. See Jung, *Symbols of Transformation*, and Campbell, *Hero with a Thousand Faces*.

4. This article is concerned only with *archetypal astrology* and the new academic discipline of archetypal cosmology, which is based on the work of Richard Tarnas and a number of other scholars connected with the *Archai* journal, myself included. Archetypal cosmology is a multidisciplinary field that draws on a range of established subject areas, including depth psychology, philosophy, cultural history, comparative mythology, religious studies, cosmology and the new-paradigm sciences. The study of astrological correlations between planetary alignments or aspects and archetypal patterns in human experience (archetypal astrology) is foundational to the field. For background on archetypal cosmology, see Le Grice, 'Birth of a New Discipline.'

5. For further detail on the relationship of astrology to Jung's theory of archetypes, see Le Grice, *Archetypal Cosmos*, 55–78, 90–94, 152–178.

6. For a discussion of the archetypal multidimensionality and multivalence inherent in astrology, see Tarnas, *Cosmos and Psyche*, 85–87.

7. For the connections between archetypal astrology and mythology, see *Archetypal Cosmos*, 34–94, 263–287.

8. The archetypal principle associated with the dwarf planet Eris – which appears to be related to themes such as the tension of opposites, evolutionary discord, cosmic justice, counterbalancing reactions and the violation of nature – might also be extremely significant for individuation. See Le Grice, *Discovering Eris*.

9. Jung, *Memories, Dreams, Reflections*, 414.

10. Campbell, *Hero with a Thousand Faces*, 51.

11. For examples of Uranus's association with individual brilliance and creative genius, see Tarnas, *Prometheus the Awakener.*

12. Nietzsche, 'Daybreak,' aphorism 575 in *A Nietzsche Reader*, 205. For Richard Tarnas's analysis of Nietzsche's Jupiter–Uranus complex, see *Cosmos and Psyche*, 335–348.

13. Campbell, interview with Bill Moyers, *The Power of Myth.*

14. Nietzsche, 'Ecce Homo' in *Basic Writings of Nietzsche*, 751.

15. See Jung, *Memories, Dreams, Reflections*, chapter IV, 194–225.

16. Bair, *Jung: A Biography*, 238.

17. Jung, *Two Essays on Analytical Psychology*, 156–171.

18. See Campbell, *Hero with a Thousand Faces*, 90–95.

19. Jung, *Mysterium Coniunctionis*, 283.

20. Jung, *Mysterium Coniunctionis*, 277.

21. See Teilhard de Chardin, *Heart of Matter.*

22. Grof, *Psychology of the Future*, 48.

23. See Eliade, *Forge and the Crucible.*

24. Nietzsche, *Thus Spoke Zarathustra*, 175, 111

25. Jung, *Memories, Dreams, Reflections*, 200–201.

26. I explore the significance of the archetypal Pluto for individual psychological development in Le Grice, 'A Last Chance Power-Drive.'

Chart Data *(courtesy of Sy Scholfield, unless stated otherwise):*

Roberto Assagioli: 27 February 1888, 12:00 Rome Time (-0:49:56), Venice, Italy (45n27, 12e21). Source: Birth certificate obtained by Grazia Bordoni, copy on file. RR: AA.

Sri Aurobindo: 15 August 1872, 05:00 LMT (-5:53:28), Calcutta, India (22n32, 88e22). Source: Marion March quotes the biography, *Auroville: City of the Future* (Fisher Books [1974?]). Sy Scholfield quotes *Sri Aurobindo: The Prophet of Nationalism* by Jyotirmati Samantaray (Orissa Review, August 2005, p. 30), '4.50 a.m'. < http://orissa.gov.in/e-magazine/Orissareview/aug2005/augreview.htm>, and *The Life of Sri Aurobindo: A Source Book* by Ambalal Balkrishna Purani (1964 [1958]), p. 2, '4-30 am, an hour before sunrise'. NB: Sunrise was at 05:40. RR: B.

Joseph Campbell: 26 March 1904, 19:25 EST (+5), White Plains, New York, USA (41n02, 73w46). Source: From his mother to Erin Cameron in 1981; place of birth from his website <www.jcf.org>. RR: A.

Neal Cassady: 8 February 1926, 02:05 MST (+7), Salt Lake City, Utah, USA (40n45, 111w53). Source: Sy Scholfield cites the birth certificate quoted in *Neal Cassady: The Fast Life of a Beat Hero* (Chicago Review Press, 2006), p. 2. RR: AA.

Bob Dylan: 24 May 1941, 21:05 CST (+6), Duluth, Minnesota, USA (46n47, 92w06). Source: Birth certificate obtained by Edwin Steinbrecher, copy on file (Robert Allen Zimmerman). RR: AA.

Allen Ginsberg: 3 June 1926, 02:00 EDT (+4), Newark, New Jersey, USA (40n44, 74w10). Source: John McKay-Clements quotes a letter from his assistant. Sy Scholfield quotes same data in *Dharma Lion: A Critical Biography of Allen Ginsberg* by Michael Schumacher (St. Martin's Press, 1992), pp. 3+7. RR: A.

Robert Graves: 24 July 1895, 04:26 GMT (+0), Wimbledon, England (51n25, 0w13). Source: The biography, *Robert Graves: His Life and Work* by Martin Seymour-Smith (Hutchinson, 1982), p. 1. RR: B.

G. W. F. Hegel: 27 August 1770, Stuttgart, Germany (48n47, 9e11). Source: Wikipedia. <http://en.wikipedia.org/wiki/Georg_Wilhelm_Friedrich_Hegel> (accessed 12 December 2011). RR: X.

Carl Gustav Jung: 26 July 1875, 19:32 LMT (Berne Time -0:29:44), Kesswil, Switzerland (47n36, 9e20). Source: From his daughter Gret Baumann, as quoted in *Carl Gustav Jung: Leben, Werk, Wirkung* by Gerhard Wehr (Kosel-Verlag, 1985); various other times around sunset have also been given (Karle Gustav Jung). 19:24 LMT has been used here. RR: A.

Jack Kerouac: 12 March 1922, 17:00 EST (+5), Lowell, Massachusetts, USA (42n38, 71w19). Source: Lois Rodden quotes *Kerouac* by Ann Charters. Sy Scholfield quotes *Subterranean Kerouac: The Hidden Life of Jack Kerouac* by Ellis Amburn (New York: St. Martin's Press, 1998): 'In a December 28, 1950, letter to [Neal] Cassady, Kerouac disclosed that his birth occurred at 5 P.M. and that [his mother] Gabrielle later gave him a blow-by-blow account of his delivery.' RR: A.

Jim Morrison: 8 December 1943, 11:55 EWT (+4), Melbourne, Florida, USA (28n04, 80w36). Source: Birth registration card obtained by Bob Garner, copy on file. RR: AA.

Friedrich Nietzsche: 15 October 1844, 10:00 LMT (-0:48:32), Rocken [Lutzen], Germany (51n15, 12e08). Source: Sy Scholfield quotes the biography *Der Junge Nietzsche* by his daughter, Elisabeth Forster-Nietzsche (A. Kroner, 1922), p. 14. Elisabeth created the Nietzsche Archive in 1894. RR: B.

Bruce Springsteen: 23 September 1949, 22:50 EDT (+4), Long Branch, New Jersey, USA (40n18, 74w00). Source: Birth certificate quoted by Janice Mackey in *Contemporary American Horoscopes* (Astrolabe 1990); Freehold, NJ, is often incorrectly listed as the birth place. RR: AA.

Rudolf Steiner: 25 February 1861, 23.15 LMT (-0:58:16), Murakirály, Austria-Hungary [now Kraljevica, Croatia] (45n16, 14e34). Source: Marion March quotes birth record cited in *Rudolph Steiner* by Gerhard Wehr (Frieberg, 1983). Astrodatabank has a copy on file of a letter written to Nandan Bosma from Steiner giving his own data as February 25, 1861, 23:07 LMT. The baptism record gives a birth date of 27 February but was issued many years after Steiner's birth. (Rudolf Joseph Lorenz Steiner). RR: AA.

Pierre Teilhard de Chardin: 1 May 1881, 07:00 LMT (-0:12), Orcines, France (45n47, 3e00). Source: Birth record quoted by Michel and Françoise Gauquelin; Sy Scholfield quotes same (No. 19). RR: AA.

Saint Teresa of Avila: 28 March 1515 (OS), 05:00 LMT (+0:18:48), Avila, Spain (40n39, 4w42). Source: The biography, *Saint Teresa of Avila* by Stephen Clissold (Sheldon Press, 1979). RR: B.

Saint Thérèse of Lisieux: 2 January 1873, 23:30 LMT (-0:00:20), Alençon, France (48n26, 0e05). Source: T. Pat Davis quotes Mayoral Register; Sy Scholfield quotes same (No. 2). RR: AA.

Alan Watts: 6 January 1915, 06:20 GMT (+0), Chislehurst, England (51n25, 0e04). Source: Dana Holliday quotes his autobiography, *In My Own Way* (Pantheon Books, 1972), p. 10. RR: B.

Bibliography

Bair, Deidre. *Jung: A Biography.* London: Little, Brown and Company, 2003.

Campbell, Joseph. *The Hero with a Thousand Faces.* 1949. Repr. London: Fontana, 1993.

Campbell, Joseph, and Bill Moyers. *Joseph Campbell and the Power of Myth with Bill Moyers.* New York: Mystic Fire Video, 1988.

Eliade, Mircea. *The Forge and the Crucible: Origins and Structures of Alchemy.* New Edition. 1978. Repr. Chicago: University of Chicago Press, 1979.

Grof, Stanislav. *Psychology of the Future: Lessons from Modern Consciousness Research.* Albany, NY: State University of New York Press, 2000.

Jung, Carl Gustav. *The Archetypes and the Collective Unconscious.* 2nd ed. *The Collected Works of C. G. Jung,* vol. 9, part I. Trans. R.F.C. Hull. Princeton: Princeton University Press, 1968.

— —. *C. G Jung Letters II: 1951–1961.* Edited by Gerald Adler and Aniele Jaffe. Trans. R.F.C. Hull. London: Routledge & Kegan Paul, 1973.

— —. *Memories, Dreams, Reflections.* 1963. Edited by Aniele Jaffe. Trans. Richard Wilson and Clara Wilson. Repr. London: Flamingo, 1983.

— —. *Mysterium Coniunctionis*. 2nd ed. 1955–1956. Vol. 14 of *The Collected Works of C. G. Jung*. Trans. R.F.C. Hull. Repr. Princeton: Princeton University Press, 1989.

— —. *Symbols of Transformation*. 2nd ed. 1967. Vol. 5 of *The Collected Works of C. G. Jung*. Trans. R.F.C. Hull. Repr. Princeton: Princeton University Press, 1976.

— —. *Two Essays on Analytical Psychology*. 2nd ed. 1966. Vol. 7 of *The Collected Works of C. G. Jung*. Trans. R.F.C. Hull. Repr. London: Routledge, 1990.

Le Grice, Keiron. *The Archetypal Cosmos: Rediscovering the Gods in Myth, Science and Astrology*. Edinburgh: Floris Books, 2010.

— —. 'The Birth of a New Discipline: Archetypal Cosmology in Historical Perspective.' In *The Birth of a New Discipline, Archai: The Journal of Archetypal Cosmology*, Issue 1, Summer 2009. Repr. San Francisco: Archai Press, 2011.

— —. 'The Dark Spirit in Nature: C. G. Jung and the Spiritual Transformation of Our Time.' In *Beyond a Disenchanted Cosmology. Archai: The Journal of Archetypal Cosmology*, Issue 3, Fall 2011. San Francisco: Archai Press, 2011.

— —. *Discovering Eris: The Symbolism and Significance of a New Planetary Archetype*. Edinburgh: Floris Books, 2012.

— —. 'A Last Chance Power-Drive: An Archetypal Analysis of Bruce Springsteen's Song Lyrics, Part 1.' In *The Birth of a New Discipline, Archai: The Journal of Archetypal Cosmology*, Issue 1, Summer 2009. Repr. San Francisco: Archai Press, 2011.

Nietzsche, Friedrich. *Basic Writings of Nietzsche*. Trans. Walter Kaufmann. New York: The Modern Library, 2000.

— —. *A Nietzsche Reader*. Selected and Translated by R. J. Hollingdale. Repr. New York: Penguin, 1984.

— —. *Thus Spoke Zarathustra*. Trans. Richard Hollingdale. New York: Penguin, 1968.

Tarnas, Richard. *Cosmos and Psyche: Intimations of a New World View*. New York: Viking, 2006.

— —. *Prometheus the Awakener: An Essay on the Archetypal Meaning of the Planet Uranus*. Woodstock, CT: Spring Publications, 1995.

Teilhard de Chardin, Pierre. *The Heart of Matter*. San Diego: Harcourt, 1978.

Connect with us on Facebook
www.facebook.com/pages/Astrology-The-New-
Generation/243754708990870

Demetrius Bagley, Project Manager
A Personal Biography

I am an internationally published astrologer as well as an award-winning events and movie producer. I wrote *Vibe* magazine's celebrity horoscope column from 2010 to 2011, while also publishing my own creation, the annual Personalized AstroDatebook. *Vegucated* is the award-winning documentary I produced; the movie is central to a grassroots program encouraging vegan eating and living. While I am an active NCGR, AFAN and ISAR member, I also am the Media and Communications Director for National Council of Geocosmic Research (NCGR), the USA's largest organization of astrologers. I may be a familiar presence from the room monitoring teams at UAC08, ISAR09 and NCGR10, or even the NCGR–NYC chapter conferences' recording station as a former associate. I am the marketing manager for State of the Art (SOTA) astrology conferences, and an instructor with the NYC Astrology Meetup. In 2010, I received the Committee for Effective Leadership Award, and recognition from U.S. Congress, U.S. Senate, New York State and New York City for my community involvement. My volunteer achievements include chairing the New York League of Humane Voters' Gala 2009 – a historic and successful fundraiser; directing NYC Vegan EatUP, a social club with a history spanning over nine years, 400+ events and nearly 1,600 members; inventing Carleton College's Annual Alumni Trivia Competition where alumni and close ones gather in various cities/time zones all competing simultaneously; plus godfathering Veggie Conquest, an amateur cooking competition that sells out tickets as fast as major music acts!

www.astrodatebook.com

Nan Geary, Editor
A Personal Biography... of sorts

Well, Nan preferred to leave the biographies to others, but she has played an instrumental role in the production of this book. The project could not have been completed without Nan's excellent editor's eye, her professionalism and dedication. So... we did a bit of detective work and discovered that Nan began studying astrology in 1970 and is married to an astronomer/telescope-maker. She is a poet, singer and songwriter – and a member of a three-woman a cappella vocal group, Harmonious Combustion. The astrological community will know her as Senior Editor of *The Mountain Astrologer*, which is widely regarded as the best astrology magazine around today.

A complete guide to horoscope synthesis – designed to help astrologers identify, prioritize and synthesize the components, themes and storylines of any chart. Packed with original ideas and observations, this textbook includes 150 horoscopes and profiles showing astrology in action.

Business astrologer Faye Cossar reveals how the birth chart can be used to create a tangible product – a Vocational Profile – which enables you and your clients to: identify talents, blocks and style; create a CV, website and logo; define goals and awaken life purpose and passion.

In *From Symbol to Substance: Training the Astrological Intuition* learn to: develop creative and spontaneous interpretations for any placement; enhance intuitive faculties when analysing charts; and think creatively when exploring symbolism and correspondences.

Sue Tompkins (*Aspects in Astrology*) presents an authoritative guide to chart interpretation, with an in-depth exploration of the planets, zodiac signs, houses and aspects. Included are biographies and step-by-step instructions for synthesizing the main horoscope factors.

From an award-winning psychological astrologer comes the definitive book on the astrological houses. This new edition of the best-selling handbook remains a firm favourite among students and professionals. With a new foreword by Dr. Liz Greene and tribute essays from astrologers.

Based on over 30 interviews with researchers and leading astrologers, this landmark, thought-provoking volume examines the lives and work of contemporary astrologers, and considers many of the issues facing this ancient and systematic art.

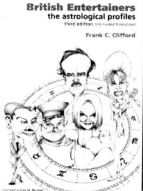
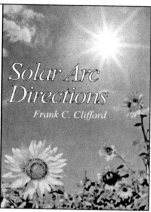
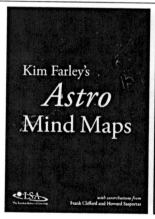